Critical Studies in Antebellum Sectionalism

Recent Titles in
Contributions in American History

SERIES EDITOR: STANLEY I. KUTLER

CONTRIBUTIONS IN AMERICAN HISTORY, NUMBER 7

Critical Studies in Antebellum Sectionalism

ESSAYS IN AMERICAN POLITICAL AND ECONOMIC HISTORY

Robert R. Russel

GREENWOOD PUBLISHING COMPANY
WESTPORT, CONNECTICUT

Library of Congress Cataloging in Publication Data

Russel, Robert Royal, 1890–
  Critical studies in antebellum sectionalism.

  (Contributions in American history, no. 7)
  Includes bibliographical references.
    1. Sectionalism (U.S.) 2. U.S.--History--Civil
War--Causes. 3. Slavery in the United States.
I. Title.
E468.R85   973.7   78-105977
ISBN 0-8371-3304-1

Library of Congress Catalog Card Number: 78-105977
ISBN: 0-8371-3304-1

Greenwood Publishing Company
A Division of Greenwood Press, Inc.
51 Riverside Avenue, Westport, Connecticut 06880

Printed in the United States of America

To my sons,
Robert H. and James M.

Contents

Introduction

It would appear that when a number of his articles are about to be republished, the author, if still alive and in reasonably full possession of his faculties (which I claim to be), should say something by way of justification or apology.

The articles presented here were written at long intervals over a period of forty-two years. Each was called forth at its time by some particular contingency, interest, or reaction. It never occurred to me when writing any of them that some day they might be assembled as a book, and, therefore, it might be well to stick to one main theme. Accordingly, if these articles have any congruity with one another, it results from the more or less fortuitous circumstance that all are in the field of antebellum history, and all are concerned to some degree with sectionalism between North and South.

The first three articles discuss episodes in the great sectional struggle over slavery in territories and do form a sequence of a sort. "What Was the Compromise of 1850?" attempts to answer the question only insofar as that compromise was embodied in the slavery provisions of the acts of Congress organizing New Mexico and Utah territories. The scope and purpose of the second article, "The Issues in the Congressional Struggles over the Kansas–Nebraska Bill, 1854," are adequately indicated by the title. The third essay, "Constitutional Doctrines with Regard to Slavery in Territories," is principally an attempt to put the Dred Scott decision and particularly the opinions of individual justices in the Dred Scott case in their setting in the long controversy over the constitutional powers of Congress and territorial legislatures with regard to slavery in territories and to show what position on that single constitutional issue each of the four political parties took in the national election campaign of 1860.

The three essays deal with old historical chestnuts, as all will readily recognize. Furthermore, they are all elementary in character; they do not attempt to go much beyond stating the basic establishable facts. They scarcely venture into the higher realm of analyzing motives and pronouncing judgments. I recognize that when it comes to finding the causes and effects of great events and to assessing the motives of leaders and masses, it is only reasonable to expect some disagreement among even the most objective and judicious students. But I am one of those students of history (the great majority, I hope and believe) who believe that there are establishable facts in history, just as there are in judicial cases, and that two or more competent historians undertaking research on the same topic, if they do their homework and observe the simple precepts as to the creditability of evidence that they learned in graduate school, should come out with quite similar statements of the ascertainable facts.

In the three essays, I point out or allege a considerable number of errors of fact in older accounts of the topics; and, while I offer little in the way of interpretation, I do contend or strongly imply that writers of history should take care to get all the essential ascertainable facts straight before venturing upon sweeping speculations and generalizations or the pronouncement of judgments upon the motives and actions of men. Of course, I know that finding flaws in other people's work is not calculated to make one popular with them and that one who does so lays himself wide open to such retorts as "And why beholdest thou the mote that is in thy brother's eye and considerest not the beam that is in thy own eye?" I can only say in defense that history is a serious business, that, judging by reviews in professional journals, it is generally considered ethical to try to correct the record, and that I have set naught down in malice.

Readers of the articles will judge for themselves whether I have made any worthwhile corrections or additions and, if so, what of it. For those who may be convinced that I have made valid corrections in matters of historical significance, I should like to be a little more explicit as to why, in my judgment, so many errors have crept into earlier accounts of the topics with which these articles deal.

One reason is that the debates and official proceedings on the subjects were long and repetitious, the contending interests and viewpoints were many and diverse, and the arguments were often subtle and not always ingenuous. The meaning and intent of proposed bills and amendments, enacted laws, and planks in party platforms are not always clear. People writing historical accounts might innocently miss important points if they failed to read the debates and official proceedings with care to the end. I am constrained to believe that only a few of the many historians who have written about the Compromise of 1850 and the Kansas–Nebraska struggle, especially, had read more than a respectable sampling of the debates and proceedings. Authors of textbooks cannot possibly read all the sources for all the numerous topics they must cover and must depend on available monographs and other specialized works or, in the absence of such, upon the longer general period histories, such as James Ford Rhodes, *History of the United States from the Compromise of 1850.* Up to the time when I wrote my essay on the Compromise of 1850, not a single monograph on that subject had been published that I could discover[1] and only a few scholarly articles. It may be that established scholars and candidates for the Ph.D. degree feared that too little grain could be found in the much threshed-over matter. There were a couple of monographs and several articles in professional journals dealing with the Kansas–Nebraska struggle, but most of them tended to emphasize questions of authorship of the Kansas–Nebraska bill and the motives of individual prominent participants, especially Stephen A. Douglas, and to neglect the great issues to be resolved.

One thing that led me to write the article on the Kansas–Nebraska struggle was exasperation with two prestigious authors whose accounts had recently appeared for having relied excessively upon the reminiscences of participants and observers and of their widows, sons, or brothers-in-law, and upon the defenses or glorifications of their own conduct made by senators or congressmen when home mending their fences among their constituents and away from their colleagues in Congress, who could soon have cut them down to size, and upon the contemporary (in this case) reports of the "usually reliable Washington correspondent" of various newspapers. I resolved to write my account from the official record and the little available contemporary correspondence of participants alone, and I almost held to that resolution, as the footnotes in the article will attest. However, after I had written it, I did go through six newspapers for the period from the assembling of the first session of the Thirty-third Congress to the signing of the Kansas–Nebraska Act, namely, the New York *Times,* the New York *Courier and Enquirer,* the New York *Herald,* the Washington *Union,* the Springfield *Illinois State Register,* and

[1] One has appeared since, however: Holman Hamilton, *Prologue to Conflict: The Crisis and Compromise of 1850* (Lexington, Ky., 1964). Professor Hamilton, however, does not give special attention to the matter of slavery in territories in his all too short book.

the St. Louis *Republican,* paying particular attention to their Washington correspondence. I also read the most commonly quoted reminiscences of the Kansas–Nebraska struggle by participants and onlookers who claimed special knowledge. While I found much that corroborated what I had found in the official records, I found very little that added thereto, and I found much that must have come from misunderstanding, faulty memory, hindsight, misrepresentation, and, in case of the newspapers, mere speculation and rumor. I realize that if I had undertaken to determine the motives of some individual participant, the part he had played in behind-the-scenes maneuvers, and the outside pressures he had been subjected to, I might have found the materials I have described to be useful, if used with insight and circumspection and in default of better.

The late Professor Andrew C. McLaughlin once, in attempting to account for one common mistaken notion about a certain issue in the sectional quarrels over slavery in the territories, gave as a possible explanation "congenital difficulty in understanding constitutional theory."[2] I do not care to commit myself to that explanation, but it would appear that one who writes about the sectional quarrels over slavery in the territories had better (among other things) first ground himself well in constitutional history and constitutional law. I believe that many of the misstatements that have found their way into books would not be there if the authors had been more familiar with elementary constitutional law and more accustomed to reading legal arguments and documents.

Inasmuch as my three articles on aspects of the sectional struggle over slavery in the territories had only limited objectives, it is perhaps improper to comment here on how their findings may be fitted into or contribute to a general account and assessment of the causes of secession and the Civil War. I will only say that I believe they tend to disprove the view stated by many historians who regard the struggle over slavery in the territories as primarily one over "mere abstractions" or as one mostly stirred up by politicians who sought to advance themselves by playing on people's emotions and prejudices. The essays, I believe, support the view of those historians who regard the issue as involving both great interests and deep convictions, emotions, and sensibilities.

While I was trying to arrange for the publication of the essay on

[2] *A Constitutional History of the United States* (Student's ed., New York, 1935), 531.

the Compromise of 1850, I had an experience which may or may not illustrate anything I have said above but which should illustrate something. I first sent the article to the managing editor of the *Mississippi Valley Historical Review*. He returned it in due season with the explanation, "The consensus of our readers is that you have threshed over a great deal of straw and come up with very little wheat." After nursing my pride a while, I sent the article to the editor of the *Journal of Southern History*. I did not hear from him for a long time and finally wrote to him saying that I hoped the essay had not been lost in the shuffle. He replied, "Our readers are evenly divided as to whether we should publish your article or not, and I shall have to read it myself and make the decision." He decided favorably. Subsequently, in 1957, the article was awarded the Charles W. Ramsdell Prize by the Southern Historical Association for having been adjudged by the committee as the best article that had appeared in the *Journal of Southern History* during a designated two-year period.

"Southern Secessionists *Per Se* and the Crisis of 1850" (chapter 4) is a paper I read at a meeting of the Mississippi Valley Historical Association, Spring, 1950. It has not been published heretofore. It defends more concisely and somewhat more baldly a couple of the theses of my book, *Economic Aspects of Southern Sectionalism, 1840–1861*. Chapter 5 of the present publication, "Economic Aspects of the Disunion Movement, 1852–1860," is taken directly from that book (chapter 7) and presents further evidence supporting the same two theses.

I wrote *Economic Aspects of Southern Sectionalism* as a doctoral dissertation at the University of Illinois, and it was published in 1924 without substantial revision as volume XI of the University of Illinois Studies in the Social Sciences.[3] As the title indicates, the book is a study of politics and public opinion and feeling, not of economics or economic history. I did, of course, have to sketch in as background a description of the Southern economy of the times. Up to the time I wrote the dissertation, I had never had an opportunity to make a systematic study of economic history, and, as I see it now, my description of the antebellum Southern economy left something to be desired.[4] But I am satisfied that, on the main themes of the book, my

[3] It was republished in 1960 by Russell and Russell, Inc., New York, with no opportunity afforded for revision.
[4] My more matured views of the economy of the antebellum South are incorporated in *A History of the American Economic System* (New York, 1964). See especially chs. 13 and 14.

research was honest and my evidence reasonably adequate, and I still believe my conclusions were sound. *Economic Aspects* has been adequately reviewed, listed in bibliographies, cited in footnotes, and quoted in support of some thesis or another, with which I may or may not have agreed. My principal disappointment in connection with the study has been that its findings have not been incorporated to a greater extent in general accounts of the causes of the secession of Southern states.

I think I have detected, since World War II, a strong tendency among historians to shy away from accepting anything that suggests a leaning toward an economic interpretation of history. This tendency, if indeed there has been such a one, is to be deplored. Historians in attempting to explain the causes of great events should explore and evaluate all possibilities, and they should know as well or better than people in other disciplines that the causes of such events are never simple or monistic and that economic motives and considerations figure importantly in the list of those that impel people to behave as they do.

Let me hasten to add, in a precautionary way, that, while I have sometimes been so categorized, I have never thought of myself as belonging to the "Beard school of economic interpretationists."[5] Beardian ideas were no doubt in the air in my graduate school days, but, if they influenced me in choosing or wording the subject for my dissertation or in the manner of handling it, I was totally unaware of the influence. The subject was suggested to me by the ample evidence I found in *DeBow's Review* while working on a master's thesis on another subject, 1914–1915, and, perhaps, more especially by Edward Ingle's *Southern Sidelights: A Picture of Social and Economic Life in the South a Generation before the War* (New York, 1896), which I happened to read in the same connection. In writing *Economic Aspects,* I was only trying to contribute my bit toward understanding a very live, complicated, and much discussed matter by presenting aspects of it which I thought had been comparatively neglected by scholars. I never purported to be writing a general account of the causes of Southern sectionalism or secession.

Professors McWhiney and Wiebe have paid me the compliment of including one of my articles in their *American Vistas* and in their introduction have classified me among the "pluralists."[6] This classifi-

[5] See below, n. 17, ch. 4.
[6] Grady McWhiney and Robert Wiebe, eds., *Historical Vistas: Readings in United States History* (2 vols., Boston, 1963), I, 404.

cation I am pleased to accept. Once when I was a graduate student at the University of Illinois, I heard a famous professor of ancient history give an advertised lecture on the fall of the Roman Empire. This eminent man summarized one after another a number of reasons various historians had advanced as causes of the fall. After each brilliant little summary he would say, "But that could not have caused the fall," and proceed in an equally brilliant fashion to tell why. All the explanations he demolished seemed to me to have a degree of validity, and as he piled one upon another I began to wonder why the rickety old structure had not fallen long before it did. Finally after summarizing number eight, as I remember it, he said, "That was *the* cause." I have been a pluralist ever since.

When, in the fall of 1914, I enrolled as a graduate student at the University of Kansas, Professor Frank Heywood Hodder assigned me "Early Projects for a Railroad to the Pacific" as the subject for my master's thesis. "Assigned" is the word, for I was so inadequately prepared at the time that I could have scarcely proposed a subject on my own. The result of my labors was unpublishable. But after I had begun my teaching career, I resumed work on the topic as circumstances permitted or invited, broadened the theme, and eventually published a monograph, *Improvement of Communication with the Pacific Coast as an Issue in American Politics, 1783–1864*.[7]

This monograph was favorably reviewed. A number of others have written monographs or specialized works on particular aspects of the subject. Our findings have been in general agreement insofar as our topics have overlapped. If my book has any features that may commend it over others, they would have to be that it is the only one that brings together under one cover all the significant aspects of the subject and that it explores the sectional aspects of the issue more thoroughly than any other.

Chapter 6, "The Pacific Railway Issue in Politics Prior to the Civil War," was originally a paper read at a meeting of the Mississippi Valley Historical Association. Although it was published long in advance of *Improvement of Communication,* it is a fairly good summary of the contents and major findings of that work. Chapter 7, "Removing an Obstacle from Northern Routes [for a railroad to the Pacific]—the Kansas–Nebraska Bill," is taken directly from the monograph (chapter 10). I believe the chapter contains a well-bal-

---

[7] The Torch Press (Cedar Rapids, 1948).

anced summary of the reasons why there was such a strong demand in the North and West about 1852–1854 to have the "Nebraska country" opened to settlement and have territorial governments organized therein. However, in the short account of the congressional struggle over the Kansas–Nebraska bill, 1854, there are a few statements that I now know to be either inaccurate or ill-considered, and they are corrected or improved in chapter 2 of this book.

The three articles on the economics of American Negro slavery (chapters 8, 9 and 10) were written in the 1930s. They were prompted chiefly by my dissatisfaction with treatments of the subject I encountered in the general histories of that time and, particularly, in textbooks in the economic history of the United States. I thought the authors of those accounts, generally, were accepting rather uncritically either the abolitionists' indictment of the institution in its economic aspects or the pronouncements of economists in Europe and America, who, it seemed to me, were theorizing with too little knowledge of slavery as it actually was or of the general economic history of the South.

In writing the essays, I borrowed much from the works of a number of Southern writers, most notably Ulrich B. Phillips. With their descriptions of how slaves were managed and treated as workers and their estimates of the effectiveness of slave labor in various occupations, especially in farming, I had and have little quarrel. However, I believed that these writers generally underestimated the profitability to slave owners of employing slave labor and accepted too readily antislavery critics' assertions as to the alleged injurious economic effects of slavery upon nonslaveholding whites in the slave states and upon the general economic development of the South as a whole. I attributed these misunderstandings, as I thought them to be, to the subtle influence of an understandable reluctance on the part of loyal Southerners to admit that the principal reason why their grandfathers (and one of mine) defended so determinedly an institution now entirely abhorrent to us all was the economic rewards that the exploitation of slave labor gave to slave owners.

My three essays were nearly completed before the publication of Lewis C. Gray's *History of Agriculture in the Southern United States*[8] or at least before I had an opportunity to read it. I read it, though, before I put the finishing touches on my articles. In the main I agreed with him (or he with me, as I prefer to think of it)

[8] 2 vols., Carnegie Institution (Washington, 1933). See especially I, 444–480.

in assessing the economics of slavery, and I was pleased to be able to support a number of my points by citations to his scholarly work. However, we disagreed to some extent on a number of consequential matters. Dr. Gray took a more favorable view than I of the plantation as a form of farm organization, of the average planter as a farm manager and businessman, and of the effectiveness of slaves as farm workers. At the same time, it seemed to me, he took a less favorable view than I of the adaptability of slave labor to nonagricultural pursuits and thought slavery to have been a greater obstacle to the diversification of agriculture and industry in general than I did. I also thought he overestimated the extent to which the institution worked to the disadvantage of nonslaveholding whites.

Professor Harold D. Woodman in a well-considered article, "The Profitability of Slavery: A Hardy Perennial,"[9] puts Dr. Gray's and my writings on the subject in their setting in the extensive historiography of slavery in its economic aspects and gives a fair summary of our views. In brief, he credits us with having delivered "the most telling of the earlier blows struck in the revisionist cause." I might quibble over "cause." I do not believe either of us undertook revision as a *cause*. In his compilation, *Slavery and the Southern Economy*,[10] Professor Woodman puts a couple of extracts from our writings in juxtaposition for the purpose of illustrating divergence of views on one material point. But differences on one point do not, of course, disprove agreement on most points.

In the long interval since I wrote the three essays on the economics of slavery, I have matured my view of it somewhat and have incorporated this more mature assessment in my *History of the American Economic System*. In the later work, I put a somewhat higher estimate upon the adaptability of slavery to industrial pursuits and tried to describe more precisely the rewards or lack of them that slaves received for their labor. Putting the economics of slavery in the setting of the whole course of American economic history, rather than in that of the sectional quarrel over slavery, tends to minimize the importance of the institution among the factors that determined the course of economic development in the great region where it so long persisted.

In this day and age when race relations and inequality of economic opportunity are being passionately discussed, these essays on the

9 *Journal of Southern History*, XIX (August 1963), 303–325.
10 Harcourt, Brace & World, Inc. (New York 1966). See pp. 116–127.

economics of slavery may seem coldly clinical. But the subject was economics and economic history and, in the background, economic causes of secession and the Civil War. We should at least be able to be objective on the economic aspects. Suffice it to say, slavery has always been utterly repugnant to me, but I have never felt that I could add anything useful to the vast literature on the morals of slavery or to that on slavery as a social institution.

The last article in this collection, "A Revaluation of the Period before the Civil War: Railroads," was originally read as a paper in one of the sections of the 1927 meeting of the American Historical Association. It was one of three revaluations of the period. The late Professor Chauncey S. Boucher did "Sectionalism." The writer and subject of the third have escaped me. The latter two papers seem not to have been published. Professor James C. Malin of the University of Kansas arranged the symposium. Upon rereading my paper in connection with the present venture, it appears largely dated. Certainly the lacunae in transportation history I deplored have been filled by a large number of excellent monographs. The challenges I threw out to authors of general economic histories to do a better job of portraying the part played by improved means of transportation in transforming farming, manufacturing, and business organization hardly seem to be in order now. I believe though that some of the suggestions I made to writers of general history or social or constitutional history may still be useful. And the paragraphs at the end of the article on the effects of improved means of transportation and communication on sectionalism still seem to me to be rather fresh and challenging.

It has been an interesting experience to me near the end of my professional career to reread these articles, some of which, at least, were written in bygone days, and to try to assess what part they may have had in the effort of a great number of historians to understand the reasons for strong antebellum sectionalism and the causes of secession and the Civil War. I hope that bringing these scattered essays together in this slender volume may prove useful to students of the period and especially to those who may undertake to write about it or its historiography. The editors and I have agreed to label this collection, "Critical Studies," using "critical" in the historian's sense. I urge those who read these essays to read critically and question whether or to what extent I have observed the canons of historical authorship which I have admonished others to observe or occasionally have charged others with not having observed.

I wish to take this opportunity to thank the publisher and the editors for undertaking this venture in republication and for many courtesies and, especially, for giving me a chance to write this introduction and explain my original motives and intent and state wherein my later researches or ponderings or the writings of others have led me to modify earlier conclusions.

ROBERT R. RUSSEL

January 1970

Critical Studies in Antebellum Sectionalism

1

What Was the
Compromise of 1850?

The following essay originally appeared in *The Journal of Southern History,* XXII (August 1956), 292–309, copyright © 1956 by the Southern Historical Association. It is reprinted here in its entirety by permission of the managing editor of *The Journal of Southern History.* The original pagination appears in brackets.

THIS PAPER IS concerned only with those provisions of the Compromise of 1850 which related to slavery in the territories, that is, the slavery provisions of the acts organizing the territories of New Mexico and Utah. Nothing is ventured here about the admission of California as a state, the fixing of the Texas-New Mexico boundary, the Fugitive Slave Law, or the law on slave trading in the District of Columbia. The slavery provisions of the territorial acts are the ones most frequently misunderstood. They were the hardest to frame and, with the possible exception of the Texas boundary, the hardest to reach agreement upon in Congress. They are the part most necessary to understand if one is to follow intelligently later phases of the sectional struggle over slavery. They represented, it is believed, the heart of the compromise.

Books treating the compromise do not agree or even approximately agree as to what were the actual provisions of the New Mexico and Utah acts relating to slavery. They agree still less as to wherein those provisions represented compromise, that is, as to who conceded what. They do not even agree in their definition of the much used term "squatter sovereignty." Take a brief look at the college textbooks; we are entitled to expect to find in them the closest approach to accuracy.

Four college textbooks blandly state that New Mexico and Utah territories were organized "without mention" of slavery or "without provisions" regarding slavery.[1] A fifth textbook states that the

---

1 Leland D. Baldwin, *The Stream of American History* (2 vols., New York, 1952), I, 724; Asa E. Martin, *History of the United States* (2 vols., rev. ed., Boston, 1946), I, 715; Avery Craven and Walter Johnson, *The United States: Experiment in Democracy* (Boston, 1947), 358, 360; Robert E. Riegel and David F. Long, *The American Story* (2 vols., New York, 1955), I, 302.

territories were organized "with no provision for slavery during the territorial period" but adds that the states which might be made from the territories were to be admitted with or without slavery as their constitutions might prescribe at the time of their admission.[2] Six other textbooks tell of the organization of the two territories without mentioning any other provision as to slavery than the statehood provision and, so, imply that there was no other.[3] Three of the six say that the territories were organized "without the Wilmot Proviso" and then give the statehood provision; they do not explain what the status of slavery would be in a territory organized "without the Wilmot Proviso."[4] Six other college textbooks state that the territorial acts provided the "popular sovereignty" or "squatter sovereignty" as to slavery during the territorial period. They mention no other slavery provision and, so, imply that there was no other.[5] These six give three substantially different definitions of popular sovereignty. Five additional textbooks, in addition to stating one, or the other, or both of the provisions heretofore mentioned, state a third slavery provision of the territorial acts, namely, one for the submission of the question of the status of slavery in the territories to the Supreme Court of the United States.[6] No two of the five in this class agree very closely, though, as to how, and when, and in what form the question might be submitted to the Supreme Court or what the

---

[2] Oliver P. Chitwood, Frank L. Owsley, and H. C. Nixon, *A Short History of the American People* (2 vols., New York, 1945-1952), I, 638-39.

[3] Arthur C. Bining and Philip S. Klein, *A History of the United States* (2 vols., New York, 1950-1951), I, 540; Harry J. Carman and Harold C. Syrett, *A History of the American People* (2 vols., New York, 1952), I, 571-73; Samuel E. Morison and Henry S. Commager, *The Growth of the American Republic* (2 vols., 4th ed., New York, 1950), I, 604, 606; James G. Randall, *The Civil War and Reconstruction* (New York, 1937), 124; Merle Curti and others, *An American History* (2 vols., New York, 1950) I, 518; Ralph V. Harlow, *The Growth of the United States* (2 vols., New York, 1943), I, 458-59.

[4] The last three textbooks mentioned in the preceding footnote. But, Randall, in a flash back on page 129, says the "principle of popular sovereignty" had been applied.

[5] Clement Eaton, *A History of the Old South* (New York, 1949), 544; John D. Hicks, *The Federal Union* (New York, 1952), 498, 525; Homer C. Hockett, *The Constitutional History of the United States* (2 vols., New York, 1939), II, 226-228; F. L. Paxson, *History of the American Frontier, 1763-1893* (Boston, 1924), 379-80; George M. Stephenson, *American History to 1865* (New York, 1940), 498; Carl B. Swisher, *American Constitutional Development* (Boston, 1943), 239, 240.

[6] Dwight L. Dumond, *A History of the United States* (New York, 1942), 390-94; A. H. Kelly and W. A. Harbison, *The American Constitution: Its Origin and Development* (New York, 1948), 374; A. C. McLaughlin, *A Constitutional History of the United States* (New York, 1935), 531-34; Jeannette P. Nichols and Roy F. Nichols, *The Republic of the United States: A History*

status of slavery was to be until the Supreme Court should have handed down its decision. In summary, twenty-two college textbooks give at least twelve substantially different descriptions of the slavery provisions of the New Mexico and Utah territorial acts of 1850.

If we turn from the textbooks to longer general accounts, we still find indefiniteness or lack of agreement. Take, for one, James Ford Rhodes's *History of the United States from the Compromise of 1850.* Surprising as it may seem, although Rhodes devotes one hundred pages to the enactment of the compromise measures, he nowhere clearly states what the slavery provisions of the territorial bills were. In one place he says the Omnibus Bill provided for territorial governments "without the Wilmot proviso" and in another says the Utah bill was "without the interdiction of slavery."[7] These glimpses are manifestly inadequate. In the good, substantial *American Nation: A History,* the appropriate volume is George P. Garrison's *Westward Extension.* It says: "The crux of the compromise was the territorial clause of the New Mexico and Utah acts, which read as follows: "Provided that, when ready for statehood, 'the said Territory . . . shall be admitted into the Union, with or without slavery, as their Constitution may prescribe at the time of admission.' "[8] Since other books state other provisions, Garrison's statement does not satisfy. Allan Nevins's account of the Compromise of 1850 is even longer than Rhodes's. Yet Nevins nowhere states clearly what provisions the compromise measures contained relative to slavery in the territories. In one place he implies that "the people of the Territories should be allowed to decide for themselves whether they should have slavery." In another place he indicates that the territorial acts were "without any stipulations for or against slavery." In the next paragraph he implies that the principle adopted was for Congress to refrain from all legislation on the subject while the territories remained in the territorial stage, "leaving it to the people of such Territory, when they have attained to a condition which entitles them to admission

---

(2 vols., New York, 1942), I, 500; Fred W. Welborn, *The Growth of American Nationality, 1492-1865* (New York, 1943), 751. I have no quarrel with the account by Kelly and Harbison or that by Wellborn on any consequential matter.

[7] James Ford Rhodes, *History of the United States from the Compromise of 1850* (7 vols., New York, 1893-1906), I, 99-198. The quotations are from pages 172 and 181.

[8] George P. Garrison, *Westward Extension, 1841-1850* (New York, 1906), 331.

as a State, to decide for themselves the question of the allowance or prohibition of domestic slavery."9

If there is a published monograph devoted to the Compromise of 1850 and including its territorial aspects, the present writer has been unable to find it. There is, however, one good scholarly article. It was by the late Frank Heywood Hodder and is entitled "The Authorship of the Compromise of 1850."10 As the title suggests, Professor Hodder was principally concerned with determining the authorship of various parts of the compromise; but incidentally he outlined the main features of the compromise and, it is believed, in a generally satisfactory manner. This article has been insufficiently noticed by those who have written on the subject.

There is no sufficient justification for the failure of our historians to agree substantially as to what were the slavery provisions of the New Mexico and Utah acts. A careful reading of the acts themselves and their legislative history seems to make them entirely clear. The legislative history of a law does not determine its meaning; but it helps us to locate the germane parts, and it usually is our best available supporting evidence as to the intent of the framers.

The New Mexico act contained eighteen sections exclusive of the one about the Texas boundary; the Utah act contained seventeen sections. Except for names and boundaries the two acts were practically identical. Most of the sections were stock; that is, they were identical, or nearly so, with the corresponding sections of earlier territorial acts, of which there had been a large number. Only those few sections which contained references to slavery need detain us here.11

One section (number 5 of the New Mexico act, 4 of the Utah) vested the legislative power and authority of the territory in "the governor and a legislative assembly." This was a stock clause. It gave the governor the veto power.

Another section (number 7 in the New Mexico act, 6 in the Utah) read as follows: ". . . the legislative power of the Territory shall ex-

---

9 Allan Nevins, *The Ordeal of the Union* (2 vols., New York, 1947), I, 229-345. The quotations are from pages 273 and 311-12.

10 Frank H. Hodder, "The Authorship of the Compromise of 1850," in *Mississippi Valley Historical Review* (Cedar Rapids, 1914-   ), XXII (March 1936), 525-36.

11 The texts are conveniently found in Francis Newton Thorpe (comp.), *The Federal and State Constitutions, Colonial Charters, and Other Organic Laws* . . . (7 vols., Washington, 1909), V, 2615-22 (New Mexico), VI, 3687-93 (Utah).

tend to *all rightful subjects of legislation*,12 consistent with the Constitution of the United States and the provisions of this act; but no law shall be passed interfering with the primary disposal of the soil; no tax shall be imposed upon the property of the United States; nor shall the lands or other property of nonresidents be taxed higher than the lands or other property of residents. All the laws passed by the legislative assembly and governor shall be submitted to the Congress of the United States and, if disapproved, shall be null and of no effect."

These were innocent-looking clauses, but they were the ones that packed the dynamite. They meant and were intended to mean that the territorial legislatures might legislate on the subject of slavery either to prohibit it, or to establish it, or to regulate it. The legislative history of the bills makes this so clear that he who runs may read.

In the Senate Henry Clay's famous eight resolutions outlining a proposed general settlement of all the matters then in dispute were referred along with sundry other resolutions and bills to a select committee of thirteen. The committee of thirteen reported two bills and an amendment to another. One bill was the so-called Omnibus Bill. It covered the matters of California, the territories of New Mexico and Utah, and the Texas-New Mexico boundary. As to the territories, the Omnibus Bill contained the stock sections just quoted, but with the insertion of six words that altered their whole character in so far as slavery was concerned. The six words were "nor in respect to African slavery," and they were so inserted as to make the bill read: ". . . the legislative power . . . shall extend to all rightful subjects of legislation . . . but no law shall be passed interfering with the primary disposal of the soil, nor in respect to African slavery."13 This wording recognized that slavery was a "rightful" subject of legislation but forbade the territorial legislatures to touch it.

This restriction on the legislatures had been put in by a bare majority of the committee over the opposition of Clay, Lewis Cass, and others.14 Efforts to get the restriction removed in the Senate were staunchly resisted. Strongly antislavery senators wanted the clause retained because they believed it would leave the Mexican laws in effect; those laws prohibited slavery. Strongly proslavery senators also favored the retention of the restriction. They believed that

---

12 All italics are mine throughout this article except where they are conventional.

13 The text of the controversial portions of the Omnibus Bill as reported from the committee of thirteen is in *Cong. Globe*, 31 Cong., 1 Sess., 947-48.

14 *Ibid.*, 948-50, 955, 1003, 1829-30, App., 902, 1463

Mexican laws had ceased to have validity when the Treaty of Guadalupe Hidalgo had gone into effect and that the courts would so hold. They believed that the territories were accordingly without valid laws prohibiting slavery at the time and the restrictive clause would prevent the legislatures from enacting any new laws inimical to the institution. Thus there was in the Senate for a time an unnatural combination of Northern and Southern extremists against moderates.

The clause forbidding the legislatures to legislate on the subject of slavery remained in the Omnibus Bill for many weary weeks. It was modified somewhat. On June 5 Stephen A. Douglas moved in the committee of the whole to strike it out. His motion was defeated 21 to 33.15 Eventually, though, the friends of compromise discovered that the retention of the restriction was likely to kill the bill. On July 30 Moses Norris, Democrat of New Hampshire, moved again, in the whole Senate, to strike it out, and this time the motion carried 32 to 19, after nearly two days of thorough debate.16 The restriction on the legislatures having been removed, it was understood by all concerned that the legislatures were left entirely free to legislate on slavery as well as on all other "rightful" subjects not expressly removed from their province by the bill. It is difficult to see how there ever could come to be any other understanding of the meaning of this provision and of the intent of the majority in Congress.

As for the veto power of the territorial governors and the provision that laws passed by the legislatures and approved by the governors might nevertheless be disallowed by Congress, little was said in the debates. A governor's veto or a congressional disallowance of a law on the matter of slavery was apparently considered a remote contingency.17 Furthermore, the veto and the disallowance had to be included to prevent Utah from legalizing polygamy.

Let us turn now to the provisions of the territorial laws that provided for or related to appeals to the Supreme Court of the United States in cases involving slaves or slavery in the territories. The provisions are rather long, but it is necessary to quote them. After the usual provisions for setting up territorial courts, prescribing their jurisdictions,

---

15 *Ibid.,* 1134, 1135.

16 *Ibid.,* 1482, 1490, App., 1463-73.

17 They were mentioned, however. *Ibid.,* App., 1469, remarks of John M. Berrien of Georgia and Solomon W. Downs of Louisiana. In order to make squatter sovereignty more nearly complete, the framers of the Kansas-Nebraska Act (1854) permitted the legislature to pass laws over the governor's veto by a two-thirds majority and omitted the requirement that laws be submitted to Congress for approval..

and regulating appeals from one to another and to the Supreme Court of the United States, the territorial acts continued:

. . . . except only that in all cases involving title to *slaves,* the said writs of error or appeals shall be allowed and decided by the said Supreme Court [of the United States] *without regard to the value* of the matter, property, or title in controversy; and except also that a writ of error or appeal shall also be allowed to the Supreme Court of the United States from the decision of the said Supreme Court created by this act, or of any judge thereof, or of the District Courts created by this act, or of any judge thereof, upon any writ of habeas corpus involving the question of *personal freedom;* . . . and the said Supreme and District Courts of the said Territory, and the respective judges thereof, shall and may grant writs of habeas corpus in all cases in which the same are grantable by the judges of the United States in the District of Columbia.[18]

Another provision that was closely related to the matter of judicial determination and appeals was, as stated in the Utah act: ". . . the Constitution and laws of the United States are hereby extended over and declared to be in force in said Territory of Utah, so far as the same, or any provision thereof, may be applicable." The corresponding provision of the New Mexico act was different in wording but identical in meaning.[19]

What did these detailed provisions mean, and why were they put in the New Mexico and Utah acts? It is again necessary to turn to their legislative history.

Southerners of the stricter states' rights school had lately espoused a view or doctrine with regard to slavery in the territories which may be labeled, in default of a better term, the property-rights doctrine. It was briefly this: Under the Constitution, the territories are the common property of the states that comprise the Union. The federal government is only the agent of the states in administering that property and must administer it for the benefit of all the states. The citizens of the several states have the constitutional right to go into the common territories and take with them the property, of whatever classes, they have legally held in their respective states. In the territories they have the right to continue to hold that property and be protected in its possession and use by the laws, the courts, and the police officers of the territories. According to this doctrine, slaveholders from slaveholding states of the Union had the right to take their slaves into the territories and there hold them as slaves and control them and have

___

18 Sec. 10 in the New Mexico act, sec. 9 in the Utah.

19 Sec. 17 in both acts.

protection for their property therein.20 Whether the proponents of this doctrine thought it also a constitutional right for citizens from slaveholding states to have property in children born of slave mothers in the territories and to buy and sell slaves there does not clearly appear; but presumably they did.

The advocates of the property-rights doctrine made persistent and determined efforts to get their view accepted by Congress and embodied in the Omnibus Bill and every other territorial bill. They were always defeated by substantial majorities. No Northern senator or representative accepted their view of the Constitution, and many Southern Whigs and Jacksonian Democrats, including Clay, Thomas Hart Benton, and Alexander H. Stephens, also rejected it. In the course of the debates, however, Clay and others frequently reminded their states' rights colleagues that the courts were open and that, if their doctrine was sound, the courts would no doubt so decide.21 Thereupon the proponents of the property-rights doctrine turned their efforts, as second best, to (1) clearing the way for an early test of their contention in the courts and (2) insuring that, if the prospective court decision should be in their favor, slavery would have the protection not only of the courts but of positive law and the police officers of the territories as well. Southern congressmen frankly admitted that, no matter what the Supreme Court might say, slavery could not exist in the territories unless sustained by positive law and effective police action.22

It will be remembered that the Omnibus Bill in its original form forbade the territorial legislatures of New Mexico and Utah to legislate *"in respect to* African slavery." After long and bitter debates the advocates of the property-rights doctrine prevailed upon the Senate to accept an amendment proposed by John M. Berrien of Georgia, which made the clause in question read: "The legislative power of said territory shall extend to all rightful subjects of legislation . . . but no law shall be passed . . . *establishing or prohibiting* African slavery." This rewording was understood to leave the territorial legislatures with the power, and presumably the duty, to enact legislation to protect

---

20 This doctrine had first been clearly stated by Robert Barnwell Rhett of South Carolina in the House, January 15, 1847. *Cong. Globe,* 29 Cong., 2 Sess., App., 244-46. John C. Calhoun embodied it in a set of resolutions, February 19, 1847. *Ibid.,* 455. During the debates on the compromise measures, the best expositions of the doctrine were made by Senator Berrien of Georgia, a former attorney general of the United States. See especially his speech of February 11-12, 1850. *Ibid.,* 31 Cong., 1 Sess., App., 202-11.

21 *Ibid.,* 31 Cong., 1 Sess., 1004, App., 424.

22 *Ibid.,* 1004 (Jefferson Davis), App., 1386 (Robert M. T. Hunter).

property in slaves if the courts should decide that under the Constitution slavery was legal in all the territories of the United States and might not be prohibited. The vote on the amendment was 30 to 27.23

On June 6 David L. Yulee of Florida proposed, also as an amendment to the Omnibus Bill: "That the Constitution and laws of the United States are hereby extended over, and declared to be in force in the said territory of Utah, so far as the same or any provision thereof may be applicable." Yulee explained his object clearly. He was trying, as he supposed those who had voted for the Berrien amendment had been, to put the bill in the same form as the proposed Clayton compromise of 1848. The idea of John M. Clayton's bill had been "to throw both parties on their constitutional rights, removing all obstructions to a fair test, and facilitating an early trial." Daniel Webster and others had contended that the Constitution did not extend to the territories *ex proprio vigore*. The courts might take the same view. To narrow the issue to rights under the Constitution and permit no side-stepping, Yulee was proposing to extend the Constitution to the territories. His amendment was adopted 30 to 24.24

Then with John P. Hale of New Hampshire, a Free Soiler, taking the leading part, the Senate adopted the careful provisions, quoted above, on appeals from the territorial courts to the Supreme Court of the United States. These were designed to insure that no conceivable sort of case involving the alleged constitutional right of slaveholders to take slaves into the territories concerned and hold them in servitude should be finally decided by any court except the highest court in the land. These provisions were adopted without a division.25 The prevailing idea seems to have been that, if the states' rights people were to have their day in court, it must be in the highest court and with no obfuscation of the issue.

As the Omnibus Bill then stood, it still forbade the territorial legislatures to establish slavery or to prohibit it, and it neither affirmed nor denied the validity of Mexican laws on the subject. But on July 31, as we have already seen, the Senate struck out the restriction on the power of territorial legislatures and left them with full power to legislate on slavery as a "rightful subject," subject to veto by a governor

---

23 *Ibid.*, 1003-1007, 1018-19, 1083-88, 1113-22, 1131-34, 1379, App., 1467 (Berrien's explanation).

24 *Ibid.*, 1144-46.

25 But after an illuminating debate. *Ibid.*, 31 Cong., 1 Sess., 1212, 1379-80, 1585, App., 897-902. The judiciary provisions as finally adopted were almost identical with those of the Clayton Bill of 1848. The text of the latter is in *Cong. Globe,* 30 Cong., 1 Sess., 1002-1005.

or disapproval by Congress itself. In what status did this leave the provision for appeals to the Supreme Court?

In the first place it should be entirely clear that Congress did not try to wash its hands of the question of slavery in the territories and leave it to the Supreme Court. It gave power to legislate upon the subject to the territorial legislatures, gave power to veto legislation upon the subject to territorial governors (officials appointed by the President with the consent of the Senate), and itself retained the right to disallow such legislation. The appeals provisions meant only that Congress recognized that a case might be got up to test the extent of its power to legislate on the subject of slavery in the territories and to confer upon a territorial legislature the power to prohibit or restrict slavery and that Congress was willing to have its powers so tested in the courts. No one in Congress suggested that the courts be denied jurisdiction of any slave cases that might arise. Such a thing has rarely been done.

The appeals provisions did not even insure that the Supreme Court would have an early opportunity to pass upon the constitutional issues that had been raised. The court must await an actual case; that might be a long time coming. Presumably a case would reach the court in some such manner as this: One of the territorial legislatures must first either confirm the Mexican laws prohibiting slavery or enact new ones to the same effect. Then a slaveowner from one of the states of the Union must bring a slave he had owned there into the territory and hold him or attempt to hold him in servitude. Next, the alleged slave must sue the master or would-be master in a court of the territory for false arrest, or charge him with assault and battery, or apply to a judge for a writ of habeas corpus directed to the person who was holding him in servitude. Finally, the territorial court must make a decision and the decision be appealed to the Supreme Court of the United States. In fact no case involving "title to slaves" or "the question of personal freedom" ever came to the Supreme Court from either New Mexico or Utah. The famous Dred Scott case, which was made to involve the powers of Congress as to slavery in the territories, came by a different route.

Congress did not give a pledge in the New Mexico and Utah acts to carry out the decision of the Supreme Court if that decision should uphold the property-rights doctrine. That is another sort of thing that is not done. Southern defenders of the doctrine did not ask for such a pledge. They had reason, however, to presume that Congress would take whatever measures might seem necessary to secure citizens in their constitutional rights as those rights should be defined by the

Supreme Court in its interpretation of the Constitution. And Southern people were entitled to be disappointed and embittered when their Northern brethren refused to abide by and carry out that decision as they did refuse to accept and implement the Dred Scott decision.

Another section of the territorial bills (number 2 of the New Mexico act, 1 of the Utah) contained this provision: ". . . when admitted as a State, the said territory, or any portion of the same, shall be received into the Union, with or without slavery, as their constitution may prescribe at the time of their admission." What did this section amount to? Let us again look at the record.

The statehood provision was first introduced, with different wording, by Senator Pierre Soulé of Louisiana, June 15, as an amendment to the Omnibus Bill. Soulé's declared object was to try to put Northern senators and representatives on record as promising not to oppose the admission of a slave state if one should apply. His amendment was adopted by a vote of 38 to 12 in the Senate after a protracted argument as to what its use would be. The House refused by a vote of 58 to 85 to strike it out.26 Only strong Wilmot Proviso men voted against the amendment. They refused to make any pledge, and they told Soulé that the amendment was useless, since one Congress could not bind a successor. Other senators seemed to think there was little likelihood that a qualified territory would be refused admission to statehood because of a constitution permitting slavery and, therefore, Soulé's amendment was immaterial. Thus the statehood part of the Compromise of 1850 was a promise by one Congress that a later Congress would not refuse to admit Utah, or New Mexico, or any part thereof for the reason that it would come into the Union as a slave state. That promise was intended to be reassuring to the South. It was certainly not the "crux of the compromise."27

The statehood provision did not mean, as so many books imply, that Congress was *conferring* upon new states the right to decide for themselves whether they should be slave or free. The Constitution gave them the right. Almost everyone in Congress recognized that they possessed the right. That had practically been demonstrated and agreed upon thirty years before at the time of the Missouri Compromise.

When informed people of the day used the term "squatter sover-

---

26 *Ibid.*, 31 Cong., 1 Sess., 1238-39, 1379, 1773, App., 902-11 (debate).

27 Those who have exaggerated the importance of this provision have perhaps been led to do so by a misleading passage in Alexander H. Stephens, *A Constitutional View of the Late War Beween the States* (2 vols., Philadelphia, 1870), II, 217-20.

eignty" or "popular sovereignty" they meant the right of a *territory* (not of a *State*) to decide for itself what to do with regard to slavery during the *territorial stage.* Congress in the Utah and New Mexico acts gave the power to make that decision to the legislatures of the respective territories. No other method of exercising "squatter sovereignty" can properly be wrung out of the acts.

The slavery provisions of the New Mexico and Utah acts differed considerably from Henry Clay's proposals in his famous eight compromise resolutions. They differed still more widely from the provisions of the Omnibus Bill as originally reported by the committee of thirteen. No one man was their author—neither Clay, nor Webster, nor Douglas.[28] They were hammered out line by line and word by word in the Senate by sixty men every one of whom had very definite ideas as to just what they should be and many of whom were among the best constitutional lawyers in the country. The House did not materially change any of these slavery provisions as they came from the Senate.[29] The House influenced them, however; for the Senate leaders in charge were in constant touch with House leaders and knew rather well what the House would accept and what it would not accept.[30] Passage in the House was recognized as the big hurdle.

Now let us summarize the slavery provisions of the New Mexico and Utah acts and their intent. *First and principally,* the territorial legislatures were given full power to legislate on slavery, subject to a possible veto by the governor or a possible disallowance by Congress. That was squatter or popular sovereignty. *Second,* if one or both of the territories should prohibit slavery and if any sort of a slave case should

---

[28] *Cf.* Hodder, "The Authorship of the Compromise of 1850," and Holman Hamilton, "Democratic Senate Leadership and the Compromise of 1850," in *Mississippi Valley Historical Review.* XLI (December 1954), 403-18.

[29] It has not seemed necessary to follow the fortunes of the various bills here. The succession is made very clear in Professor Hodder's article. Briefly: The Committee on Territories, Stephen A. Douglas, chairman, put California in one bill and the matters of the Texas-New Mexico boundary and the organization of New Mexico and Utah territories in another. The committee of thirteen, not Clay, put all these matters in one bill, the so-called Omnibus. The provisions in regard to slavery in the territories were hammered out in perfecting the territorial parts of the Omnibus Bill. The Senate, not Douglas, broke up the Omnibus Bill into four, not five, bills. The House united the Senate Texas Boundary and New Mexico bills, and the Senate accepted this combination. The matters of fugitive slaves and slave trading in the District of Columbia had never been in the Omnibus Bill. These are simple and not very important matters; but most books mention them, and few get them straight.

[30] Hodder, "The Authorship of the Compromise of 1850," and George Fort Milton, *The Eve of Conflict: Stephen A. Douglas and the Needless War* (Boston, 1934), chs., iv, v, give numerous illustrations.

arise under that prohibition, the case could go on appeal to the Supreme Court, could not be withheld therefrom because of any technicality Congress had been able to foresee, and the Supreme Court would then have to pass on the question whether Congress had the power under the Constitution to exclude slavery from the territories or to confer upon a territorial legislature the power to do so. *Third*, a promise was given that a future Congress would not refuse to admit New Mexico, Utah, or any part thereof as a state for the reason that it would be a slave state or that it would be a free state.

These were the slavery provisions of the New Mexico and Utah acts. It is understood, of course, that the provisions were not the compromise. The essence of compromise is mutual concessions for the sake of agreement. To know what the compromise was, we must know who conceded what. But one cannot determine what the Compromise of 1850 was until he knows what the provisions of the compromise measures were.

It is admitted, as a possibility, that the slavery provisions of the territorial acts could have been themselves a concession by one side to secure the consent of the other to the passage of one or more of the other compromise measures. It is believed, however, that the territorial acts did contain mutual concessions, that these concessions were an important part of the Compromise of 1850, and that in the main the territorial bills stood on their own merits. It is true that a number of senators and representatives voted for them as a part of a general scheme of adjustment who would not have done so if they had stood entirely alone.

Let us look first at the slavery provisions of the territorial acts from the viewpoint of the proslavery people. Strongly proslavery men had been determined that the territories should be opened to slavery. They were striving desperately to get new slave states into the Union so that they could maintain a balance in the United States Senate friendly to their "peculiar institution." They had long since lost control of the House. They thought they must maintain a balance, or something approaching a balance, in the Senate if they were to continue to ward off federal legislation inimical to slavery. They believed slaveholders had a constitutional right to take slaves into the territories and hold them and that neither Congress nor a territorial legislature could constitutionally deny them that right. Slaveholders did not want to be denied any rights. They did not want to be denied the opportunity to settle in the territories if the territories should prove attractive. Most proslavery people saw nothing in the climate or soil of Utah and New Mexico or in the occupations or probable occupations of the settlers to make slavery impractical or unprofitable there; and, indeed, there was nothing.[31] They believed that if these territories could be opened to slavery, slaveholders would move into them with their slaves, and, in due course of time, the majority of the people there would come to accept slavery and the territories would become slave states. The territorial acts held out only a modicum of hope to these men.

The territorial acts did not open the territories to slavery. They neither explicitly nor implicitly recognized the alleged constitutional right of slaveholders from states of the Union to take slaves into the territories and hold them in slavery there. The territories had been free under Mexican laws and were likely to remain free. There was only a bare chance that a large enough number of Southern people friendly to slavery would migrate into the territories to get laws enacted in one or both territories legalizing slavery. There was also only a bare possibility that the appeals provisions would bear fruit. Some slaveholder might assume the risk of taking slaves into one of the territories and trying to hold them there in violation of the laws against slavery, which in all probability would prevail. In such an event, a test case would go to the Supreme Court. If then the Supreme Court should decide that the property-rights view of the Constitution was valid, as extreme states' rights people hoped and professed to believe it would, the territories would be legally open to slavery. Then, if the Supreme Court decision could be implemented by territorial or federal legislation, the territories would actually be open to slavery. Then, if slavery should flourish there, the territories might someday become slave states.[32] These possibilities were slender comfort to the South.

Only one feature of the territorial acts, in so far as they affected slavery, was entirely satisfactory to all proslavery men: There was nothing in the acts which pronounced or even implied a moral judgment against slavery.[33] Practically all the Southern people had been determined that nothing should be put in an act of Congress stigma-

---

31 I have argued at some length the point of what determined the profitability of slaveholding in "The Economic History of Negro Slavery in the United States," in *Agricultural History* (Chicago, 1927-   ), XI (October 1937), 308-21. *Cf.* Charles W. Ramsdell, "The Natural Limits of Slavery Expansion," in *Mississippi Valley Historical Review*, XVI (September 1929), 151-71.

32 After the Dred Scott Decision (1857) had been made, the legislature of New Mexico enacted a law for the protection of slave property. The Census of 1860 showed no slaves in New Mexico, 29 in Utah, 2 in Kansas, and 15 in Nebraska.

33 One of Clay's compromise resolutions had implied a reproach: "as slavery does not exist by law, and is not likely to be introduced into any territory acquired . . . from Mexico, it is *inexpedient* for congress to provide by law either for its introduction into, or exclusion from, any part of said territory."

tizing slavery as an institution unfit to be extended to new territory. That would have been almost universally regarded in the South as an insult which was "not to be borne" and which would call for resistance to the "last extremity." With the Senate constituted as it was in 1850, there had never been any considerable danger that the Wilmot Proviso itself would be adopted. The largest vote that it received in any form in the critical session was twenty-five in a possible sixty, and that not-withstanding the fact that thirty senators were under instructions from state legislatures to vote for it.34 The danger had been that California would be admitted with its free-state constitution and nothing would be done about settling the territorial question. But the absence from the bills of any sort of "taunt or reproach" was a matter of genuine satisfaction to the Southern people generally. It was sufficient to satisfy that large number who believed the best strategy to pursue in defense of slavery was to refrain from any aggressive campaign to extend the limits of slave territory.

Now let us consider the territorial acts from the viewpoint of antislavery people. Strongly antislavery men had been determined that slavery should not go into the territories under any circumstances. They made it a matter of conscience to vote against any provision that would create even a bare possibility of the extension of slavery. They believed slavery would thrive in Utah and New Mexico if permitted there35 and the only way to be sure of keeping it out was by an act of Congress absolutely prohibiting it. They were greatly disappointed, therefore, by their failure to attach the Wilmot Proviso to the territorial acts.

Milder antislavery people could reconcile themselves to squatter sovereignty in the two particular territories; though not as a general principle applicable to all territories. They could persuade themselves that the existing populations—Mexicans in New Mexico, Mormons in Utah—were so firm in their opposition to slavery that they would never let it get started among them. They were strongly reassured on this point when a convention held in New Mexico during the very time the great struggle was going on in Congress framed a constitution for the prospective state which forbade slavery.36 Or antislavery men of

---

34 Lewis Cass and Alpheus Felch of Michigan, Daniel S. Dickinson of New York, and Webster made no pretense of obeying their instructions. Several other senators, Douglas for one, technically obeyed them but worked for compromise. They often absented themselves when the Proviso was being voted on.

35 See, for example, statement of William H. Seward in his "Higher Law" speech, March 11, *Cong. Globe,* 31 Cong., 1 Sess., App., 266.

36 Roger S. Baldwin, Whig of Connecticut, gave this as a reason why he had reversed his position on the proposed squatter-sovereignty provision between June 5 and July 31. *Ibid.,* App., 1472.

the milder sort could persuade themselves, as Webster seems to have, that slavery was excluded from these territories by "an ordinance of nature." Still milder antislavery men could further salve their consciences, if that was necessary, by rationalizing that they might as well leave the determination of the status of slavery to the territorial legislatures in the first place, for those bodies would determine it in the long run anyway.[37] As for the possibility under the territorial acts that a case might be taken to the Supreme Court and the court might decide in favor of the property-rights view of the Constitution, antislavery people could reassure themselves in several ways: The likelihood that a case would get to the court was remote. At any rate a citizen must have the opportunity to take a question of constitutional rights to court. That could have been done even though the Wilmot Proviso had been in the laws, and the issue would have been substantially the same.[38] In any event the Supreme Court was not likely to accept the property-rights doctrine; for the power of Congress to legislate for the territories in the matter of slavery or let them legislate for themselves was sustained by the practice of over sixty years.

It is a testimonial to the great skill with which the slavery provisions of the territorial bills had been framed that no one, North or South, had to vote contrary to his deep-seated feelings or convictions on slavery in order to get the bills passed. No antislavery man had to vote affirmatively to permit slavery where it was already prohibited. No Northern representative could have brought himself to do that, and several Southerners, including Clay and Benton, could not have done it either. No antislavery man had to feel that by his vote he was even making probable the establishment of slavery in a region where it did not already exist. No proslavery man had to vote directly to exclude slavery anywhere. No proponent of the property-rights view of slavery in the territories had to betray his views. Of course, many members of both houses and of both sections could not bring themselves to make even the limited concessions of principle or interests necessary to vote for these acts, and they opposed them to the end. The acts, passed over their stubborn opposition by substantial majorities in the Senate and narrow in the House.

It would be futile to attempt to say which side came off the better in the territorial acts. They were a compromise. The late Professor

---

37 This was the line taken by Douglas and William A. Richardson of Illinois. *Ibid.*, App., 369-70, 423.

38 The Dred Scott case actually arose in Missouri, and judges examined the constitutionality of the provision in the Missouri Compromise of 1820 prohibiting slavery in a portion of the Louisiana Purchase.

Hodder thought "The Compromise was more largely . . . a southern measure than a northern one." He had reference to the compromise measures as a whole.39 As to the territorial bills alone, there is no question that a larger proportion of Southern Congressmen than of Northern voted for them. In the Senate 21 Southerners voted for the Utah bill, and only 2 against it; 11 Northern men voted for it, and 16 against it. In the House 56 Southerners voted for it, and 15 against it; 41 Northerns voted for it, and 70 against it.40 But this distribution by no means proves that the territorial acts were more favorable to the proslavery cause. The proslavery party was the weaker of the two. Proslavery men had to make greater concessions to effect a settlement. They were more in need of an immediate settlement. Time and the trend of events favored the other side.

---

39 Hodder, "The Authorship of the Compromise of 1850," 535.

40 *Cong. Globe*, 31 Cong., 1 Sess., App., 1485 (Senate vote), 1776 (House). The votes on the Utah bill were more of a test on the slavery provisions than those on the New Mexico bill, for the latter was always involved with the Texas boundary dispute.

2

The Issues in the Congressional Struggle over the Kansas–Nebraska Bill, 1854

The following essay originally appeared in *The Journal of Southern History*, XXXIX (May 1963), 187–210, copyright © 1963 by the Southern Historical Association. It is reprinted here in its entirety by permission of the managing editor of *The Journal of Southern History*. The original pagination appears in brackets.

I T IS THE PURPOSE IN THIS ARTICLE TO DISCUSS ONLY THE PUBLIC issues in the congressional struggle over the Kansas-Nebraska bill. It is not proposed to discuss the personal or political motives of Stephen A. Douglas, Salmon P. Chase, Franklin Pierce, Jefferson Davis, and other central figures. It is intended to imply, however, that one can not write satisfactorily on these latter matters unless he understands what the public issues were, what the provisions of the Kansas-Nebraska bill were in its successive versions, and how those provisions were calculated to affect the resolution of the issues involved.

The struggle over the Kansas-Nebraska bill involved other important matters besides slavery in the territories, namely, territorial government in general, public lands policy, Indian policy, and the choice of a route or routes for railroads to the Pacific coast. But here we shall be concerned only with the paramount matter of slavery. On the final passage of the bill probably not as many as five votes in both houses together turned principally or even largely on the bearing the bill might be expected to have on any issue other than slavery.

All of the territory proposed to be organized by the Kansas-Nebraska bill lay north of the parallel of 36° 30′, and nearly all of it lay within the limits of the Louisiana Purchase.[1] And by the eighth section of the Missouri Enabling Act of 1820, commonly called the Missouri Compromise, slavery had been "forever prohibited" in all the Louisiana Purchase north of the parallel of 36° 30′ except within the limits of the contemplated state of Missouri. The general issue in the Kansas-Nebraska struggle was, accordingly: Should the Missouri Compromise settlement be disturbed and, if so, what other provisions with regard to slavery should be substituted?

The debates and the voting in Congress on the Kansas-Nebraska bill make it abundantly clear who in that body wanted what with regard to slavery in the territory involved and why. And, as a

[1] The southwest corner west of the 100th meridian and south of the Arkansas River was not a part of the Louisiana Purchase.

matter of fact, Douglas and every other knowledgeable politician knew in advance what various leaders, factions, and groups wanted, for they had all been through the long struggle over slavery in the Mexican Cession, the bitter contests over whether the Compromise measures of 1850 should be accepted in various parts of the country, and more recently the Presidential campaign of 1852.

Southern state rights Democrats and a considerable faction of Southern Whigs had come to hold what may, perhaps, best be denominated the common-property doctrine of the powers of the federal government in the territories. This doctrine or view was briefly as follows: The territories are the common property of the several states, not of the United States as an entity. The federal government necessarily governs the territories but only as agent of or trustee for the common owners, the states. As agent or trustee, it may not discriminate among the states and, accordingly, must allow citizens of the several states to enter the territories freely and on equal terms and take with them any property —slaves, for example—of which they had been lawfully possessed in the respective states from which they had come and must afford such property owners due protection in their property while in the common territories. People who subscribed to the common-property doctrine considered the slavery prohibition of the Missouri Compromise and all similar restrictions to be unconstitutional. They also considered it unconstitutional to leave the decision as to slavery to the territorial governments, for, as they pointed out, a principal—the federal government in this case— could not delegate to its creature, a territorial government, a power of which it was not itself possessed. The only power with regard to slavery Congress might confer upon territorial governments was the power, indeed the obligation, to protect slaveowners in their property rights.[2]

[2] Among the best reasoned statements of the common-property doctrine in the Thirty-Third Congress were those of Senators Robert M. T. Hunter of Virginia and Andrew P. Butler of South Carolina and of Representative William T. S. Barry of Mississippi. *Congressional Globe*, 33 Cong., 1 Sess., app., 221-26, 232-40, and 612-19. In an earlier article (to which I intend this to be a sequel), I denominate the doctrine, the "property-rights doctrine." That term now seems ill-chosen, for it suggests reliance on the protection of property under the due-process-of-law clause of the Fifth Amendment. See R. R. Russel, "What Was the Compromise of 1850?" *Journal of Southern History*, XXII (August 1956), 292-309. See also Arthur Bestor's critique of the common-property doctrine—which he calls "the extra-jurisdictional principle"—in "State Sovereignty and Slavery: A Reinterpretation of Proslavery Constitutional Doctrine, 1840-1860," Illinois State His-

If Southern state rights senators and representatives could have had their way entirely, they would have written into the Kansas-Nebraska Act and into every other territorial measure a declaration of the validity of the common-property doctrine and a requirement that the territorial courts and legislatures afford slaveowners due protection in their property. Such a provision, if enforced in the territories for, say, ten or twenty years might well have resulted in several of them developing into slave states. The common-property doctrine was no mere abstraction. As has been true with many constitutional contentions, it had no doubt been invented because of the practical advantages that might follow its application.[3] Strongly proslavery people had been striving to get new slave states into the Union so as to maintain strength enough in the United States Senate to ward off the passage of legislation inimical to the peculiar institution.

Southern Jacksonian Democrats, of whom there were still many left, especially in the Upper South, did not accept the common-property doctrine. But such had been the shifts and fortunes of politics in recent years that of the large Democratic delegation in the Thirty-Third Congress only one senator, Sam Houston of Texas, was a Jacksonian, and only one representative, Thomas Hart Benton, now in the House after thirty years in the Senate, can be clearly recognized as belonging to that faction. Of thirteen Southern Whig senators at least three, Archibald Dixon of Kentucky, Robert Toombs of Georgia, and John M. Clayton of Delaware, held constitutional views difficult to distinguish from those of the state rights Democrats, and of the twenty-three Southern Whig representatives at least one, John R. Franklin of Maryland, was of the same persuasion.[4]

Not one Northern senator or representative who spoke on the Kansas-Nebraska bill accepted the common-property doctrine or was willing to write it into a piece of legislation. All but a few from the North took the position that Congress had the power to legislate for the territories in all matters and accordingly to

---

torical Society, *Journal,* LIV (Summer 1961), 117-80, and also published separately.

³ The doctrine had first been clearly stated by Robert Barnwell Rhett of South Carolina in the House of Representatives, January 5, 1847; and John C. Calhoun had presented it in a set of resolutions in the Senate, February 19, 1847. *Congressional Globe,* 29 Cong., 2 Sess., app., 244-46, 455.

⁴ So was Thomas L. Clingman of North Carolina who had long been a Whig but now claimed to belong to no party. *Ibid.,* 33 Cong., 1 Sess., app., 489. The party affiliations in the Thirty-Third Congress are taken from *ibid.,* 33 Cong., 1 Sess., 1-2.

delegate to a territorial legislature the power to legislate on slavery and other rightful subjects of legislation.[5] Senator Lewis Cass of Michigan was one of the exceptions. He argued with much learning that Congress had no power whatever to legislate for the territories in matters of local concern except to give each a frame of government and start it on its way.[6] A few other Northern Democrats in Congress, of whom Douglas was not then one, agreed with Cass.[7] All that Cass's view and the common-property doctrine had in common was that according to each the slavery prohibition of the Missouri Compromise was unconstitutional; they differed widely in supporting reasoning. Senator Salmon P. Chase of Ohio presented but did not press the idea, later popular with the new Republican party, that it would be a violation of the due-process-of-law clause of the Fifth Amendment for the federal government to permit slavery in any of the territories.[8]

The large majority of Southern Whigs agreed with the great majority in the North in their view as to the constitutional powers of Congress over slavery in the territories, although they agreed with their state rights colleagues in wanting the Missouri Compromise repealed and the territories opened to slavery.

Next to congressional acceptance and implementation of the common-property doctrine the state rights people wanted most the repeal of the slavery restriction in the Missouri Compromise; and in wanting this they were joined by nearly all other Southerners. The debates on the Kansas-Nebraska bill make it starkly clear that a principal reason Southerners wanted the restriction repealed was that they had come to regard it as an insult and a reproach to their section, a stigma implanted on their institutions by an act of the Congress of their own country. Southerners' denunciations of the Missouri restriction in 1854 were as bitter as their denunciations of the Wilmot Proviso had been in its time. Senator Andrew P. Butler of South Carolina termed it "a festering thorn" in "the side of the South."[9] Senator David R. Atchison of

[5] The best statement of the majority view was that of Senator John Pettit of Indiana, a former judge. *Ibid.*, app., 212-21.

[6] *Ibid.*, 33 Cong., 1 Sess., 456-58; app., 270-79.

[7] Senators Augustus C. Dodge of Iowa, Moses Norris, Jr., of New Hampshire, and Isaac Toucey of Connecticut took the same line. *Ibid.*, 375-83, 305-310, 313-21. Lewis Cass said Jesse D. Bright of Indiana, who was absent because of illness, also agreed. *Ibid.*, 279.

[8] *Ibid.*, 138. Those familiar with Chief Justice Roger B. Taney's opinion in *Dred Scott v. Sanford*, 19 U. S. 393 (1857) will remember that Taney also relied on the due-process clause but used it to protect the master in his "property" rather than the Negro's "liberty," as Chase would have done.

[9] *Congressional Globe*, 33 Cong., 1 Sess., 1309; app., 240.

Missouri called it "infamous"[10] and Representative Philip Phillips of Alabama, a "miserable line, containing as it does a congressional imputation against one half the states."[11] Some Northerners could understand the Southern feeling. Cass said that if he were a Southerner he would regard the restriction as "invidious." "And certainly to remove this bar sinister from the national escutcheon," he continued, "may well furnish a more powerful motive of action to a great community jealous of its honor, than any hope or expectation that its accomplishment will lead to the introduction of slavery into these territories."[12] Senator Truman Smith of Connecticut, who made the most powerful speech against repeal, said, "We know that legislation like the act of 1820 has ever been to them a stumbling block and an offense."[13]

Those Northern senators and representatives who opposed the repeal of the Missouri Compromise restriction or its weakening in any way also made its proposed repeal a matter of conscience but in the opposite way. Slavery was such a violation of the rights of man, they said, such a moral and social evil, that they could not in good conscience vote to permit it to enter or even vote to give it indirectly a chance to enter a territory in which it was not already established. They further said that slavery was so degrading to the dignity of labor that, if slaves should be taken into the territory, even in comparatively small numbers, free workers from the North and immigrants from Europe would shun it and in effect be excluded.[14] The "Appeal of the Independent Democrats" asserted that opening the territory to slavery would "exclude from a vast unoccupied region immigrants from the Old World and free laborers from our own States, and convert it into a dreary region of despotism inhabited by masters and slaves."[15] Of the many Northern members of Congress who for the sake of

[10] *Ibid.*, 33 Cong., 1 Sess., 1303.
[11] *Ibid.*, app., 533.
[12] *Ibid.*, 278.
[13] *Ibid.*, 173.
[14] *Ibid.*, 155, 162, 262-70. In a long teaching career in Northern colleges I have presented the substance of this and the preceding paragraph to thousands of students. A rough estimate is that half understood how it might be a matter of conscience with many congressmen to vote to exclude slavery from the territories and one in ten could believe that Southern congressmen might regard exclusion by law as an insult and a reproach and understand how and why they could do so. Yet no one who can not understand both of these conflicting attitudes and the reasons why people maintained them can understand the causes of secession and civil war.
[15] *Ibid.*, 281-82. Adequate extracts are in Henry Steele Commager (ed.), *Documents of American History* (New York, 1934), 329-31.

national and party harmony were willing to make concessions to the South, not one was willing to vote for any provision of law that would *directly* establish or protect slavery in a territory.

The legislative history of the Kansas-Nebraska Act may be characterized briefly as the territorial aspects of the great congressional slavery struggle of 1846-1850 all over again, but compressed into five months and with most of the bargaining and compromising done in closed committee meetings, conferences of leaders, and caucuses instead of on the floors of the Senate and House, as had been true of the Compromise of 1850.

On December 14, 1853, early in the first session of the Thirty-Third Congress, Augustus C. Dodge of Iowa introduced a bill in the Senate to organize a territory of Nebraska embracing all of the then unorganized territory of the United States lying between the parallels of 36° 30′ and 43° 30′ north latitude.[16] The bill made no mention of slavery, and it was assumed that if enacted it would leave the slavery prohibition of the Missouri Enabling Act in force. Dodge's bill was properly referred to the Committee on Territories, of which Douglas was chairman.

On January 4, 1854, Douglas on behalf of the committee reported the Dodge bill back to the Senate with important amendments and submitted a committee report which explained provisions likely to be controversial and gave or purported to give the reasons why the committee had included those provisions.[17] One amendment pushed the northern boundary of the proposed territory up to the forty-ninth parallel, the national boundary. Other amendments gave the bill provisions with regard to slavery that were all but identical with those of the Utah and New Mexico acts of 1850, provisions which, in those acts, embodied a very significant part of the Compromise of 1850.[18] Putting these provisions in the Nebraska bill, of course, represented considerable concessions to the South.

The most significant slavery provision of this first version of the committee Nebraska bill was as follows: "The legislative power of the territory shall extend to all *rightful subjects* of legislation *consistent with* the Constitution of the United States and the provisions of this act . . . ." A few matters were excluded from

[16] For a description of the Dodge bill, see *Congressional Globe*, 33 Cong., 1 Sess., 221-22.

[17] *Report on Nebraska Territory, Senate Reports*, 33 Cong., 1 Sess., No. 15 (Serial 706). An adequate extract is in Allen Johnson (ed.), *Readings in American Constitutional History, 1776-1876* (Cambridge, Mass., 1912), 426-29.

[18] For a description of the bill, see *Congressional Globe*, 33 Cong., 1 Sess., 222.

this sweeping grant but slavery was not one of them. This provision remained unchanged in the later versions of the bill.[19] It meant that the territorial legislature would have power to legislate on the subject of slavery, either to establish it, exclude it, or make other provision regarding it, unless perchance such legislation should be held unconstitutional by the courts. That this was the meaning of the provision was made unmistakably clear by an explicit statement to that effect in the committee's report and by another section of the bill itself, the germane portion of which reads as follows:

That in order to avoid all misconstruction, it is hereby declared to be the true intent and meaning of this act, so far as the question of slavery is concerned, to carry into practical operation the following propositions and principles, established by the compromise measures of . . . [1850], to wit: First, that all questions pertaining to slavery in the Territories, and in the new States to be formed therefrom are to be left to the decision of the people residing therein, through their appropriate representatives.[20]

The provisions just described, be it noted, would not have repealed or abrogated the slavery prohibition of the Missouri Compromise but would have left it in effect, enforceable in the courts, until the time, if that should ever come, when the territorial legislature should have superseded it with other legislation or the courts should have held it unconstitutional. The said provisions, if enacted, would have left the Missouri Compromise in precisely the same legal position that the Utah and New Mexico acts left the Mexican laws prohibitive of slavery which were in effect in those territories at the time of cession to the United States. These acts left the Mexican laws in effect but gave the territorial legislatures the power to change them and recognized that their constitutionality might be tested in the courts.

The provisions just cited, insofar as they related to territories,

---

[19] All italics except conventional ones are mine throughout the article. See sections 6 and 24 of the Kansas-Nebraska Act, *ibid.*, 1249-53, or in Francis Newton Thorpe (comp.), *The Federal and State Constitutions, Colonial Charters, and Other Organic Laws* . . . (7 vols., Washington, 1909), II, 1161-76. For the New Mexico and Utah acts of 1850, see *ibid.*, V, 2615-22, and VI, 3687-93.

[20] *Congressional Globe*, 33 Cong., 1 Sess., 222. Section 21 did not appear in the bill as originally printed but did in later printings. As it appeared before the debate began and before any amendments were proposed and did not change the meaning anyway, the reason for the delay need not concern us. See Allan Nevins, *Ordeal of the Union* (2 vols., New York, 1947), II, 94-95. Nevins says, "This significant section gave it [the bill] an entirely new meaning"; but he had overlooked the section on legislative power and its intended meaning.

not states, provided, in short, for squatter sovereignty. The term *squatter sovereignty*, which has come to be respectable, is the most satisfactory term in use to designate the thing it designated for both *popular sovereignty* and *nonintervention* applied to states as well as to territories. Furthermore, nonintervention applied to slavery only, not to all "rightful subjects," as did the other two terms, and, as applied to slavery in the territories, it had in 1854, as we shall see, a different connotation in the South from what it had in the North.

Another provision in the committee Nebraska bill relating to slavery was, "and when admitted as a State or States, the said Territory, or any portion of the same, shall be received into the Union, with or without slavery, as their [*sic*] constitution may prescribe at the time of their admission . . . ." This provision did not mean, as so many history books have implied, that the committee was proposing that Congress waive a constitutional power to decide whether a new state should be a free state or a slave state, for only a very few congressmen believed that Congress possessed such a power.[21] Its enactment would simply represent an attempt on the part of the Thirty-Third Congress to pledge future congresses not to refuse to admit a new state from the region involved either because it would be a slave state or because it would be a free state, as the case might be. This provision remained unchanged in the later versions of the bill.[22] It occasioned little controversy.

A third slavery provision in the committee Nebraska bill, copied verbatim from the Utah and New Mexico acts, was designed to insure that any sort of court case that might arise in the proposed territory "involving title to slaves" or "any writ of habeas corpus, involving the question of *personal freedom*" might be appealed to the Supreme Court of the United States; the stock judiciary provision in earlier territorial acts did not insure that a slave case, even though it might involve a constitutional issue, could go any higher than the supreme court of the territory in which it might arise. The more careful appeals provision had been put in the Utah and New Mexico acts to insure that, if the constitutional issue of the powers of Congress over slavery in the territories should be decided in a court, that court would be the highest in

[21] The only identifiable ones are Senator William H. Seward of New York and Representative E. Wilder Farley of Maine. *Congressional Globe*, 33 Cong., 1 Sess., app., 154, 679.
[22] See sections 1 and 19 of the Kansas-Nebraska Act.

the land.[23] This provision also remained unchanged in later versions of the Nebraska bills, and it also occasioned no controversy.[24]

The explanation the Committee on Territories gave in its accompanying report for proposing to disturb the settlement of the slavery question embodied in the Missouri Compromise and substitute the provisions we have just described was to this effect: The "prevailing sentiment" in the South is that the slavery restriction of the Missouri Compromise is unconstitutional and that under the Constitution "every citizen [has] a right to remove to any territory of the Union, and carry his [slave] property with him under protection of the law . . . ." Some "eminent statesmen" in the North hold that "Congress is invested with no rightful authority to legislate on the subject of slavery in the territories" but must leave it to the people of the territories. (This last plainly was a bid for the support of Cass and probably for that of President Pierce.[25]) The prevailing view in the North is that the Missouri restriction is constitutional. "These controverted questions . . . involve the same grave issues which produced the agitation, the sectional strife, and the fearful struggle of 1850." The Compromise measures of that year provided a solution then *and were intended to be applied in similar circumstances in the future*. Both national political parties have endorsed the Compromise of 1850 "with singular unanimity." So let us adopt the slavery provisions of that compromise as the best solution in the present crisis.

If Douglas and his collaborators had ever expected that the committee bill in its original form would be acceptable to a majority in Congress or to a majority of the Democratic members, they were quickly disillusioned. On January 16, Senator Dixon gave notice that he would introduce an amendment providing that the eighth section of the Missouri Compromise Act

shall not be so construed as to apply to the Territory contemplated by this act, or to *any other* Territory of the United States; but that the citizens of the several States or Territories shall be at liberty to take and *hold* their slaves within *any* of the Territories of the United States,

[23] Russel, "What Was the Compromise of 1850?" 292-309.

[24] See sections 9 and 27 of the Kansas-Nebraska Act. The bill also contained provision for the return of fugitive slaves. It caused no debate.

[25] Pierce's views seem not to have been well known. Roy F. Nichols gives only a few hints in his *Franklin Pierce, Young Hickory of the Granite Hills* (Philadelphia, 1958), 139 especially. Another eminent Northern statesman who held the Cass view was former Senator Daniel S. Dickinson, leader of the New York Hards, a faction of the Democratic party of the state which at the time was warring on the Pierce administration over patronage matters.

or of the States to be formed therefrom, as if the said act . . . had never been passed.[26]

It is not likely that Dixon had been authorized to act as spokesman for any faction or group. But, it will be noted, except that he did not demand a congressional declaration of the validity of the common-property doctrine, he had voiced the extreme Southern demands. If his proposed amendment had been adopted *in toto* (it was not), it would not only have repealed the Missouri Compromise but would also have nullified the main feature of the committee bill, namely, squatter sovereignty, and the laws of Oregon, Minnesota, Utah, New Mexico, and Washington territories prohibitive of slavery in addition; for it would have estopped any territorial legislature from prohibiting slaveowners to bring their slaves into that territory and hold them there.

Just what other pressures were applied upon Douglas and his committee off the Senate floor by proslavery representatives does not clearly appear. But that such pressures were applied is evident from what happened later, was freely charged at the time by opponents of the Kansas-Nebraska bill, and was more or less frankly acknowledged by Southern leaders. Said Senator R. M. T. Hunter, of Virginia, for one, "Was it not then an inevitable consequence of the course of events I have depicted that the South should make this request for the repeal of the Missouri Compromise?"[27]

At any rate, on January 23, and still before debate on the bill had formally begun, Douglas on behalf of the Committee on Territories reported a substitute for its first bill that was distinctly more favorable to the proslavery views. The substitute would create two territories (instead of one) in the Nebraska region, one, Kansas, lying between the thirty-seventh and fortieth parallels, the other, Nebraska, extending from the fortieth parallel to the forty-ninth. Except for the names and boundaries, the slavery and other provisions relating to the one territory were identical with those for the other. The substitute retained intact, for each of the proposed territories, the slavery provisions already described, including squatter sovereignty. But a new provision stated that the eighth section of the Missouri Enabling Act "was *superseded* by the *principles* of the legislation of 1850, commonly called the compromise measures, and is declared inoperative."[28]

---

[26] *Congressional Globe*, 33 Cong., 1 Sess., 175.
[27] *Ibid.*, app., 221.
[28] For a description of the substitute, see *ibid.*, 33 Cong., 1 Sess., 222.

The inclusion of the provision declaring the Missouri Compromise inoperative was a great concession to the sensibilities of Southern people and an added shock to those of antislavery folk. But with squatter sovereignty left intact, it is highly questionable that the virtual repeal of the Missouri Compromise would in actual practice increase the likelihood that Kansas and Nebraska or the one or the other would become slaveholding. Under the original committee bill, had it been enacted, a slaveowner presumably would have been afraid to migrate into either territory and take slaves along until and unless the territorial legislature first legalized slavery, for otherwise territorial judges might set their slaves free under the eighth section of the Missouri Act. People from the free states, presumably hostile to slavery, and nonslaveholders from slave states, who might prove also to be opposed to the establishment of the institution, would not be taking such property risks in coming to the territory and would, therefore, be less likely to be deterred from coming. This difference in risks would militate against the legalization of slavery by the very important first legislature or by any subsequent one. Under the committee substitute, if it should be enacted, slaveowners might well be just as hesitant about moving into the territory with their property until and unless the legislature should have first legalized slavery; for until then they could have little assurance that the territorial legislature would not prohibit slavery when it should come to act on the subject or that meanwhile the judges would protect them in their property in the absence of any statute law on the subject—as the majority in Congress certainly assumed would be the case. Indeed, the judges might even enforce the common law principle that slavery can not exist where there is no statute positively establishing it. In short, squatter sovereignty with the Missouri Compromise repealed would have about the same practical result as squatter sovereignty without repeal. In either case squatter sovereignty would weight the scales considerably in favor of freedom. However, the creation of the two territories instead of one, as proposed in the first committee bill, whether designed for that purpose or not, would greatly improve the chances that the South would eventually get another slave state. The proposed Territory of Kansas would lie directly west of Missouri, and it might well be that people friendly to slavery would move into the new territory from that state in sufficient numbers to dominate the early legislatures and get slavery firmly established. But, if the district lying west of Missouri should be included for a time with that lying west of Iowa in a single territory, that single territory almost certainly would choose to be free. Free state people moving into the upper district from and through Iowa would certainly overbalance any majority of slave state people that might enter the lower portion from or through Missouri, and accordingly the critically important early legislatures would almost certainly have free state majorities.[29]

Formal debate on the Kansas-Nebraska bill, as it now was, began in the Senate on January 30. The next day, William A. Richardson of Illinois, chairman of the House Committee on Territories, introduced in the House of Representatives a Kansas-Nebraska bill almost identical with the one before the Senate.[30] Neither bill came regularly before the House until May 8, but many members managed to speak on the bills while other less exciting measures were technically before the House. The House debates were about as long and as able as those in the Senate.

The debates soon revealed that the provision in the bills that virtually repealed the Missouri Compromise was unfortunately worded to say the least. If declaring the Compromise "inoperative" was equivalent to repealing it, why not say "repealed"? And how could a specific prohibition in an act of 1820 have been superseded by the "principles" of the legislation of 1850? Opponents of disturbing the Missouri Compromise had a field day in showing by long quotations from the speeches of the framers of the Utah and New Mexico acts of 1850 that not one of them had at the time believed or even suggested that anything in those acts would supersede, or render inoperative, or weaken the slavery prohibition of the Missouri Compromise. And the influential Senator Cass and other supporters of the bill were unwilling to countenance what they considered a misrepresentation. Furthermore and more serious, Southern state rights members were far from satisfied with the squatter-sovereignty feature of the bills and the lack of any recognition of the common-property doctrine other than the minor provision for insuring a test in the Supreme Court if a case should ever arise in one of the territories involving the constitutionality of an act of its legislature inimical to slavery.[31]

At this critical juncture, the senators favorable in general to the Kansas-Nebraska bill, both Democrats and Whigs, now caucused

[29] *Ibid.*, 1238; app., 645, 871.
[30] *Ibid.*, 33 Cong., 1 Sess., 294-97.
[31] *Ibid.*, 280-81, 337-45; app., 133-45.

several times and worked out a rewording of the troublesome sections. Douglas moved the revised version in the Senate on February 7, with, so he said, "the general concurrence of the friends of the measure."[32] We know next to nothing of what was said in the caucuses. John Pettit of Indiana and Cass were the chief talkers among the Northern Democrats; Albert G. Brown of Mississippi, state rights Democrat, seems to have talked a lot.[33] But "by their fruits ye shall know them." The caucus amendment bears all the earmarks of having been the product of hard bargaining between Northern Democrats and Southern state rights Democrats and Whigs. Other Southern Whigs probably exercised a moderating influence on their state rights colleagues.

For the clause in the pending bill that ran "which [the Missouri Compromise] was *superseded* by the *principles* of the legislation of 1850, commonly called the compromise measures, and is hereby *declared inoperative*," the caucus amendment would substitute, "which *being inconsistent with* the *principle of nonintervention* by Congress with slavery in the States and Territories, as recognized by the legislation of 1850, commonly called the compromise measures, is hereby declared *inoperative and void*." The caucus amendment did not modify the sections of the pending bill giving the territorial legislatures the power to legislate on "all rightful subjects," slavery included. But for the sections saying it was the true intent and meaning to carry into effect the principle, "that all questions pertaining to slavery in the Territories, and in the new States to be formed therefrom, are to be left to the decision of the people residing therein, through their appropriate representatives," the caucus amendment would substitute the following: "it being the true intent and meaning of this act not to legislate slavery into any Territory or State, nor to exclude it therefrom; but to leave the people thereof perfectly free to form and regulate their *domestic institutions* in their own way, subject *only to the Constitution of the United States*."[34]

Declaring the Missouri Compromise "inoperative and void" would appear more decisive to Southern minds than "inoperative" alone but still would not grate as harshly on Northern ears as "repeal." Declaring the Missouri Compromise void because it

[32] *Ibid.*, 33 Cong., 1 Sess., 353.

[33] On caucuses, see *ibid.*, 1310-11; app., 939 ff; New York *Times*, February 4, 6, 1854; and Robert Toombs to W. W. Burwell, February 3, 1854, in Ulrich B. Phillips (ed.), *The Correspondence of Robert Toombs, Alexander H. Stephens, and Howell Cobb* (Washington, 1913), 342.

[34] *Congressional Globe*, 33 Cong., 1 Sess., 353.

was "inconsistent with" the Compromise of 1850 instead of because it had been "superseded by" the Compromise would satisfy the scruples of Cass and others with regard to historical accuracy but would still carry the injunction to the faithful that they were under some sort of moral compulsion to apply the solution of 1850 to the problem of 1854. The assertion in the caucus amendment that the Compromise of 1850 recognized the principle of "nonintervention by Congress with slavery in the States and Territories" was plainly, insofar as it applied to territories, a sop to the state rights wing. While to Northern men and the majority of Southern Whigs "nonintervention in the territories" meant permitting squatter sovereignty—which the Utah and New Mexico acts did plainly permit [35]—to state rights men it meant recognizing a constitutional right of slaveholders to take their slaves into the territories and hold them and to be protected in their property therein. Another concession to the state rights group was the insertion of the phrase, "subject only to the Constitution of the United States," qualifying the grant of squatter sovereignty. This phrase, if enacted, would mean that Congress was admitting that its power to prohibit slavery in the territories or to grant territorial legislatures the power to do so was questionable and that it was not trying to influence a prospective decision of the Supreme Court by asserting or even assuming the constitutionality of its action. No such admission was in the Utah and New Mexico acts.

Northern Whigs and anti-Nebraska Democrats had not attended the caucuses that framed the compromise amendment just described. The Northern Democrats in the caucuses had been outnumbered by Southern Democrats and Whigs approximately two to one. There can be only one reason, therefore, why the Southerners had not forced more concessions, namely, the understanding that to do so would result in the defeat of the bill in the House, if not also in the Senate, and the disruption of the Democratic party. The caucus amendment was approved in the Senate, February 15, 35 to 10.

On the Senate floor, Chase, the most active leader of the opposition, promptly jumped on the principal concession the caucus amendment would make to the South: the qualifying clause, "subject only to the Constitution of the United States." To this he proposed to add, "under which the people of the Territory, through their appropriate representatives, may, if they see fit, *prohibit* the existence of slavery therein." Several Northern Demo-

[35] See Russel, "What Was the Compromise of 1850?"

crats and Southern Whigs friendly to the bill indicated a willingness to support Chase's amendment provided the words "or introduce" were inserted after "prohibit." The amendment thus
changed would have amounted to an assertion by Congress of
its constitutional power to legislate on the subject of slavery in
the territories and of the constitutionality of squatter sovereignty.
The state rights people would have none of that; those friends of
the bill who had indicated an inclination to support the change
shied away; and, when Chase's amendment came to a vote, in
its original form, caucus lines held and it was defeated 36 to 10.[36]

Even after the caucus agreement, in both houses state rights
members continued to expound their common-property doctrine
at every turn. Their objects probably were to try to persuade
themselves and the public that the Missouri Compromise was
being repealed because a majority in Congress believed it to be
unconstitutional—which was not so—and to influence the thinking of Supreme Court justices against the day of decision.

There was naturally some speculation in the course of the
struggle as to how the Supreme Court would decide when and
if a case involving the constitutional issue should come before it.
A few on each side expressed misgivings.[37] But the remarkable
thing is how confident most members seemed to be that the
Court would sustain their particular views. Neither faction or
group tried to exact a pledge from the others to abide by the
expected decision. A few members declared that the bill would
pledge Congress to accept the decision whatever it might be,
and a few promised to abide by it.[38]

The opponents of the Kansas-Nebraska bill employed as their
chief talking point the contention that the substitution for the
Missouri Compromise of another settlement of the slavery question was a gross violation of a "sacred" sectional compact. According to that compact, ran the argument, the North was to consent
to Missouri entering the Union as a slave state and allow Arkansas
to remain open to slavery, and in return the South agreed that

[36] *Congressional Globe*, 33 Cong., 1 Sess., 421-22, 519. Similar amendments
were also defeated in the House. *Ibid.*, 1238-39.
[37] Representatives John R. Franklin of Maryland, Laurence M. Keitt of South
Carolina, Wiley P. Harris of Mississippi, and Henry Bennett of New York did.
Ibid., app., 419, 467, 549, 692.
[38] Taking the position that the bill would pledge Congress to accept the decision were Senator Charles E. Stuart of Michigan and Representatives Laurence
M. Keitt and Wiley P. Harris; promising to abide by the decision were Representatives William H. English of Indiana and William T. S. Barry of Mississippi. *Ibid.*,
286, 467, 549, 606, 618.

forever after slavery should be excluded from all of the Louisiana Purchase north of the line 36° 30′ excepting Missouri. The North had lived up to its agreement. Missouri had been admitted as a slave state. Arkansas had remained a slave territory and in due time had been admitted as a slave state. Now that Kansas and Nebraska are ready for settlement and organization as territories, the South demands that the prohibition on slavery be repealed. How can Southern senators and representatives honorably make such a demand?

Southerners were very sensitive to the charge of broken faith, but their spokesmen were at no loss for a reply. One reasoned reply was that the Missouri Compromise had never been a compact between the sections in any proper sense of the term. The South had been forced by a numerically superior North to accept an unconstitutional and discriminatory prohibition of slavery in the remainder of the Louisiana Purchase in order to prevent a palpably unconstitutional limitation from being imposed on the new state of Missouri as a condition of admission, namely, the gradual abolition of slavery. The most effective Southern reply, however, to the charge of broken faith was *tu quoque.* If, ran this reply, division along a parallel of latitude was a fair settlement for the Louisiana Purchase, it was also a fair settlement for the acquisitions farther west. The South had repeatedly offered to extend the line to the Pacific. President Polk had proposed it. Even John C. Calhoun, Jefferson Davis, and the Nashville Convention had been willing to make such a division, in spite of their view that exclusion of slaveholders with their property from the common territories was clearly unconstitutional. But Northerners would not agree. They had insisted for four years on applying the hateful Wilmot Proviso to all the territory acquired from Mexico, that part south of the line 36° 30′ as well as that north of it, and in the end they had forced the South to accept another compromise which admitted all of California as a free state without its ever having gone through the territorial stage and left the South only the barest chance of ever introducing slavery into Utah or New Mexico. Therefore, the South had been released by the actions of the North from any obligation it may ever have had to regard the Missouri Compromise as a binding contract.[39]

[39] Good arguments on whether or not the Missouri Compromise was still morally binding were those of Salmon P. Chase and William H. Seward, *pro,* and Senator George E. Badger of North Carolina and Representative Alexander H. Stephens, *contra. Ibid.,* 133-40, 150-55, 145-50, 193-97.

It is not likely that the extended arguments as to whether the Missouri Compromise had been a solemn compact or not and, if so, which side had first broken faith changed *directly* a single vote in Congress. But that the South was guilty of a breach of faith certainly gained wide acceptance in the North and contributed powerfully to the outburst of righteous indignation there, and that outburst, in turn, caused many Northern Democrats in Congress, especially in the House, to withdraw their support from the Kansas-Nebraska bill and a small number of cautious Southern members to draw back in dismay.

Another issue in the Kansas-Nebraska debates was, of course, the merits of squatter sovereignty. Few senators or representatives from either section showed any enthusiasm for squatter sovereignty as a proper principle for governing territories. A few supporters extolled it as being in accord with American principles of democracy and contended that the people, native born and foreign born, who would settle the territories were just as capable of choosing their "domestic institutions" as people in the states were and had as good a right to do so.[40] Some Northern Democrats who were supporting the Kansas-Nebraska bill admitted that they were choosing squatter sovereignty only as a way of taking the accursed subject of slavery in the territories out of Congress and, thus, relieving themselves of the necessity of voting for exclusion. To vote for outright exclusion would give deep offense to their Southern brethren and might well result in disrupting the Democratic party and endangering the Union. Douglas added the argument, not very flattering to the efficacy of our federal government, that in our history the people of the several territories had always in actual practice decided the slavery question to suit themselves so Congress might as well give them authority to do so in the first place.[41]

Northern Whigs and free soil Democrats exposed the weaknesses and hypocrisies of squatter sovereignty unmercifully. How would it quiet slavery agitation to transfer the controversy from Congress to territorial legislatures? What would supporters do in the event Utah, or Kansas, or Nebraska should legalize polygamy? Marriage was certainly a "domestic institution." Furthermore, it was only a pretense that the bill granted squatter sovereignty, for

[40] See remarks of Senators Stephen A. Douglas and Lewis Cass and of Representatives Alexander H. Stephens and Christian M. Straub of Pennsylvania. *Ibid.*, 337, 278, 195, 746.

[41] *Ibid.*, 278-79. Those familiar with Douglas' career will recall that he continued to take this line even after the Dred Scott decision.

it contained the stock governmental provisions making the territorial governor, secretary, and principal judges appointive by the President, giving the governor an absolute veto of bills passed by the legislature, requiring that the laws enacted be reported to Congress, and stipulating that legislation disapproved by Congress would be null and void.[42] The supporters of the bill met these sallies in silence for the most part. But they did finally amend the bill by giving the Kansas and Nebraska legislatures power to override governors' vetoes by a two-thirds majority and by striking out the requirement that laws passed by the legislatures be submitted to Congress.[43] Pettit explained that, while Congress could not divest itself of the power to disallow territorial laws, the amendment would "show . . . what our intention is."[44]

To state rights Democrats and some of the Southern Whigs, squatter sovereignty was a bitter pill, for reasons already explained. When they were called upon by opponents of the Kansas-Nebraska bill to explain how they could support a measure containing a feature so distasteful to them, they replied variously: The territorial legislatures would recognize their constitutional duty and provide for the protection of slave property (even though Congress was not meeting its obligation!). If the legislatures should fail to meet their constitutional obligation, surely the territorial courts would meet theirs. The bill would give the South a "chance" to get a new slave state. If it would accomplish nothing but the removal of the intolerable stigma of the eighth section of the Missouri Enabling Act, it would be justified.[45] "Our honor is saved," said Senator James M. Mason of Virginia. "Nothing is saved but our honor; and yet we agree to it."[46] After all, said some, we can not press the Northern Democrats too far lest we disrupt the party and endanger the Union. A number of state rights men who were supporting the bill simply refused, in the face of all the evidence, to recognize openly that squatter sovereignty was in it.

The tendency of some Southern senators to refuse to recognize that the squatter sovereignty provisions of the bill meant what they said exasperated some Northern Democrats, and in the last days of the Senate debate Charles E. Stuart of Michigan demanded with some asperity that his Southern colleagues state in

[42] *Ibid.*, 175, 154-55, 662, for examples.
[43] *Ibid.*, 33 Cong., 1 Sess., 423, 520.
[44] *Ibid.*, app., 212.
[45] *Ibid.*, 239-40; 33 Cong., 1 Sess., 1303, 1309, 1311.
[46] *Ibid.*, app., 299.

unequivocal language that they had the same understanding of
the provisions that Northern Democrats had.[47] Under catechism
most of the Southern leaders admitted, although not all in unequivocal language, that under the bill the territorial legislatures
would have the power to exclude slavery.[48] But some, notably
Senators Toombs and Dixon, avoided making the unpleasant admission.[49] And in the House a number of members persisted in
asserting that, if squatter sovereignty was in the bill, they could
not find it.[50]

Apparently because of just such avoidances and intransigencies
and because of the efforts of opponents of the bill to take advantage of them to foment dissension in the ranks of the bill's supporters, some historians have concluded that the terms of the bill
were understood one way in the North and another in the South
and, even, that the terms had been deliberately made ambiguous
to maintain unity among the bill's supporters.[51] Now this simply
can not be true, in the light of the terms of the bill, the extended
debates on the merits of squatter sovereignty, and the admissions
of Southern leaders. Even men in the street understood the
squatter-sovereignty feature. Witness the well-known fact that
even before the final passage of the bill arrangements were being
made in the North and in Missouri to contest the control of the
first legislature in Kansas.

It is obvious that the votes of members whose consciences were
not too strict or principles too doctrinaire might turn on whether
they believed that, under the provisions of the bill and other
factors which would operate, the territories or the one or the other
would more likely become a free state or a slave state. The re-
corded debates in Congress are about the last place one should
look to try to find out what the beliefs of individual members
were on this score. When supporters of the bill, Northern and
Southern, were appealing to Northern waverers, they argued that

47 *Ibid.*, 285.

48 Among these were state rights Democrats R. M. T. Hunter, A. P. Butler,
Albert G. Brown, James M. Mason, and James A. Bayard and Whigs George E.
Badger, John M. Clayton, Thomas G. Pratt of Maryland, John Bell of Tennessee,
and William C. Dawson of Georgia. *Ibid.*, 289, 239, 292, 228-32, 299, 776, 286,
291, 937, 939, 303; 33 Cong., 1 Sess., 691.

49 *Ibid.*, 1311, 240; app., 346-51, 140-45.

50 At least Representatives W. T. S. Barry of Mississippi and James F. Dowdell
of Alabama did so. *Ibid.*, 618, 704.

51 Allan Nevins, for example, says, "Supporters of the bill were themselves bit-
terly divided as to the point at which popular sovereignty was to be applied . . . .
Only by a sharp suppression of debate on this vital point was unity maintained."
Ordeal of the Union, II, 101.

both territories would become free states. When they were appealing for the votes of Southern waverers, they asserted that under the bill there was a good prospect that Kansas, at least, would become a slave state. Northern opponents of the bill in appealing for Northern votes against it commonly asserted that, if the bill should pass, the territories would become slave states. But when Northern Whig leaders were trying to persuade Southern Whigs not to vote for the bill, they said, Why violate a compact and arouse antislavery passions when the territories will both become free states anyway? [52] In a more or less unguarded moment Senator John Bell of Tennessee divulged to the Senate that Senator Atchison of Missouri had been assuring Southern colleagues privately that Kansas would become a slave state and that the Southern people were being told that such would be the case.[53] At any rate senators and representatives remained uncertain enough and concerned enough about the outcome in the territories, especially Kansas, that they continued to the end to weigh carefully every proposed amendment that might affect the choice in the territories.

Opponents of the Kansas-Nebraska bill alleged that the Committee on Territories in its second version of the bill had divided the originally proposed Nebraska Territory into two with the deliberate purpose of improving the chances for the South to get a new slave state. They could offer only circumstantial evidence, namely, the fact that division would improve Southern chances. Dodge of Iowa and Douglas in the Senate and Richardson and Bernhart Henn of Iowa in the House explained that the division had been made at the request of the Iowa delegation and with the consent of the Missouri delegation. The former feared, they said, that with only one territory, the valley of the Kaw, being somewhat more accessible than the valley of the Platte, would be settled somewhat earlier and would get the seat of government and these advantages, in turn, would give the Kaw Valley route an advantage over the Platte Valley route in the struggle which was going on over the choice of route for the first railroad to the Pacific. There can be no doubt of the keenness of the rivalry over railroad routes and the extent of the interests involved.[54] But whether the divi-

---

[52] *Congressional Globe*, 33 Cong., 1 Sess., app., 162, 176.

[53] *Ibid.*, 939-40.

[54] *Ibid.*, 33 Cong., 1 Sess., 221; app., 382, 795, 886-88. See Frank Heywood Hodder, "The Railroad Background of the Kansas-Nebraska Act," *Mississippi Valley Historical Review*, XII (June 1925), 3-22; and Robert R. Russel, *Improve-*

sion into two territories had been made originally for the one purpose or the other or for both we may never know for certain. However, we are certain that every senator and representative understood that the division of the original Nebraska into two would greatly increase the likelihood that the South would get a new slave territory subsequently to become a new slave state; and we can be reasonably certain that, whether a bargain had been made in the first place or not, the friends of the bill who met in the caucuses and conferences at least agreed to support the proposed division. For, when Chase proposed in the Senate to amend the bill by combining the two proposed territories into one, every Southern senator present and every Northern senator present who later voted for the bill voted to retain the division; and every Northern senator present (with two exceptions) who later voted against the bill voted to combine. When a similar amendment was proposed in the House, the totals *against* and *for* the amendment on a voice vote were so close to the totals *for* and *against* the bill on its final passage that it is reasonable to conclude that practically all the friends of the bill had voted to retain provision for two territories and practically all the opponents had voted for only one.[55]

As the Senate debate neared its close, it developed that several Southern senators believed that the abrogation of the Missouri Compromise would have the effect of reviving in the proposed territories the old Spanish laws of Louisiana; and these laws sanctioned slavery. Northern supporters of the bill reacted sharply. They had understood that the abrogation of the slavery restriction of the Missouri Compromise would leave the proposed territories without any law on slavery or on anything else until the legislatures should have filled the void. Revival of the old Spanish laws might give a slight temporary advantage in Kansas to the proslavery people, and, of more concern, it would have put Northern men in the position of having voted positively to legalize slavery in the territories, a position no Northern man dared be caught in. In this minor crisis, George E. Badger of North Carolina, the leader of the Southern Whigs, offered the following amendment: "Provided, That nothing herein contained shall be construed to revive or put in force any law or regulation which may have existed prior to the act of . . . 1820, either protecting,

---

ment of Communication with the Pacific Coast As an Issue in American Politics, 1783-1864 (Cedar Rapids, Iowa, 1948).

[55] *Congressional Globe*, 33 Cong., 1 Sess., 520, 1238.

establishing, prohibiting, or abolishing slavery." This proviso was adopted without debate by a vote of 35 to 6, five of the six being state rights Democrats.[56] Later there were bitter recriminations among Southern representatives over the proviso. Badger and some other good Southern lawyers said the provision was no concession to the North, for the repeal of the Missouri Compromise would not otherwise revive earlier laws. Other Southern members disagreed and insisted the proviso was a concession to the North that should not have been made.[57]

On March 2 Senator Clayton of Delaware, up to then a supporter of the bill, moved to amend it by striking out a provision that would give the rights of suffrage and holding office to aliens who had declared their intention of becoming citizens of the United States. Striking this out would leave only citizens eligible. The Senate approved Clayton's amendment 23 to 21 with every Southern senator present voting aye and every free state senator but one voting nay. Although the new Know-Nothing movement may have influenced a few votes, the alignment and the accompanying discussion make it clear that the main consideration was not the proper treatment of immigrants but how the suffrage requirements would affect the slavery question in the first territorial legislatures: Immigrants were predominantly strongly antislavery, and giving them the suffrage would strengthen the free state cause.[58] In the House, where the Northern majority was large, Richardson in moving to substitute the Senate bill for the House bill omitted the Clayton amendment, and no one tried to restore it. After the bill without the Clayton amendment passed the House and was returned to the Senate, a large majority of those who had voted for the amendment now voted against restoring it lest insistence on the amendment kill the bill in the House, where the vote had been very close.[59]

In the Senate the final division on the Kansas-Nebraska bill, counting all who were paired and all who were absent but later indicated how they would have voted had they been present, was 41 to 17. Northern Democrats voted 15 for the bill, 5 against it; Southern Democrats, 15 for to 1 against. Northern Whigs voted none for, 7 against; Southern Whigs voted 11 for, 2 against. The two Free Soilers, of course, voted "Nay." The lone Southern Dem-

[56] *Ibid.*, 520; app., 289-96, 836.
[57] *Ibid.*, 33 Cong., 1 Sess., 686-91; app., 488, 583, 419, 427-28, 549, 618, 796.
[58] *Ibid.*, 33 Cong., 1 Sess., 520, 1300 ff; app., 297-98.
[59] *Ibid.*, 33 Cong., 1 Sess., 1132, 1300-1309, 1321; app., 765 ff.

ocrat who voted against the bill was Sam Houston of Texas; his principal reason seems to have been that he thought the South was making a grievous mistake in making demands that were rousing antislavery passions while receiving so little practical advantage in return.[60] The two Southern Whigs who voted against the bill were Bell and Clayton. Both had joined with other Southern senators in earlier votes. Bell voted "Nay" at the last because of the rising storm in the North and Clayton, ostensibly, because he could not swallow squatter sovereignty.[61]

The House, counting as above for the Senate, passed the bill 115 to 104.[62] Northern Democrats voted 44 to 44; Southern Democrats, 57 for, 2 against. Northern Whigs voted none for and 45 against; Southern Whigs, 14 for and 7 against. The six Free Soilers voted against, of course. The two Southern Democrats who voted against the bill were John S. Millson of Virginia and Thomas Hart Benton. Millson, a state righter of the strictest sort, could not stomach squatter sovereignty.[63] At least three other Southern Democrats and one Whig who disliked this feature refused to vote.[64] The seven Southern Whigs who voted against the bill in the House gave explanations similar to those of Senators Bell and Houston.[65]

The slavery provisions of the Kansas-Nebraska bill were not the work of any one man or clique. They were a compromise, hammered out with great difficulty in committee, conferences, and caucuses and on the Senate floor, between a majority of the Northern Democratic senators and representatives on the one hand and nearly all the Southern senators and representatives, both Democratic and Whig, on the other. Although quite similar to the slavery provisions of the Utah and New Mexico Acts of 1850, the provisions of the Kansas-Nebraska Act included two new concessions to Southern sensibilities, principles, and interests. They abrogated the slavery prohibition of the Missouri Compromise, whereas the Utah and New Mexico acts did not abrogate

[60] *Ibid.*, 33 Cong., 1 Sess., 520, 521, 550, 1321, 1324; app., 788, 338-42, 550; 33 Cong., 1 Sess., 691-92; app., 383-93.

[61] *Ibid.*, 407-15.

[62] *Ibid.*, 33 Cong., 1 Sess., 1254-55.

[63] *Ibid.*, app., 425-29.

[64] Democrats John McQueen and Laurence Keitt of South Carolina and Wiley Harris of Mississippi and Whig John R. Franklin of Maryland. *Ibid.*, 419-22, 463-68, 547-50.

[65] Robert M. Bugg, William Cullom, Emerson Etheridge, Nathaniel G. Taylor, all of Tennessee, Theodore G. Hunt of Louisiana, and Richard C. Puryear and Sion H. Rogers of North Carolina. *Ibid.*, 434-39, 538-43, 811-16, 830-37.

the Mexican laws prohibitive of slavery; and they admitted that the prohibition of slavery in a territory by Congress or by the territorial legislature was of questionable constitutionality. Considering that the region being organized had long been "dedicated to freedom" by a federal statute, the Northern Democrats who voted for the Kansas-Nebraska bill made great sacrifices of sentiment, interests, principles, and personal political advantage in their states and districts for the sake of party unity and sectional accommodation. But, and this is perhaps the point most frequently overlooked in accounts of the struggle, the Kansas-Nebraska Act fell far short of meeting what the great majority of Southern congressmen thought were the South's just demands.

3

Constitutional Doctrines with Regard to Slavery in Territories

The following essay originally appeared in *The Journal of Southern History*, XXXII (November 1966), 466–486, copyright © 1966 by the Southern Historical Association. It is reprinted here in its entirety by permission of the managing editor of *The Journal of Southern History*. The original pagination appears in brackets.

THIS ARTICLE ATTEMPTS TO DESCRIBE THE VARIOUS DOCTRINES THAT were advanced and subscribed to in our ante-bellum period with regard to the constitutional powers of Congress and territorial legislatures as to slavery in territories, briefly appraise them, and tell in a general way who espoused each and why. It is not supposed that the matters here presented will induce anyone to modify materially his view of the general causes of secession and civil war. But people at the time debated these doctrinal matters at great length; they attached great importance to them. Historians in venturing their explanations of the causes of secession should at least consider these constitutional issues for what they are worth and, if they mention them at all—as nearly all do—should get them straight.

It is very uncertain what powers the framers of the Constitution intended the federal government to have in territories. The provisions of the Constitution that may have been intended to relate to the matter are capable of differing interpretations, and the available records of proceedings in the Constitutional Convention shed surprisingly little light on the subject.[1] However, all students of our history have agreed that within a few years after the Constitution had gone into effect it had come to be the prevailing view in all the states, although not in the territories themselves, that Congress had complete or almost complete legislative power in the territories and could not only apply to them the laws applicable to the country generally, such as revenue laws, currency laws, and navigation laws, but could also legislate for them in all matters on which state legislatures might legislate for their respective states.

[1] Francis S. Philbrick has done as much with this matter as one can reasonably expect to be done in his long introduction to *The Laws of Illinois Territory, 1809-1818* (Illinois State Historical Library, *Collections*, XXV, Springfield, 1950). See especially pages lxiv-cxxix.

In accord with this view of its power, Congress continued the practice begun in the Confederation period of organizing portions of the "territory" of the United States into political units, which shortly came to be called "territories," and providing for the organization of "territorial" governments therein. And it also early came to be the practice of Congress when organizing a territory to provide for an elective legislature and to authorize that body to legislate on "all rightful subjects" except for a short list of reserved matters. However, bills passed by a territorial legislature might be vetoed absolutely by the territorial governor, an official appointive by the President of the United States with the advice and consent of the Senate, and those bills approved by the governor must nevertheless be sent to Congress for review and possible disallowance.

Chief Justice John Marshall accepted this prevailing view of the powers of Congress in the territories and lent it the support of his great prestige; he seemed to assume that the matter was so clear as not to require argument or demonstration. In *American Insurance Company* v. *Canter*, 1828, he said, that until it should become a state,

. . . Florida [in this case] continues to be a territory of the United States; governed by virtue of that clause in the Constitution, which empowers Congress "to make all *needful rules and regulations,* respecting the territory, or other property belonging to the United States."

Perhaps the power of governing a territory belonging to the United States, which has not, by becoming a state, acquired the means of self-government, may result necessarily from the facts, that it is not within the jurisdiction of any particular state, and is within the power and jurisdiction of the United States. The right to govern, may be the inevitable consequence of the right to acquire territory. Whichever may be the source, whence the power is derived, the possession of it is *unquestioned.* . . .

. . . .

. . . . In legislating for them [the territories], Congress exercises the *combined powers of the general, and of a state government.*[2]

As to the particular subject of Negro slavery in territories, it was the *early prevailing view,* in accord with the prevailing view

---

[2] 1 Peters 511-46. The passages quoted appear on pages 542-43 and 546. An adequate extract is in Henry Steele Commager (ed.), *Documents of American History* (6th ed., New York, 1958), I, 248. The italics in the quotation are mine, as are all other italics throughout this article except those that are conventional or specifically credited to others.

of the general powers of Congress in the territories, that Congress could exclude slavery from a territory, or legalize it there, or continue in effect the laws on the subject that had been in effect there prior to the annexation to the United States of the district involved, or delegate to the territorial legislature the power to legislate in regard to slavery. It was entirely in accord with the then prevailing view of its power that Congress by the famous eighth section of the Missouri Enabling Act, 1820, prohibited slavery "forever" in that portion of the Louisiana Purchase which lay north of 36° 30′ north latitude and was not within the bounds set for the contemplated state of Missouri. Of all those whom President James Monroe consulted before he signed the Missouri Compromise and for whom we have records, only former President Madison said that he did not think the imposition of such a restriction was "within the true scope of the Constitution," and even he said no blame could attach to "those acquiescing in a conciliatory course . . . ."[3]

In the 1840's three virtually new views of the powers of Congress as to slavery in territories were presented to the public; and each of these in the troublous years that followed gained a considerable number of adherents among concerned citizens generally as well as among constitutional lawyers.

The first of these new views to appear may, perhaps, best be denoted the *free-soil doctrine*. In its more specific form the doctrine was briefly this: That portion of the Fifth Amendment of the Constitution which says, "No person shall be . . . deprived of . . . *liberty* . . . without due process of law," prohibited and was intended to prohibit slavery in territories, the District of Columbia, and all other places under the exclusive jurisdiction of the federal government. Congress, the executive department, and the courts were under a constitutional obligation to give effect to this provision.[4] A variant of the doctrine was that the prevailing view at the time of the making of the Constitution was that freedom, not slavery, was the natural and proper status of people of African descent, as well as of white people, therefore the framers of the Constitution must have intended to embody this idea of liberty

[3] Madison to Monroe, February 23, 1820, in Gaillard Hunt (ed.), *The Writings of James Madison* (9 vols., New York, 1900-1910), IX, 23-26. Madison had stated his reasoning at greater length in a letter to Robert Walsh, November 27, 1819. *Ibid.*, 1-13.

[4] The best-reasoned statement of this form of the doctrine I have seen is in the national platform of the Liberty party for 1844. Kirk H. Porter (comp.), *National Party Platforms* (New York, 1924), 7-15.

in the Constitution and therefore Congress was under a constitutional obligation to exclude slavery from the territories and other places under the exclusive jurisdiction of the federal government.[5]

Those who espoused this free-soil doctrine did not, for they could not, advance one bit of direct historical evidence that the framers of the Fifth Amendment or the members of the legislatures which ratified it—those of seven slave states and four free states—intended, expected, or even suspected that it would be interpreted to prohibit slavery in the territories. And adherents of the doctrine never bothered to explain how or why the phrase "due process of law" could or should be construed to govern the *substance* of the laws affecting life, liberty, or property as well as the procedures by which the laws were enforced.[6] Nor could those who held the free-soil doctrine in its more general form advance one scrap of direct historical evidence that the framers intended to incorporate in the Constitution any rule as to who might be held in bondage and who might not or as to what might be held as property and what might not. The free soilers could advance, and did advance at great length, strong historical evidence that Thomas Jefferson and his colleagues meant all men, white or black, when they wrote, "all men are created equal," that the common law at the time of the making of the Constitution did not sanction slavery but that wherever slavery existed in the country it did so under special statute laws, and that the framers generally hoped and expected that the institution would die out.

This free-soil doctrine as to slavery in territories became the official doctrine of the Liberty party in 1844 and of the Free Soil party in 1848 and 1852.[7] Senator William H. Seward subscribed to it in his famous "Higher Law" speech of March 11, 1850,[8] and Sena-

---

[5] See, for examples, speeches of Lewis D. Campbell of Ohio and Gerrit Smith of New York in the House of Representatives February 17 and April 6, 1854, respectively. *Congressional Globe,* 33 Cong., 1 Sess., Appendix, 244-47, 519-30.

[6] Students of our constitutional history will recognize that this was one of the earlier assertions of what came to be known as substantive due process of law, a form of law which courts both federal and state came in the 1880's and subsequent decades to employ frequently and extensively.

[7] Porter (comp.), *National Party Platforms,* 7-15 (1844), 22-25 (1848), 32-36 (1852).

[8] Seward did not say or imply, as his critics asserted at the time and many historians persist in asserting, that Congress should disregard the Constitution in order to observe a higher law. After a long disquisition designed to show that the Constitution did not embody the idea of property in man, he said, "The Constitution regulates our stewardship [in the territories]; the Constitution devotes the domain to union, to justice, to defence, to welfare, and to liberty. But there is a higher law than the Constitution, which regulates our authority over

tor Salmon P. Chase, a future Chief Justice, briefly expounded it during the debates on the compromise measures of 1850 and the Kansas-Nebraska Bill.[9] It was taken up by a large portion of the early Republican party when that party appeared. It, perhaps, should go without saying that strongly antislavery people liked the doctrine because it allowed them to feel that in opposing the spread of slavery into territories they were not only acting on moral principles but obeying a constitutional injunction as well.

The second virtually new view of the powers of Congress as to slavery in territories presented in the 1840's was that which has most commonly been called the *Calhoun doctrine* but whose subscribers chose to call "nonintervention." It could perhaps better be called the "common-property-of-the states" doctrine. It was first stated publicly in something like its final form by Robert Barnwell Rhett of South Carolina in the House of Representatives January 15, 1847, and then, more logically, by John C. Calhoun in a set of Senate resolutions on February 19.[10] The doctrine was briefly this: Sovereignty is indivisible. The states were sovereign; the United States was not. The federal government was only the agent or trustee of the states in matters expressly delegated to it by the Constitution. The territories were the common property of the states, as co-owners, not of the United States as an entity. The government of the territories was necessarily left to the federal government, as agent or trustee for the states. But in governing territories the federal government was under obligation not to discriminate in any way among the various states or among their citizens. It must admit into the territories and protect there as property anything, slaves, for example, which a citizen of any state might choose to bring with him and of which he had been legally possessed in the state whence he had come; for to do otherwise would be discrimination between states and between citizens of different states and, therefore, unconstitutional. And if Congress could not prohibit slaveowners from bringing their slaves into the territories but must protect them there in their property rights, a territorial legislature could not exclude slaves or deny

---

the domain, and devotes it to the same noble purposes." *Cong. Globe*, 31 Cong., 1 Sess., Appendix, 265.

  [9] *Ibid.*, 471 (March 26, 1850); 33 Cong., 1 Sess., Appendix, 138 (February 3, 1854).

  [10] *Ibid.*, 29 Cong., 2 Sess., 455; Appendix, 244-47. Perhaps the best exposition of the doctrine ever made was that of Senator John M. Berrien of Georgia, a former attorney general of the United States, February 11-12, 1850. *Ibid.*, 31 Cong., 1 Sess., Appendix, 202-11.

protection to slave property, for a territorial legislature was but a creature of Congress and could not be authorized to do what its creator could not do.

Subscribers to the Calhoun doctrine seldom bothered to defend its main premise, that the states were sovereign and that the federal government was merely their agent or trustee in specified matters. That view had been more or less tentatively stated by Jefferson and Madison in their Kentucky and Virginia resolutions and reports of 1798-1800 and fully developed by John C. Calhoun, Robert Y. Hayne, and others at the time of the South Carolina nullification episode, 1828-1833. Thereafter it was simply dogma to all extreme state-rights people. As every student of our constitutional history knows, some good historical evidence can be advanced in support of this premise.[11] but that evidence has not been sufficient to convince many historians or a single federal judge. Subscribers to the Calhoun doctrine, also, seldom deigned to reply to its opponents' contention that the legalization and protection of slavery in the territories would repel from the territories a far greater number of people from free states than the number of slaveowners who would care to migrate to the "common territories" under any circumstances and would, therefore, work a far greater discrimination against free states and their citizens than prohibition of slavery would work against slave states and their citizens.

Almost as soon as it was pronounced by the great master, the Calhoun doctrine gained the acceptance of the entire extreme state-rights, or Calhoun, wing of the Democratic party in the South and of the comparatively small number of "Nullifiers" that the accidents of politics had left in the Whig party. It never gained the acceptance of the Jacksonian Democrats of the South or of the great majority of Southern Whigs, who looked to Henry Clay as their great exemplar. It probably never won the adherence of a majority of the thinking people of the South as a whole. But in the tempestuous years before the Civil War the Calhoun wing gained ascendancy in the Democratic party in almost all the Southern states, and the Democratic party rather consistently

[11] Most notably and in very brief: The delegates to the Constitutional Convention were chosen by state governments. The voting in the convention was by states, each state delegation having one vote. The Constitution was ratified by conventions in the several states. It was not to go into effect until at least nine states should have ratified it and then only in those states which had ratified it. Three states in ratifying adopted resolutions which were capable of the interpretation that those states reserved the right to withdraw their adherence.

carried the elections in most of them; so the Calhoun doctrine had spokesmen in Congress in numbers out of proportion to its subscribers among the people.

No doubt the great majority of those who espoused the Calhoun view became honestly convinced of its validity. But it is not being cynical to suggest that strongly proslavery people were influenced to accept it by the fact that it lent strong support to a political objective. They feared the rising antislavery sentiment in the North. They desperately wanted more slave territories that they might become slave states and send senators and representatives to Congress to help their colleagues from older slave states ward off legislation inimical to the peculiar institution. If the Calhoun doctrine could be vindicated and slavery be legalized and protected in all the territories, it might well become so firmly established in at least some of them that eventually they would become confirmed slave states.

A third new view of the constitutional powers of Congress as to slavery in territories—or perhaps one should say a view that was revived in the 1840's after a long period of dormancy—was the "squatter-sovereignty" or, better, the *Cass doctrine*. It was first prominently advanced by Senator Lewis Cass of Michigan in a well-publicized letter to A. O. P. Nicholson of Tennessee dated December 24, 1847,[12] and was refined and elaborated by Cass and others in the next several years.[13] Very briefly, the doctrine was this: While from the very necessities of the case, Congress must have power to mark off new territories and provide and ensure them, as incipient states, republican forms of government, it had no constitutional authority to regulate their internal policies in matters not put under federal jurisdiction by the Constitution. The regulation of these latter matters must be left to the people of the territories themselves acting through their elected representatives; and whether or not to permit slavery was one of these matters of local, internal concern.

It should not be overlooked that the term "squatter sovereignty," although it has become conventional in the books, was never employed by subscribers to the Cass doctrine but was ap-

---

[12] An adequate extract is in Allen Johnson (ed.), *Readings in American Constitutional History, 1776-1876* (Boston, 1912), 411-14.

[13] The best exposition and defense of the doctrine was by Cass himself in speeches in the Senate February 20, 21, 27, 1854. *Cong. Globe*, 33 Cong., 1 Sess., 449-51, 456-58; Appendix, 270-79. A good, brief summary of the Cass doctrine is in Andrew C. McLaughlin, *A Constitutional History of the United States* (New York, 1935), 520.

plied to it in derision by its opponents—its coinage has most frequently been attributed to Calhoun. Proponents of the Cass view never asserted that a territory had sovereignty in the sense that a state of the Union had. And they did not claim or believe that a district in the territory of the United States with a population consisting principally of squatters on the public domain should be allowed to have an elective legislature. They did assert that a territory with an established and reasonably stable population must under the Constitution be allowed to have a very large measure of self-government.

If one was inclined to a strict construction of the Constitution, the Cass doctrine was the one—of all—which could most logically be derived from the actual wording of the Constitution. With the exception of the *long prevailing view* already described, it was better supported than any other by the historical setting of the Constitutional Convention and the scanty records we have of the proceedings in the convention relating to the matter. The most convincing single piece of historical evidence proponents of the Cass doctrine could advance was simply that it was inconceivable that men of the Revolutionary generation could have intended to establish a territorial (colonial) system which allowed the territories smaller powers of self-government than the old British system had allowed the Thirteen Colonies. Their best single witness among the Fathers was James Madison.[14] The most damaging piece of historical evidence against the Cass doctrine was simply that the early Congresses, including the Confederation Congress, did in fact frame a territorial system modeled closely on the old British system, and many of the men who wrote the Constitution also sat in those Congresses and participated in framing it.

The Cass constitutional doctrine should by no means be confused with squatter sovereignty supported only as a political expedient. It was possible for people who held the *prevailing view* of the constitutional powers of Congress as to slavery in the territories to favor leaving the question to the territorial legislatures as the most acceptable way of taking the divisive issue out of Congress or of preventing it from disrupting their national political party. A much larger number of people accepted squatter sovereignty as a practical compromise than ever subscribed to the Cass doctrine as a valid interpretation of the Constitution. Stephen A. Douglas himself, who became the leading champion of squatter

[14] Especially his letter to Robert Walsh, November 27, 1819, in Hunt (ed.), *Writings of James Madison,* IX, 1-13.

sovereignty, did not, publicly at least, accept and defend it as a constitutional doctrine until 1859. The Cass doctrine was likely to appeal more to people who had rather strong feelings about slavery, either against it or for it, and who liked to feel that in voting to leave the decision to territorial legislatures they were not compromising their principles or bowing to political expediency but simply obeying a requirement of the Constitution.

The Utah and New Mexico territorial acts, 1850, and the Kansas-Nebraska Act, 1854, provided for practical squatter sovereignty in the territories to which they applied. The congressional debates during the proceedings leading to the passage of these acts contributed nothing toward agreement on the constitutional issues involved. But incidents during the debates and proceedings and some of the actual provisions of the acts, especially the Kansas-Nebraska Act, were almost tantamount to an invitation by majorities in Congress to the Supreme Court to step in and settle the constitutional controversy if opportunity should afford.[15]

No slave case reached the Supreme Court under either of the statutes mentioned; but a Missouri case, the Dred Scott case, which could be made to involve at least some of the constitutional issues did reach the Court and was there heard and decided, the decision being announced in March 1857.[16] Eight of the nine justices found it either necessary or convenient in deciding this case to pass upon the constitutionality of the Missouri Compromise, that is to say, upon the power of Congress to exclude slavery from a territory, or at least from the particular territory to which the Missouri Compromise act applied. One justice, Samuel Nelson of New York, avoided passing upon that critical issue.

Of the eight justices who passed upon the constitutionality of the Missouri Compromise, two said it had been constitutional, that is, that Congress had power to exclude slavery from the territory concerned; six said it had been unconstitutional, that is, in effect, that Congress did not have power to exclude slavery from the territory. The two minority justices, John McLean of Ohio and Benjamin R. Curtis of Massachusetts, wrote elaborate opinions. So also did four of the majority justices, Chief Justice Roger B. Taney of Maryland, Peter V. Daniel of Virginia, John A. Campbell of

---

[15] I have explained at length the points made in this and the preceding paragraph in two articles, "What Was the Compromise of 1850?" *Journal of Southern History*, XXII (August 1956), 292-309, and "The Issues in the Congressional Struggle Over the Kansas-Nebraska Bill, 1854," *ibid.*, XXIX (May 1963), 187-210.

[16] 19 Howard 393-633.

Alabama, and John Catron of Tennessee. Justice James M. Wayne of Georgia was content to say that he agreed with the Chief Justice both in his conclusion and supporting argument. Justice Robert C. Grier of Pennsylvania simply said he agreed that the Missouri Compromise had been unconstitutional. He carefully avoided giving any indication of what line of reasoning he had followed, if any. It seems desirable to analyze briefly the six argued opinions just mentioned to see what they contributed, if anything, toward resolving the constitutional controversies under discussion and how much respect they were and are entitled to as constitutional doctrine.[17]

Justices McLean and Curtis in their opinions presented the older, prevailing view as to the powers of Congress in territories, and Curtis gave perhaps the most thorough argument in support of it that has ever been made. It is the view which, with minor qualifications, has prevailed in court and out since the Civil War and requires no further description here.

The four majority justices who wrote out their opinions reached the conclusion that the Missouri Compromise had been unconstitutional by *four distinctly different* lines of reasoning, only one of which—that of Justice Catron—resembled at all closely any one of the four constitutional doctrines described thus far in this article. Chief Justice Taney's opinion was labeled the "Opinion of the Court" in the official report of the case and was understood to be that by many people at the time. But in fact it was the opinion of the Court only in the sense that six other justices agreed that Dred Scott was not entitled to his freedom.

Chief Justice Taney (Justice Wayne concurring) said Congress possessed extensive power to legislate for territories acquired since 1789.[18] Its power to do so was limited only by the specific prohibitions imposed upon the federal government by the Constitution. The specific prohibition pertinent to the case before the court was, he said, that portion of the Fifth Amendment which reads, "No person shall be . . . deprived of . . . *property*, without due process

[17] The analyses of the justices' opinions given in this article have been made independently. Their necessary brevity may do injustice to subtleties of argument. The numerous accounts of the Dred Scott decision have by no means agreed upon what various justices said in their opinions. It is believed that the analyses given here agree substantially with those given by Vincent C. Hopkins in *Dred Scott's Case* (New York, 1951).

[18] For reasons and in ways which need not concern us here, Taney distinguished between the powers Congress had in territories within the original boundaries of the United States and those it had in territory acquired after the new Constitution had gone into effect.

of law . . . ." Without saying that he was making such an assumption, he assumed that the Fathers had somehow embodied in the Constitution the rule that things of every class of things commonly regarded as property at the time the Constitution was made should be so regarded by the federal government. He cited at length evidence designed to show that at the time of the making of the Constitution our people generally in all parts of the country regarded slavery as the proper and normal status of persons of African descent and that both the common law and the law of nations at the time sanctioned slavery. From these alleged facts, and from the fact that the Constitution in two—he said two—separate clauses recognized the existence of slavery in the country, and without offering one scintilla of direct historical evidence to show that a single member of the Constitutional Convention had ever thought of doing any such thing, and with complete disregard of a great deal of historical evidence that the convention intended the Constitution to be neutral in the matter, he concluded that the Fathers had incorporated into the Constitution the recognition that persons of African descent were among the objects normally and rightly held as property. Slave property, he said, was as much entitled to protection as any other class of property. And to deprive a citizen of property (Dred Scott and his wife Harriet), as the Missouri Compromise had undertaken to do, just because he had taken it across the line into a territory into which he had a legal right to go certainly was not due process of law. Therefore, the Missouri Compromise had been unconstitutional and void.

It will have been observed that the Chief Justice was employing substantive due process of law, just as the free soilers would do; but whereas they invoked it to protect a *liberty*—freedom from slavery—which they claimed was recognized by the Constitution as the rightful condition of all human beings, the Justice resorted to it to protect a right of *property* in persons of African descent held in slavery, which right, he said, was recognized by the Constitution. Taney, as was also true of the free soilers, offered no explanation as to how or why the phrase, "due process of law," could or should be construed to govern the substance of laws affecting life, liberty, and property as well as the procedures by which the laws were enforced. He did not cite a single precedent.[19]

---

[19] He could have cited a few precedents for employing substantive due process, including one by his colleague Justice Curtis. See Hopkins, *Dred Scott's Case*, 134; Alfred H. Kelly and Winfred A. Harbison, *The American Constitution, Its*

Justice Daniel said Congress had only a limited amount of power to legislate for territories. Just how much it was unnecessary to determine. But it did not have the power to exclude slave property. By a line of reasoning almost impossible to follow he concluded "that the only private property which the Constitution has *specifically recognised,* and has imposed it as a direct obligation both on the States and the Federal Government to protect and *enforce,* is the property of the master in his slave . . . ." "Congress was made simply the agent or *trustee* for the United States, and could not, without a breach of trust and a fraud," exclude from the territories any portion of the citizens of the United States because they were owners of slaves. The Missouri Compromise, therefore, had been unconstitutional and void.[20] Daniel, be it noted, did not have to resort to a history of the times of the Fathers, as did Taney, to find that the Constitution recognized that persons of African descent were normally property; he somehow found the right to hold such persons as property specifically guaranteed by the Constitution. He did not have to resort to substantive due process of law as a means of invalidating an act of Congress; he said the act in question had violated an express mandate of the Constitution.

Justice Campbell, as had Daniel, found that the Constitution gave Congress only a limited amount of power to legislate for territories. The history of the times, which he reviewed, indicated, he said, that the Fathers did not intend Congress to have power to determine the internal "polity" of the territories or to adjust the domestic relations of the people there or to determine who might lawfully enter them. At this point logic would seem to require him to have said that such matters must be left to the territories themselves as bodies politic—as the Cass doctrine had it. Instead, he took a different tack. Both the state and federal governments, he said, were "agents and trustees of the *people* of the several States, appointed with different powers and with distinct purposes, but whose acts, within the scope of their respective jurisdictions, are *mutually obligatory.*" It was left to the *states* to determine what might and what might not be held as property. Whatever they or any of them recognized as property [slaves in this case], it was the duty of the federal government to recognize

---

Origin and Development (3rd ed., New York, 1963), Chap. 19; Edward S. Corwin, *The Doctrine of Judicial Review: Its Legal and Historical Basis and Other Essays* (Princeton, 1914), 146-49.

[20] 19 Howard 489, 490. The italics were Justice Daniel's.

as property in the territories; for to do otherwise would *endanger* the *"social system"* of one or more states and would, therefore, be repugnant to the federal compact and accordingly unconstitutional.[21] The Justice neglected to suggest that permitting slavery in all the territories might endanger the "social system" of one or more free states and, therefore, also be repugnant to the federal compact. Presumably he saw no such danger.

Justice Catron agreed with Taney that Congress had extensive legislative powers in the territories. However, he said, the Missouri Compromise had been void from the start because Article III of the Louisiana Purchase treaty had stipulated that the property laws in effect in the region at the time of the purchase by the United States should remain in effect, and those laws recognized and protected slavery. But the Justice did not stop there; *the treaty aside,* he said, the Missouri Compromise had been unconstitutional: The territories were "the common property of all the States united." The citizens of any state derived the right to go into the territories and "enjoy the common property" not from the United States but from their state. The federal government governed the territories as trustee for the *states.* The Constitution made the states equal in political rights and the right to participate in the common property. For Congress to exclude slavery from the territories would in effect exclude slaveowners, and to do that would violate the "great fundamental condition of the Union —the equality of the States."[22] Catron's view, it will be noted, was quite similar to the Calhoun doctrine except that he did not assert the sovereignty of the states.

Both Justices Curtis and McLean in their written opinions acknowledged the weight of Campbell's and Catron's contention as to the equality of the states and their citizens under the Constitution. Curtis said it may have been unfair to slave states and to slaveholders to prohibit slavery in the territory concerned, but whether it was or not was a political question to be decided by Congress. The Court could only decide as to the constitutional power of Congress, and Congress had acted within its powers. McLean went a little farther. He said, ". . . with one-fourth of the Federal population of the Union, they [our Southern brethren] have in the slave States a larger extent of fertile territory than is included in the free States . . . ." As for the territories, "The repugnancy to slavery would probably prevent fifty or a

21 *Ibid.,* 515-16.
22 *Ibid.,* 518-29; quotations appear on pages 526 and 527.

hundred freemen from settling in a slave Territory, where one slaveholder would be prevented from settling in a free Territory."[23]

The Supreme Court cannot justifiably be criticized for taking the opportunity afforded by the Dred Scott case for passing upon the constitutionality of an act of Congress excluding slavery from a territory, for it had virtually been invited to do so by two Congresses. And individual judges cannot justifiably be criticized for spreading on the record their own deeply pondered and reasoned-out views. But it almost goes without saying that such a disparate set of opinions as the justices produced could contribute little or nothing towards resolving differences on issues involving great interests and deep emotions. Looking back, it is little wonder that the opinions of the justices convinced few people of anything of which they were not already convinced. No friendly lawyer or publicist could make a convincing defense of the majority decision because it is logically impossible to defend four different lines of reasoning at the same time. A considerable number of those people who could not agree that the decision was good law nevertheless counseled acquiescence in it out of respect for the authority of the Court and in the vain hope of bringing an end to the sectional controversy over slavery in the territories. But the great majority of the unconvinced decided to "treat it as not having yet quite established a settled doctrine for the country," as Abraham Lincoln mildly put it.[24]

The state-rights people of the South hailed the Dred Scott decision as a complete vindication of their constitutional view. And it is true, of course, that the decision upheld the main substantive contention of the Calhoun doctrine, namely, that Congress lacked the constitutional power to prohibit citizens lawfully possessed of slaves to take them into any territory and hold them there in servitude. But that is almost the extent of the similarity between the Calhoun doctrine and the opinions of majority justices. It is significant in this regard that when, after the Dred Scott decision, constitutional lawyers of the state-rights school undertook full-dress expositions of slaveholders' rights in territories, while they quoted when convenient from the justices' opinions, especially Taney's, they never followed at all closely any one

[23] *Ibid.*, 529-633; quotations appear on page 543.
[24] Speech at Springfield, Illinois, June 26, 1857. Roy P. Basler *et al.* (eds.), *The Collected Works of Abraham Lincoln* (8 vols. and index, New Brunswick, 1953-1955), II, 401.

justice's line of reasoning but continued to follow the familiar Calhoun line.[25]

Only one justice, Catron, had taken the position that the territories were the common property of the states, not of the United States as an entity, and that citizens got the right to go into the territories and take slaves with them from their states, not from the federal government. And although logic may have required him to say it, even Catron stopped short of saying the states were sovereign—the basic premise of the Calhoun doctrine. This premise, be it noted, was also the basic premise of the contention that a state had a constitutional right to secede, which extreme Southern sectionalists of the time were trying to establish, and the failure of even one judge to give it countenance must have been a disappointment to them. Of the majority justices, Chief Justice Taney was especially nationalistic.[26]

Strongly proslavery people liked the pronouncements of Taney (Wayne concurring) and Daniel that the Constitution itself recognized people of African descent normally to be property. But good state-rights doctrine was that only states could define what might and what might not be held as property. On this particular point the opinions of Nelson, Curtis, and McLean, Northerners, as well as those of Campbell and Catron were more in accord with state-rights tenets.

The state-rights people promptly assumed and were very insistent upon the point that, since a majority of the Court had ruled that Congress could not prohibit slavery in a territory, it had also ruled that, as they had long contended, a territorial legislature could not do so either. It soon appeared, however, that a large number of Northern Democrats and some Southerners refused to accept this interpretation of the Court's decision and contended, on the contrary, that the Court had not yet decided upon the constitutionality of acts of territorial legislatures prohibitive of slavery.

It will be recalled that according to the Cass doctrine Congress did have power to confer upon territorial legislatures the power to legislate on matters of internal policy which Congress did not itself possess and that, according to the doctrine, even if Congress could not confer such power, the territorial legislatures would still

[25] See, for examples, the speeches of Jefferson Davis and Louis T. Wigfall in the Senate May 7 and 23, 1860, respectively. *Cong. Globe*, 36 Cong., 1 Sess., 1937-42, 2270-78.

[26] See also Corwin, *Doctrine of Judicial Review*, 140 ff.; McLaughlin, *Constitutional History*, 558, n. 13.

have it under the inherent right of self-government. The Supreme Court had not been called on to pass upon these contentions. The Dred Scott case had not arisen out of an act of a territorial legislature. Neither the plaintiff nor the defendant in the case had claimed any right under a territorial law. Not one of the able counsel on either side had raised the issue.[27] Chief Justice Taney, to be sure, had gone out of his way to say, ". . . if Congress itself cannot do this [exclude slaves from territories] . . . it will be admitted, we presume, that it could not authorize a Territorial Government [to do it]."[28] Justice Curtis, also in obiter dicta, had said, in substance, that a territorial legislature could have no legislative power not conferred upon it by Congress.[29] No other justice even mentioned territorial legislatures. To be sure the reasoning of Taney, Wayne, Daniel, and Catron was such as to have logically required them to hold a territorial act excluding slaves to be unconstitutional. But that was not clearly true of Campbell's opinion. Nelson and Grier had given no indication at all of how they would have ruled on such a law. And Curtis and McLean, if they followed the logic of their position, would have had to uphold such a law; for they held the older, traditional view of the powers of Congress, and Congress had authorized all the territorial legislatures to legislate on "all rightful subjects," not excepting slavery. So the Cass doctrine had not had its day in court, the Supreme Court had not ruled against it, and it had not even clearly indicated how it would have ruled if Scott or someone else had claimed his freedom under a territorial statute. Sharp politicians committed to squatter sovereignty as a solution of the question of slavery in territories detected this opening and proceeded to take advantage of it.[30] The great majority of Northern Democrats, it appears, felt they had gone as far as their consciences and interests would permit toward meeting the demands of their Southern brethren when they had compromised on leaving the question of slavery in the territories to the territorial legislatures. They were determined to go no further no matter what

[27] Hopkins, *Dred Scott's Case*, 33-40, 47-50, analyzes counsels' arguments. Reverdy Johnson, one of the counsel for Sanford, said the issue had not been before the court. *Cong. Globe*, 36 Cong., 1 Sess., 417, 2152, 2242 (January 13, May 17, 22, 1860).

[28] 19 Howard 451.

[29] *Ibid.*, 620.

[30] Senator George Pugh of Ohio did the best job of it in a running debate with Jefferson Davis and others. *Cong. Globe*, 36 Cong., 1 Sess., 176-87, 415-23, 2241-48 (December 19, 1859; January 12, May 22, 1860).

the Dred Scott decision may have been, and were easily convinced, therefore, that the decision had left squatter sovereignty
intact.

The predicament in which the Dred Scott decision put most
Northern Democrats is well illustrated by the case of Stephen A.
Douglas, the most prominent Northern aspirant for the Democratic nomination for the Presidency in 1860. As the popularly
reputed and self-proclaimed author of the Kansas-Nebraska Act,
he was more prominently identified with squatter sovereignty
than any other man. Before the Supreme Court announced its decision, he had never publicly endorsed the Cass doctrine. All he
had ever said or done with regard to slavery in territories indicated that he believed territorial legislatures possessed only those
powers on that subject, or any other, which Congress itself possessed and which it might choose to delegate to them.[31] Logic,
therefore, required him to conclude that since the Supreme Court
had decided that Congress could not prohibit slavery in a territory it had also decided that a territorial legislature might not do
so. In this tight spot his first expedient was his indefensible Freeport doctrine.[32] Stripped of verbiage that doctrine amounted to
this: *If* the Court has decided that a territorial legislature may
not legally prohibit slavery, it will make no practical difference
anyway, for such a decision cannot be enforced in a territory
whose people are opposed to slavery. As the Freeport Doctrine
was mercilessly assailed and exposed by Abraham Lincoln, Judah
P. Benjamin, and others,[33] Douglas gradually explained it away,
or tried to, and finally, with many other Northern Democrats,

[31] The evidence is negative and inferential; Douglas had theretofore always
refused to participate in the long debates on the constitutional issue. But he had
introduced and as chairman of the Senate Committee on Territories reported
many a bill which delegated legislative powers to territorial legislatures with
lists of *excepted* matters and subject to possible vetoes by territorial governors
(federal officers) and possible disallowance by Congress. He had never said he
thought the Missouri Compromise was unconstitutional (as Cass had done). He
had joined in efforts of compromisers in 1847-1848 to extend it across the Mexican cession to the Pacific. And he had introduced or reported and supported
several Nebraska bills before 1854 which, if enacted, would either have left the
Missouri Compromise permanently in effect or until, if ever, a territorial legislature should have superseded it by other legislation.

[32] He stated the "doctrine" many times, but the version frequently quoted is
that he gave at Freeport, August 27, 1858, in a debate with Lincoln. Basler *et
al.* (eds.), *Collected Works of Lincoln*, III, 51; Commager (ed.), *Documents,*
I, 348.

[33] See especially the bitter debate in the Senate February 23, 1859, between
Douglas and friends and Southern assailants. *Cong. Globe*, 35 Cong., 2 Sess.,
1241-74.

opted for the Cass doctrine. In the fall of 1859 in a long and labored article in *Harper's New Monthly Magazine* entitled "The Dividing Line Between Federal and Local Authority: Popular Sovereignty in the Territories,"[34] he attempted to show that even though, as the majority of the Supreme Court had ruled, Congress could not prohibit slavery in the territories, territorial legislatures nevertheless could constitutionally do so and that this contention was not inconsistent with the Court's decision.

In 1860 the Democratic party in national convention at Charleston and Baltimore split on the single issue of *what* the Supreme Court had decided as to slavery in the territories and what to do about the matter of slavery in the territories.[35] The platforms of the two wings of the party were all but identical except on that one issue.[36]

The platform of the Northern, or Douglas, wing assumed, without actually saying so, that the Supreme Court had not yet rendered a decision "as to the nature and extent of the powers of a Territorial Legislature, and as to the powers and duties of Congress, under the Constitution of the United States, over the institution of slavery within the Territories," and that until the Court should have decided adversely, if it ever should, the territories would continue to have squatter sovereignty on the question. It promised, "That the Democratic Party will abide by the decision [presumably a future decision] of the Supreme Court of the United States upon these questions of Constitutional law." Another resolution, included apparently in the hope of enabling Buchanan Democrats to subscribe to the platform, said, with some neat double talk, that "every branch" of the federal government

[34] XIV (September 1859), 519-37; reprinted in Harry W. Jaffa and Robert W. Johannsen (eds.), *In the Name of the People: Speeches and Writings of Lincoln and Douglas in the Ohio Campaign of 1859* (Columbus, 1959), 58-125. See also Johannsen, "Stephen A. Douglas, 'Harper's Magazine,' and Popular Sovereignty," *Mississippi Valley Historical Review*, XLV (March 1959), 606-31. I believe Professor Johannsen and I are in substantial agreement as to when and wherein Douglas changed his constitutional view, but he is considerably more kindly towards that gentleman than I in ascribing motives for the switch.

[35] Those writers who contend that the great objective of the Southern delegates in the Charleston convention was to prevent the nomination of Douglas and that the platform was of minor concern to them seem to have overlooked the simple fact that under the well-established two-thirds rule they had more than enough votes to block his nomination and force the nomination of a compromise candidate. The highest vote Douglas received at Charleston was 152½. That was 50 votes short of a two-thirds majority. See Allan Nevins, *The Emergence of Lincoln* (2 vols., New York, 1950), II, 211, 213, 224, 226, 227.

[36] Porter (comp.), *National Party Platforms*, 53-55; Commager (ed.), *Documents*, I, 365-66.

should enforce with "promptness and fidelity" whatever the Supreme Court had already decided or might finally determine on the matter. Thus the Douglas platform *did not* denounce the Dred Scott decision. It *did not* endorse the Freeport doctrine. It did not endorse popular sovereignty *unconditionally*. In short, considering the realities of Northern public opinion, the Douglas platform made remarkable concessions to the demands of the state-rights faction

The platf⸗ m of the Breckinridge wing of the Democratic party assumed, also without saying so, that the Supreme Court had already settled the constitutional issues and had decided that "all citizens of the United States have an equal right to settle with their property in the Territory, without their rights, either of person or property, being destroyed or impaired by Congressional or Territorial legislation." The platform then asserted, "That it is the duty of the Federal Government in all its departments, to protect, *when necessary*, the rights of persons and property in the Territories . . . ." The Breckinridge platform, thus, *did not* demand the passage of a congressional slave code for the territories, as has so often been carelessly asserted.[37] It *did* contain a resolution which would justify making a demand for a congressional slave code *if* and *when* such a code should seem *necessary*.

No doubt the Democrats, as they loved their party and the Union, should somehow have bridged the gap between the two platforms. But the gap was pretty wide. And the gap between the Breckinridge platform and the Republican platform was as wide as such a gap could be.

The Republican party in its 1860 national platform, with special relevance to Chief Justice Taney's opinion, justifiably denounced the Dred Scott decision as "a dangerous political heresy, at variance with the explicit provisions [of the Constitution], with contemporaneous exposition, and with legislative and judicial precedent . . . ." It then inconsistently plumped for the doctrine that

[37] For that matter, Jefferson Davis' famous Senate resolutions, which are supposed to have been designed as a guideline for Southern delegates to the Charleston convention, did not call for a blanket slave code either. They called upon Congress to supply the necessary means to protect the property rights of slaveholders in any individual territory "if experience should at any time prove that the judiciary and executive authority do not possess means to insure adequate protection . . . , and if the territorial government shall fail or refuse" to do so. *Cong. Globe,* 36 Cong., 1 Sess., 935 (March 1, 1860). Efforts of Senator Albert Gallatin Brown of Mississippi to amend Davis' resolutions to make them say that experience had already proved the need for congressional action received the support of only five other senators, all from the deep South. *Ibid.,* 36 Cong., 1 Sess., 2343, 2349 (May 25, 1860).

the due-process-of-law clause of the Fifth Amendment forbade slavery in the territories, and it denied "the authority of Congress, of a territorial legislature, or of any individuals, to give legal existence to slavery in any territory of the United States."[38] That is, the platform adopted the *free-soil* doctrine. As stated earlier, this was a position for which no justification whatever could be found in "contemporaneous exposition" or in "legislative and judicial precedent." Whether any of the grave men who framed this platform appreciated the nice irony of doing in one plank what they had in the preceding plank condemned the Chief Justice for doing, the records do not reveal.

The Republican platform of 1856 had contained not only a resolution stating the free-soil doctrine but also one saying that Congress had "sovereign" power over the territories "and that in the exercise of this power, it is both the right and the imperative duty [moral, that is] of Congress to prohibit in the Territories those twin relics of barbarism—Polygamy and Slavery."[39] The phrase "relics of barbarism" was insulting, but the constitutional position was in accord with the older prevailing view and was accepted by far more people. Why the Chicago convention chose to drop that position in favor of the other indefensible and more intransigent view[40] has never been satisfactorily explained. But of one thing we may be certain, it was not done to meet the views of the man the convention nominated for President of the United States.

Abraham Lincoln never accepted or endorsed the free-soil doctrine, except as he may be considered to have done so when, in accepting the presidential nomination, he endorsed the platform in general.[41] In all the public speeches in which he discussed the matter, he endorsed the old traditional view. On one occasion at least he specifically endorsed the arguments employed by Justices McLean and Curtis in the Dred Scott case and said he could not improve upon them.[42] He even, guardedly to be sure, advised acquiescence in the Dred Scott decision (understanding it as he

[38] Porter (comp.), *National Party Platforms*, 57; Commager (ed.), *Documents*, I, 364.

[39] Porter (comp.), *National Party Platforms*, 47-48.

[40] Many books regard the slavery resolutions in the 1860 platform as more conservative and conciliatory than those in the 1856 platform. See, for examples, Reinhard H. Luthin, *The First Lincoln Campaign* (Cambridge, 1944), 148-53, and Nevins, *Emergence of Lincoln*, II, 254. But this cannot be if we regard the meanings of words and the substance of the constitutional argument of the preceding thirteen years.

[41] Basler *et al.* (eds.), *Collected Works of Lincoln*, IV, 52.

[42] *Ibid.*, II, 400, 403.

did to protect slavery in the territories) until it should be overruled by a more responsible court.[43] His statement in his inaugural address of his willingness to acquiesce in that decision for the time being was not inconsistent with his earlier statements.[44]

The Constitutional Union party, that is, the remnant of the Whig party, was so divided upon what the Dred Scott decision was and what to do about it that it could not agree on any specific platform. There can be little doubt, however, that the great majority of its adherents still held the old traditional view of the powers of Congress as expounded by Henry Clay and later by Justice Curtis and hoped for a settlement along the lines of the old Missouri Compromise.[45]

After Lincoln's election, Southern secessionists both of the *per se* and conditional varieties insisted that slaveholders and slave states had been or were being or were about to be deprived of their constitutional rights in the common territories as those rights had been affirmed by the highest court in the land. The Northern people generally, except for the comparatively small Buchanan faction, denied that the South had been deprived of a single constitutional right in the territories.

In conclusion, this writer has no disposition to try to magnify the constitutional controversies herein described into a major explanation of the causes of secession and civil war.[46] However, not only did great constitutional lawyers grapple with the constitutional issues described, but also hundreds of thousands of their fellow citizens took these issues seriously and debated or pondered them earnestly and intelligently. Historians should strive to understand these constitutional matters and the positions individuals and parties took upon them and treat them neither lightly nor carelessly in their general accounts of the causes of secession.

[43] *Ibid.*, II, 495; III, 255 (speeches at Chicago, July 10, and Quincy, October 13, 1858).

[44] A long paragraph a little beyond the middle of the address starting "I do not forget the position assumed by some that constitutional questions are to be decided by the Supreme Court . . . ." *Ibid.*, IV, 268.

[45] See, for examples, statements of John J. Crittenden and John Bell in the Senate March 18, 1858. *Cong. Globe*, 35 Cong., 1 Sess., Appendix, 130, 140.

[46] Arthur Bestor, "The American Civil War as a Constitutional Crisis," *American Historical Review*, LXIX (January 1964), 327-52.

4

Southern Secessionists Per Se and the Crisis of 1850

The following essay was originally read at the Spring 1950 meeting of the Mississippi Valley Historical Association. It has not been published previously.

An attempt will be made in this essay to support two principal contentions: namely, that historians have not, in general, adequately assessed the activities and influence of Southern secessionists *per se* in bringing about and trying to take advantage of the sectional crisis of 1850, and that they have not, in general, attached sufficient importance to economic motives in explaining the rise of secession *per se* sentiment. It is believed that historians have not, in general, found enough secessionists *per se*, have not found them early enough, and have not paid enough attention to their propaganda and maneuvers.[1] It is believed that *a* (not *the*) principal cause of the rise, growth, and spread of secession sentiment in the South was an early, persistent, and widespread belief that the Union operated in such a way as to build up the North at the expense of the South, thus preventing the

---

[1] The author does not disagree with all histories and historians of secession. He does find himself in disagreement, though, with practically all the textbooks, nearly all the general histories, and a goodly portion of the monographs and scholarly articles. Years ago Edward Ingle gave adequate recognition to the economic causes of secession in his *Southern Sidelights: A Picture of Social and Economic Life in the South a Generation Before the War* (New York, 1896). R. S. Cotterill, *The Old South* (Glendale, Ca., 1939), finds a large number of secessionists and recognizes that the secession movement was of "ancient ancestry." Avery Craven, *The Coming of the Civil War* (New York, 1942) and *Edmund Ruffin, Southerner* (New York, 1932), names secessionists *per se* and describes their propaganda and maneuvers. The author of this essay once tried to evaluate the economic motives for secession in a monograph, *Economic Aspects of Southern Sectionalism, 1840–1861* (University of Illinois, *Studies in the Social Sciences*, XI, 1924). John G. Van Deusen, in his *Economic Bases of Disunion in South Carolina* (New York, 1928), attached still greater weight to economic causes. Economic reasons for secession were set forth with a vengeance by the late B. B. Kendrick in "The Colonial Status of the South," *Journal of Southern History*, VIII (February 1942),3–22. Professor Kendrick's paper was read as a presidential address before the Southern Historical Association in Atlanta, November 7, 1941. The above list is by no means exhaustive.

South from attaining the wealth and prosperity to which its natural resources and the industry and enterprise of its people entitled it.

Secessionists *per se* are understood to have been people who became convinced well in advance of their fellow citizens that their region's best interests and chance for happiness lay in separation and independence, no matter what might be the outcome of specific controversies of the moment, and labored persistently to achieve their great objective.

In a short essay on such a large subject, one can only sample the evidence and outline the arguments. Readers who have long studied our tragic sectional conflict can readily supply further evidence in support of the theses presented here or in refutation thereof.

Let us start at the beginning. The two sections fought together in the American Revolution and formed a "perpetual" union under the Articles of Confederation with remarkably little jealousy and friction; however, the making of the Constitution presented sectional difficulties.

The principal matters of sectional dispute in the Constitutional Convention were the foreign slave trade, commerce, and taxation. The sharpest division on the slave trade was between the Upper South and the Lower South. The division on commerce and taxes, however, was more sharply South versus North. In those times, the Southern states were often referred to as the "exporting states" and the Northern as the "commercial states." The exporting states, being in a minority, feared that the commercial states would try to use their power in the new Congress to obtain favorable navigation and commercial laws and to throw the burden of taxation on exports. Southern delegates accordingly tried to have provisions put in the new Constitution requiring a two-thirds majority in both houses of Congress to enact commercial laws or to ratify commercial treaties.[2] They failed to get this, but they did secure the prohibition of export duties and the requirement that treaties must be ratified by a two-thirds vote in the Senate.[3]

In Virginia and North Carolina, two of the principal reasons for opposition to ratification of the new Constitution were a belief that the commerce clauses did not adequately protect the interests of the South and fear as to how Virginia or North Carolina would fare in

[2] Max Farrand, ed., *Records of the Federal Convention of 1787* (New Haven, 1911), II, 359–65, 374–75, and 448–53, especially.
[3] This was one of the compromises of the Constitutional Convention that historians have often neglected.

the impending settlement of the federal debt and the federal–state accounts.[4] Patrick Henry opposed ratification and, in all probability, preferred a separation from the Union and the formation of a Southern confederacy. He had been outraged, especially, by a proposed treaty with Spain that John Jay had negotiated, which would have abandoned free navigation of the Mississippi for certain commercial concessions.[5] Many others in the South seem to have shared Patrick Henry's views.

Shortly after the new government was inaugurated, events occurred which caused many Southerners to feel that their worst fears had been realized. The measure for refunding the federal domestic debt was passed in a form unacceptable to the South, and the assumption of state debts was carried over the strong opposition of every Southern delegation except South Carolina's. Southern dissatisfaction was not allayed when it was learned that five dollars in interest on the new funded debt went to Massachusetts for every dollar that came to Virginia.[6] When the Revolutionary War pensions were computed, it was found that, for some reason or other, four times as many dollars went to the North as to the South.[7] When Jefferson presented the Southern complaints to Washington, the father of his country only said that all the debt was "honest" debt.[8] Henry Lee wrote Madison that all Patrick Henry's dark forebodings were coming true and that he would submit to a dissolution of the Union rather than submit to "a fixed, insolent Northern majority."[9] Dozens of similar complaints might be cited.

Thus, there *early came to be a set belief* in the older South that in its financial operations and commercial arrangements the federal government worked to benefit the North at the expense of the South. Southerners were still complaining of the allegedly ill effects of assumption and the funding measures long after the debts were paid. Muscoe R. H. Garnett of Virginia repeated the story in 1850 in his

[4] Madison to Washington, October 18, 1787, to Jefferson, October 24, 1787, *Writings of James Madison,* ed. Gaillard Hunt (9 vols., New York, 1900–1910), V, 11, 17.

[5] Madison to Thomas Jefferson, March 19, 1787, to Randolph, January 10, 1788, to Edmund Pendleton, February 21, 1788, to Jefferson, April 22, 1788, *Writings of James Madison,* II, 328, V, 80, 107, 120.

[6] Charles A. Beard, *Economic Origins of Jeffersonian Democracy* (New York, 1915), 189.

[7] Van Deusen, *Economic Bases of Disunion in South Carolina,* ch. 6.

[8] Jefferson to Washington, May 23, 1792, and notes of conversation, July 10, 1792, *Works of Thomas Jefferson,* ed. P. L. Ford (12 vols., New York, 1904–1905), II, 227–31, VI, 487–95.

[9] The letter was dated April 3, 1790. *Writings of James Madison,* VI, 10.

influential pamphlet, *The Union, Past and Future: How It Works and How to Save It.*

Jefferson, Madison, and others built up the Republican party, which captured control of the government. Under the Republican banner, three great Virginians in succession held the presidency for twenty-four years. But the "Old Republicans" of the older South felt that Jefferson and Madison had made too many compromises for the purpose of winning friends in the North and continued to carry on the tradition of unequal benefits between the sections. Three prominent Virginians, John Taylor, John Randolph, and the latter's half brother, Beverly Tucker, were notable examples of Old Republicans.

Then came the beginnings of the industrial revolution and the revolution in transportation. Older regions of the country watched expectantly to see where the lightning would strike and to a degree tried to direct it. For reasons which cannot be examined here, the new textile mills, factories, and machine shops sprang up chiefly in southern New England and in the Middle Atlantic states. Household and shop manufacturing declined everywhere—East, West, and South. New York, Philadelphia, Boston, and the border city of Baltimore became the assembling and distributing centers for the goods of the rising industrial belts and also became great manufacturing centers themselves. *They* got the shipping. They got radiating turnpikes, canals, and railroads. They (especially New York) came to do nearly all the importing for the entire nation, including the South. They got the central banks and the investment brokers. Alexandria, Richmond, Norfolk, Wilmington, Charleston, and Savannah languished by comparison.[10]

The manufacturing interests of the North demanded and secured protective tariffs. The shipping interests demanded and gained a monopoly of coastwise carriage, as against foreign shipping. Various interests involved demanded federal funds for improving harbors, building lighthouses, dredging rivers, and constructing "internal improvements" of various sorts. Even the commercial fisherman claimed and secured bounties for their catches.

The older staple exporting districts of the South reacted sharply to the accentuated sectional economic divergence and to the system of plunder and privilege which seemed to benefit other sections at their expense. When their representatives in Congress failed to defeat

[10] Richmond, however, did quite well as a manufacturing town.

the obnoxious legislation, one state, South Carolina, resorted to the device of nullification. The nullifiers of that state received much moral and political support from the commercialized farming belts of Virginia, North Carolina, Georgia, and even the infant state of Alabama. The nullification movement had strong secession over-tones.[11] The party in South Carolina opposed to nullification sig-nificantly took the name "Unionist." Andrew Jackson's famous toast was, "The Federal Union—It must be preserved."

After the Compromise Tariff of 1833 had been enacted, the Nulli-fiers, with few exceptions, never regained an affection for the Union. There came to be a saying in the South, "Once a Nullifier, always a Nullifier." The saying was substantially true, it being understood, of course, that nullification was abandoned as a specific remedy. The great majority of the Nullifiers, in South Carolina and out, by easy stages and at different times became secessionists *per se.* They gained converts as they went along.

In national politics, the Nullifiers of South Carolina and other states first aligned themselves with the Whig party when it was formed. This proved to be an unnatural alliance. In 1840 Calhoun led the great majority of the Nullifiers back into the Democratic fold. A minority, especially in Virginia and Georgia, long stayed in the Whig party without changing their views on economic issues. John Tyler is the most notable example. Within the Democratic party in the South, the line of cleavage between the Old-Nullifier, or Calhoun, wing and the Jackson–Benton–Van Buren, or Union, wing remained distinct until the Civil War. In several states, the factional strife within the Democratic party was almost as violent as that be-tween Whigs and Democrats.[12] The story of factional differences within the Democratic party in the South has never been adequately

[11] It is believed that this statement is amply supported by the standard works on nullification by David F. Houston, *A Critical Study of Nullification in South Carolina* (New York, 1896), and Chauncey S. Boucher, *The Nullification Controversy in South Carolina* (Chicago, 1916).

[12] Virginia, Georgia, Alabama, Mississippi, and Tennessee, at least. The state-ments made herein can be verified by an almost casual reading of *Correspondence of John C. Calhoun,* ed. J. F. Jameson (Washington, 1900); *Correspondence of Robert M. T. Hunter,* ed. C. H. Ambler (Washington, 1918); J. F. H. Claiborne, *Life and Correspondence of John A. Quitman* (2 vols., New York, 1860); and *Correspondence of Robert Toombs, Alexander H. Stephens, and Howell Cobb,* ed. U. B. Phillips (Washington, 1913). The statements concerned are also amply supported, it is believed, by T. H. Jack, *Sectionalism and Party Politics in Alabama, 1819–1842* (Menasha, Wis., 1919); C. H. Ambler, *Thomas Ritchie: A Study in Virginia Politics* (Richmond, 1913); H. T. Shanks, *The Secession Move-ment in Virginia, 1847–1861* (Richmond, 1934); and numerous other mono-graphs and biographies.

presented for the section as a whole. Someone should do for the Democratic party in the antebellum South what A. C. Cole has done for the Whig in his *The Whig Party in the South* (1913) and Arthur M. Schlesinger, Jr., has done for the Democratic party in the Northeast in *The Age of Jackson* (1945).

The Calhoun or Nullifier wing of the Democratic party held these tenets: the federal government was being too extravagantly administered; the Southern people were paying far more than their proportionate share of the federal taxes and receiving far less than their proportionate share of the federal disbursements; they were being compelled by government to pay tribute to Northern manufacturers, merchants, fishermen, and shipowners by virtue of tariffs, fishing bounties, shipping subsidies, and the exclusion of foreign vessels from the coasting trade; otherwise, through the tricks of trade, the legerdemain of finance, the shrewd Yankees were somehow getting the Southerners' hard-earned dollars away from them; and these continued and uncompensated drains upon the Southern people were building up the North and keeping the South impoverished.

"Abolish Custom Houses," wrote Calhoun in a private letter in 1845, "and let the money collected in the South be spent in the South and we would be among the most flourishing people in the world. The North could not stand the annual draft, which they have been making on us 50 years, without being reduced to the extreme of poverty in half the time. All we want to be rich is to let us have what we make."[13] "The South is nothing else now, but the very best colony of the North any people ever possessed," said Robert Barnwell Rhett in his famous disunion speech in the United States Senate, December, 1851.[14] The following quotation from an Alabama newspaper of 1851 is typical:

At present, the North fattens and grows rich upon the South. We depend upon it for our entire supplies. We purchase all our luxuries and necessaries from the North. . . . With us, every branch and pursuit in life, every trade, profession, and occupation, is dependent upon the North; for instance, the Northerners abuse and denounce slavery and slaveholders, yet our slaves are clothed with Northern manufactured goods, have Northern hats and shoes, work with Northern hoes, ploughs, and other implements, are chastised with a Northern-made instrument, are working for Northern more than Southern profit. The slaveholder dresses in Northern goods, rides in a Northern saddle,

[13] Calhoun to J. H. Hammond, August 30, 1845, *Correspondence of John C. Calhoun.*
[14] *Congressional Globe,* 32 Cong., 1 Sess., Appx., 42–8.

sports his Northern carriage, patronizes Northern newspapers, drinks Northern liquors, reads Northern books, spends his money at Northern watering-places. . . . The aggressive acts upon his rights and his property arouse his resentment—and on Northern-made paper, with a Northern pen, with Northern ink, he resolves and reresolves in regard to his rights! In Northern vessels his products are carried to market, his cotton is ginned with Northern gins, his sugar is crushed and preserved by Northern machinery; his rivers are navigated by Northern steamboats, his mails are carried in Northern stages, his negroes are fed with Northern bacon, beef, flour, and corn; his land is cleared with a Northern axe, and a Yankee clock sits upon his mantelpiece.[15]

The Jacksonian Democrats and a majority of the Whigs of the South never more than half believed the thesis of unequal operation of the Union. If they admitted Southern "decline" at all, they were more likely to attribute it to natural causes or to Southern "lethargy." They were willing to compromise on the tariff, scramble for the section's share of the federal appropriations, and fight each other over Jacksonian democracy, banks, public-lands policies, the chartering of joint-stock companies, public aid to railroads, manifest destiny, and other national and state issues.

As time went by, the states' rights wing of the Democratic party gradually gained ground at the expense of the Jacksonians. It eventually gained control of the party in all the cotton states and equal strength with the Union wing in several of the border states.

The steady gains of the states' rights wing may be attributed to several circumstances and developments. As time went by, the economic and social organization and conditions of the newer Southwestern states came to approximate those of the older planting districts; and, as they did so, the economic interests and political views of people in the Southwest tended to be like those of people in the older South. The industrial, commercial, and financial supremacy of the East became more pronounced; and, as it did so, Southern discontent with the South's dependent position became keener. Old Nullifiers conducted a persistent and effective propaganda of discontent with the Union. Charleston was the main center of emanation, and the Lower South was the most fertile field. Many South Carolinians moved into the newer cotton states, gained positions of influence in society and politics, and seldom failed to disseminate the orthodox doctrines of the South Carolina school.[16] And certainly the exacerba-

---

[15] Quoted in F. A. P. Barnard, *An Oration Delivered before the Citizens of Tuscaloosa, Alabama, July 4th, 1851* (Tuscaloosa, 1851).

[16] J. M. and A. P. Calhoun and J. A. Elmore in Alabama, J. D. B. DeBow in New Orleans, and L. T. Wigfall in Texas come most readily to mind.

tion of sectional feeling by the quarrels over slavery contributed greatly to the triumph of the states' rights wing. That wing, having other grounds for dissatisfaction, was more disposed to take sharp issue on slavery.

It is not denied for a moment that the slavery question came to overshadow other sectional issues. Actual fears for the security of the institution of slavery in the Union and feelings of outrage and wrong because of Northern denunciations of slaveholding and slaveholders and Northern denials of what most Southerners considered their constitutional rights in the premises quite probably made secessionists faster than any other cause. But one cause of discontent did not supplant another. One rather reinforced the other. Why does it seem necessary to find *one* cause?[17]

It is most illuminating in this connection that, in the great slavery crises, the Southern people divided along very much the same lines that they divided on in economic matters. The crisis that followed the introduction of the Wilmot Proviso and led to the Compromise of 1850 is a good example. The Whigs tried to avoid agitation of the slavery question. They would not take an advanced position. They were willing to accept almost any face-saving compromise. The Jacksonian Democrats also were willing to accept a formula that did not require their Northern brethren to vote against their consciences. Not so of the Democrats of the states' rights school. They took the extreme position and refused to compromise.

It was old Nullifiers that were most instrumental in calling the Nashville Convention of 1850. The published correspondence of John C. Calhoun and the papers of Whitemarsh B. Seabrook,[18] then governor of South Carolina, make this clear. These papers, the James H. Hammond Papers,[19] and numerous other sources[20] make it just as clear that most of the old Nullifiers hoped to use the Nashville

[17] Howard K. Beale in his excellent article, "What Historians Have Said about the Causes of the Civil War" (in *Theory and Practice in Historical Study: A Report of the Committee on Historiography,* Charles Beard et al., eds [Social Science Research Council Bulletin 54, 1946, pp. 55–102; New York, 1946, pp. 71–2]) decries, or seems to decry, the tendency of historians, professional as well as amateur, to seek one cause for secession. I agree. Professor Beale pays me the compliment of a reference and facilely catalogs me in the "Beard school of economic interpretationists." That I am not and never have been. I tried to evaluate the economic *aspects* of Southern sectionalism in my book (see n. 1 of my introduction) and am here protesting their neglect by professional historians.

[18] Deposited in the Library of Congress.

[19] Deposited in the Library of Congress.

[20] See especially Laura White, *Robert Barnwell Rhett: Father of Secession* (New York, 1931), ch. 7.

Convention to make demands upon the North that would not be acceded to and, thus, to provide the occasion for secession.[21]

After the passage of the Compromise Measures of 1850, there were sharp contests over their acceptance in four states—South Carolina, Georgia, Mississippi, and Alabama. The alternative to acceptance was secession. Again we find the familiar alignment. The great majority of the Whigs and the Jackson Democrats united to form the Unionist party, and the States' Rights Democrats and the small element of States' Rights Whigs formed the Southern Rights, or Secession, party. The Unionists won but had a clear-cut victory only in Mississippi.

In South Carolina there were three parties—the Separate Actionists, the Cooperationists, and the Unionists. The Separate Actionists favored secession even though no other state seemed so disposed at the same time. The Cooperationists also advocated secession, but only if other Southern states could be persuaded to go along. The Unionists were the smallest of the three parties, although probably a number of Unionists represented themselves as Cooperationists for tactical reasons. It is interesting and illuminating to note that, with only one exception,[22] every prominent Unionist of 1850 who had been active in politics in nullification times had been a Unionist in the earlier crisis, that, with only the one exception, every prominent Nullifier of 1832 still living in 1850 was an active secessionist at the latter date, and that, of the comparatively few Unionists of 1832 who had become professed secessionists by 1850, all identified themselves with the Cooperationists rather than with the more radical Separate Actionists.

The alignments which have been described show remarkable persistence. It is hard to escape the conclusion, therefore, that people who had come to believe that the South occupied a position of "economic vassalage" to the North were more easily persuaded than others to believe that slavery was endangered in the Union and that Northern insults could no longer be borne. No doubt it was also true that people who had become greatly excited by the slavery con-

---

21 Whether Calhoun himself had become a secessionist *per se* by the last years of his life will probably long continue to be debated. The present writer believes not. Calhoun never seems to have so described himself. He was still longing for the presidency a few months before his death. His proposal for two presidents, one Northern and Southern, each armed with the veto, reminds one of Galloway's Plan of Union advanced in 1774 as a means of saving the political connection between the thirteen colonies and Great Britain. But Calhoun certainly did more than any other man to creat secession sentiment.

22 Waddy Thompson, a Whig.

troversy were more ready to believe that the South was economically oppressed by the North.

Now the facts have not been overlooked that the alignment between the Calhoun Democrats and the Jackson–Benton Democrats was largely along class lines, and the former were more closely identified with slavery than the latter. The great majority of the Union Democrats were nonslaveholders and consequently had less at stake in the slavery controversy. But this by no means proves that slavery was the sole basis for the difference in attitudes toward the Union. The alignment between the factions was along geographic and occupational lines as well. The Calhoun Democrats were to be found very largely in the commercialized farming belts and were economically interdependent with the outside world; therefore, they were more likely to feel "colonial status." The Union Democrats were to be found mostly in the back-country districts where people were more economically self-sufficient and less dependent on the outside world and, accordingly, had less reason to be concerned about economic vassalage.

Even if differing degrees of interest in slavery should be accepted as an adequate explanation of the differing attitudes of the Democratic factions toward the value of the Union, they would hardly suffice to explain the differences between the Calhoun Democrats and the Southern Whigs in that respect. The Whigs almost certainly included more large slaveholders than the Democrats did. The Whigs were, nevertheless, nearly all Unionists. Only a few were secessionists *per se*. Whigs of the black belts did not agree with their States' Rights Democrat neighbors on the proper tactics to pursue to meet the antislavery menace, to be sure, and there was plenty of room for disagreement. But neither did they agree with them as to the causes and remedies for "Southern decline." There was a subtle but logical relation between choice of tactics in the slavery struggle and calculations of the economic value of the Union.

During a quarter-century before secession, there was a great deal of discussion in the South on the desirability of making the section less dependent on the North. Praiseworthy efforts were made to encourage manufacturing, establish direct trade with Europe, connect different parts of the section by railroads, and, in general, promote the economic development of the South. These movements for economic independence were a bona fide attempt on the part of public-spirited citizens to remedy the ills of their economy. In general, Unionists were more active in these efforts than disunionists, for their analysis of the causes of Southern "decline" gave them greater faith in the efficacy of state and local remedies, and Unionists believed alleviation of economic ills would allay dissatisfaction with the Union. The secessionists believed or professed to believe that little could be done in the Union to free the South of its economic dependence on the North and, accordingly, took less part in the movement for the economic regeneration of the South in the Union.

The movements to make the South more economically independent in the Union have sometimes been described as an effort on the part of Southern fire-eaters to prepare their section for a separation which they believed or hoped to be inevitable.[23] This is not a correct interpretation. It is true that the secessionists *per se* managed to take over the Southern Commercial Convention, which met annually in the 1850s, and use it to advance their great cause. But under them it ceased to be a commercial convention.[24]

Considerable credence should be accorded to the evidence given by Southern Unionists as to the motives of the secessionists *per se* in the crisis of 1850. They were their contemporaries—their friends and neighbors. Southern Unionists commonly refused to believe that the secessionists were more concerned than themselves for the preservation of slavery or the maintenance of Southern honor. They persisted in ascribing other motives to the secessionists, economic ones principally. For example, F. A. P. Barnard of Alabama, in 1851, said he believed there were causes much deeper than the slavery agitation for the war to the knife which had recently been waged against the Union. He retold the story of South Carolina nullification. The people of that state were still smarting from the old feud, he said. He told of Southern dependence upon the North and of the sensitivity of Southern people about that condition. "From this condition of things our people have become impatient to be free; and this it is . . . more truly than any other existing evil, which has caused the word disunion to be of late so often and so lightly spoken among us. . . ."[25]

The limits of this essay will not permit us to carry the story down to actual secession. During the 1850s there were developments and conditions that tended to make the people of the South more content

---

23 See, for example, Craven, *The Coming of the Civil War*, ch. 12.
24 The author has traced the change in the personnel and objectives of the Convention in chapter 5 of his *Economic Aspects of Southern Sectionalism.*
25 Barnard, *Oration Delivered before the Citizens of Tuscaloosa, Alabama, July 4, 1851.*

with their economic system and position. A comparatively few former secessionists *per se* decided the Union could now be endured. But the belief that the Union was unequal in its benefits was too deeply ingrained to be quickly overcome, and the bitter quarrels over slavery made secessionists faster than any brightening economic prospects could unmake them. During the decade and especially the latter half, the secessionists *per se* stepped up their propaganda and diligently sought an occasion for secession. Finally in Lincoln's election, to which they had contributed so greatly, they found the occasion that enabled them to "fire the Southern heart—instruct the Southern mind—give courage to each other, and . . . precipitate the cotton States into a revolution."[26]

[26] William Yancey to James S. Slaughter, June 15, 1858, in J. W. DuBose, *The Life and Times of William Lowndes Yancey* (2 vols., Birmingham, Ala., 1892, reprint ed., New York, 1942), I, 376.

5

Economic Aspects of the Disunion Movement, 1852–1860

The following essay originally appeared in *Economic Aspects of Southern Sectionalism, 1840–1861,* University of Illinois Studies in the Social Sciences, XI (Urbana, 1924), 179–198. The original pagination appears in brackets.

After the defeat of the disunion movement of 1850-1851 the disunionists were comparatively quiet for a few years. The struggles over slavery were temporarily abated. All parties seemed to turn with more or less earnestness to efforts to see whether something could not be done in an organized way to hasten the economic and social progress of the South—a policy which Unionists had earlier supported as a substitute for disunion. It was during this short period that the Southern Commercial Convention was instituted, and went about its work with a hope of accomplishing results. Meanwhile, however, the Southern Rights wing strengthened its control of the reunited Democratic party. In doing this it was aided materially by the Pierce administration. In his distribution of the patronage Pierce tried to conciliate the Southern Rights faction, and failed to recognize the more conservative element. He submitted himself largely to the guidance of the radical Southern leaders in the formulation of policies. Meanwhile, too, the Whig party began to dissolve.

In 1854 the lull in the quarrel over slavery was rudely interrupted by the repeal of the Missouri Compromise—the motives of which we shall not pause to discuss. The repeal served as the occasion for the organization of a sectional party in the North, which in turn reacted to strengthen the hands of the extremists in the South. The Kansas troubles and the presidential campaign of 1856, with its threat of the election of the candidate of a sectional party, called forth again threats of disunion, and once more the subject was canvassed in all its aspects. From this time on little reserve was shown in expressing disunion sentiments.

The session of the Southern Commercial Convention held in Savannah a month after the election showed unmistakably the growth of disunion sentiment, and proved to be the last controlled by the conservative element; its successors were little more than gatherings of disunionists. A large proportion of the representative newspapers of the South, especially of the cotton states, openly and almost constantly advocated disunion. The Richmond *Enquirer,* in the summer of 1857, complained that the Charleston

Mercury "does nothing from year's end to year's end but to announce the speedy dissolution of the Union."[1] Among others scarcely less open in their advocacy of disunion were, not to mention South Carolina journals, the Richmond *Examiner,* Roger A. Pryor's Richmond *South,* the Columbus (Georgia) *Corner Stone,* the Mobile *Register,* the Mobile *Mercury,* the Montgomery *Advertiser and Gazette,* the New Orleans *Crescent,* the New Orleans *Delta,* the Vicksburg *True Southron,* and the Memphis *Appeal.* J. D. B. DeBow had by this time become an avowed disunionist, and *DeBow's Review* was disunionist in the whole tendency of its teaching. The *Review* had some quite able writers among its contributors, had won for itself a considerable circulation and much prestige, and exercised great influence in the South. The avowed secessionists in Congress had come to be a considerable group, which included Miles, Keitt, and Bonham, of South Carolina, Iverson, of Georgia, Roger A. Pryor, of Virginia, John A. Quitman, J. D. McRae, Reuben Davis, and Barksdale, of Mississippi, C. C. Clay and J. L. Pugh, of Alabama, and Wigfall, of Texas. Many who did not publicly avow themselves secessionists were known to lean strongly in that direction. Outside of Congress were dozens of men of reputation and influence, most conspicuous of whom was William Lowndes Yancey, of Alabama, who devoted their best energies to advancing the cause of disunion. Through public agitation and discussion and the later meetings of the Southern Commercial Convention,[2] through private conferences and the wide correspondence carried on by various individuals— some unsuccessful attempts were made at organization[3]—the disunionist leaders in the several states became acquainted with each other, came to have a good understanding of the state of public

---

[1]August 13.

[2]*Edmund Ruffin's Diary* gives a good understanding of the way in which the Southern Commercial Convention, aside from the formal meetings, was used to promote the cause. See entries covering the session at Montgomery, which Ruffin attended.

[3]League of United Southerners. Hodgson, *Cradle of the Confederacy,* 393-396; DuBose, *Life and Times of Yancey,* 377; Charleston *Mercury,* Aug. 3, 1858; Montgomery *Daily Confederation,* May 21, 1859, quoting an editorial in the Mobile *Mercury; DeBow's Review,* XXV, 250.

sentiment in all quarters of the South, and strove to approach an agreement in regard to the proper policies to be pursued.[4]

Disunionists frankly expressed their hope that a pretext could be found which would precipitate the cotton states into a revolution.[5] Their desire to make an issue in part explains the agitation for repealing the laws against the foreign slave trade. When the Southern members in Congress compromised the Kansas question, in April, 1858, by accepting the English bill, several prominent disunionists expressed their disappointment that an issue had not been made.[6] Finally, the issue was presented when, largely through the agency of the disunionists, the Democratic party was split in twain at Charleston and Baltimore, and the triumph of a sectional party made inevitable.

The discussion of disunion during the several years preceding the actual launching of the experiment left no phase of the subject untouched. Every possible angle of the question was explored— the ability of the Southern states to support a separate government; the probability of their being permitted to secede without war; the attitude the border states would take in case the cotton states should secede; the most desirable boundary line; the division of the territories; the policies the new confederacy should pursue with respect to commerce with the North and Europe, the tariff, the navigation of the Mississippi, the Pacific railroad, immigration, the slave trade, expansion of the confederacy to the southward, and the military establishment; the effect of dissolution

[4]In a letter to Roger A. Pryor, Yancey said he did not expect Virginia to take the initiative. "Her position as a border state, and a well considered Southern policy—(a policy which has been digested and understood and approved by some of the ablest men in Virginia, as you yourself must be aware)—would seem to demand that, when such movement takes place by any considerable number of Southern states, Virginia . . . . should remain in the Union." Hodgson, *op. cit.*, 397; *National Intelligencer*, Sept. 4, 1858.

[5]W. L. Yancey to James S. Slaughter, June 15, 1858, in Hodgson, *op. cit.*, 393; DuBose, *Yancey*, 376.

[6]Yancey to Thos. J. Orme, May 22, 1858, in Montgomery *Daily Confederation*, June 5, 1858; DuBose, *Yancey*, 366-75; M. L. Bonham, of South Carolina, in the House of Representatives, June 9, *Cong. Globe*, 35 Cong., 1 Sess., Appx. 509-11. A correspondent of the Charleston *Mercury* wrote of the Southern Commercial Convention at Montgomery: "I have not met a single man except the Virginians who approves the late compromise in Kansas." May 15, 1858.

upon the prosperity and development of the South as a whole and of particular classes, interests, and localities.

The various arguments in favor of disunion did not appeal with equal force to all disunionists. Many emphasized the greater security of slavery in a separate republic and the freedom from the quarrels over slavery, which seemed interminable in the Union; and there can be no doubt that, could the slavery quarrel have been hushed, and the issue amicably settled, disunion sentiment would never have reached alarming proportions or have been translated into action. Others were prone to contemplate the glories of a great republic stretching from the Ohio to Panama and encircling the Gulf of Mexico. Others were influenced by the possibility of reopening the foreign slave trade. Too many politicians, it must be said, felt that their political careers had been blighted in the Union, and hoped for better fortune in the narrower confines of a Southern confederacy. But almost all disunionists believed, or professed to believe, that the South in the Union was being exploited economically for the benefit of the North; that the Southern states had somehow become tributary provinces of the Northern; that Northern wealth largely represented the product of Southern labor; and that, could the Southern states but cut loose from their Northern connections and be permitted to work out their own destiny in their own way, their prosperity would be greater and their development quickened.

The arguments advanced in support of these propositions were similar to those used in 1850 and 1851, but had been modified to some extent by circumstances. Since that time there had been much discussion of diversification of industry and development of varied resources; commercial conventions had been held and public opinion educated; and various plans for regenerating the South had been tried or proposed, and, in general, had failed. Whereas in the earlier period most of those who hoped for a diversification of Southern pursuits had held aloof from or had opposed the disunion movement, in the latter many of that class, despairing of success in the Union, lent it their support.

The doctrine that the South paid more than her share of the taxes and received less than her share of the disbursements had been so frequently repeated that it was becoming generally accepted. One estimated at $50,000,000 the sum the South paid annually, and at $10,000,000 the amount returned in the form of expenditures; $40,000,000 annually would be saved by going out of the Union. Such a sum distributed among the states would give an enormous impetus to manufactures and all other branches of industry which suffered from a deficiency of capital in the South.[7] Southern men did not cease to attribute Southern decline to unequal taxation and disbursements.[8]

Direct trade with Europe would follow, it was said, closely upon the heels of separation; for importers would never pay the duties imposed by the North in addition to the moderate duties imposed by the Southern confederacy. "With a horizontal duty upon all imports it would be impossible for foreign products to come to us by way of the cities of the North."[9] If necessary, navigation laws could be enacted discriminating against Northern shipping. Foreign ships would flock to Southern ports; Northern ships would be transferred to the South. Northern seaports would decline; Southern would flourish.[10] The South, having control of its own commerce, would control the "exchanges" also, and thus become financially independent. The establishment of direct trade would give an impulse to every other pursuit: "Manufactories would then grow up, commerce would extend, mechanical arts would flourish, and, in short, every industrial and every professional pursuit would receive a vivifying impulse."[11]

Of all those who speculated in regard to the proper policy of a new confederacy, it is worthy of note that very few proposed that the government should be supported without resort to duties on

[7] *DeBow's Review*, XXI, 543. Similar statements are in the Charleston *Mercury*, Feb. 25, 1858, quoting the Mobile *Mercury; DeBow's Review*, XXX, 252; *ibid.*, XXI, 532; speech of J. A. Jones, of Georgia, in Vicksburg, New York *Herald*, May 21, 1859.

[8] John Forsyth's lecture on "The North and the South," Mobile, 1854, *DeBow's Review*, XVII, 368-73; *ibid.*, XIX, 383-4; *ibid.*, XXVI, 476 (A. P. Calhoun, 1859); *ibid.*, XXX, 436 (DeBow, 1858); W. P. Miles, of South Carolina, in House of Representatives, Mar. 31, 1858, Charleston *Mercury*, Apr. 17; *Southern Literary Messenger*, XXXI, 238; "Barbarossa" [John Scott], *The Lost Principle, or the Sectional Equilibrium*, Pt. I, ch. V; Claiborne, *Life and Correspondence of John A. Quitman*, II, 186-7.

[9] *DeBow's Review*, XXI, 543.

[10] *Ibid.*, XXI, 519; XXV, 373; XXIII, 604; *Cong. Globe*, 33 Cong., 1 Sess., 375 (Preston S. Brooks).

[11] *DeBow's Review*, XXIX, 462.

imports. It is true many spoke of a free trade republic; but "free trade" was generally equivalent to "tariff for revenue only." Almost all would have had low duties; but while some told how low they would be and emphasized the blessings of free trade, others dwelt upon the incidental protection which would be afforded by a tariff for revenue. Said Willoughby Newton, a Virginia disunionist of long standing, "A tariff for the support of the new government would give such protection to manufacturers that all our waterfalls would bristle with machinery."[12] Men from border states were more inclined to speak of the advantages of protection against Northern competition than were men from the cotton states, though the latter often held out as an inducement to Virginia and North Carolina to go with the Gulf states the probability that they would supplant New England in manufacturing for the South. There were free traders, however, who thought it might be well to leave the Northern slave states out of the confederacy lest they should demand protection for their industries. Disunionists believed that, in case of separation, the North would have to resort to direct taxation to support her government; for she would no longer be able to import on Southern account, and she could not tax imports from the South, since they were chiefly raw materials.[13] The consequences of direct taxation would be the transfer to the South of much capital invested in manufactures.

The disunionists often took a somewhat skeptical attitude toward the efforts which were being made to promote Southern commerce and industry while the Union continued. Each failure confirmed their opinion that such efforts were futile. The Charleston *Mercury* said that in the Union "Direct trade with the customers of the South in Europe is an impossibility....Norfolk, Charleston, Savannah, Mobile, are only suburbs of New York."[14] According to a contributor to *DeBow's Review*, the process of development went on much more slowly than in the North, and must as long as the South remained in the Union with the North to lean upon. Disunion would call for and foster a variety of home products. Pride would demand protection for home indus-

[12]*DeBow's Review*, XXV, 373 (Sept., 1858).
[13]*Ibid.*, XXI, 541-44.
[14]May 20, 1858.

tries. Diversification would develop and unfold the wealth of the South. "True, we *might*, in the course of time, unfold this wealth *in the Union*, but not till the teeming North has 'embellished all her slopes,' and of her superabundance and for lack of other lands to conquer, empties her surplus on us, . . . With all these aids and stimulants we must advance with equal or faster steps than they."[15] A. J. Roane, of Virginia, wrote: "Experience has demonstrated that direct trade to Southern ports cannot be established to any considerable extent in the Union. It can only be accomplished by the stress of the necessity which separation would create."[16] In Virginia the opinion was held that in case of disunion the very necessity of her condition of estrangement from the manufacturing North would impel her to add a manufacturing phase to her already innumerable sources of wealth.[17]

As we have seen, certain south Atlantic ports, particularly of Virginia, which was slowly building the Chesapeake and Ohio railroad, aspired to export and import for the Ohio and the upper Mississippi valleys, and had high expectations of the beneficial effects of such a commerce upon the prosperity of the seaboard regions. A considerable part of the exports and some of the imports of the Northwest still followed the Mississippi river with New Orleans as their port of entry and departure. The people of New Orleans, furthermore, hoped to retain or increase her share of the Western commerce by the building of north and south railroads. There continued to be considerable exchange of products between the South and the West. It was to be presumed that the people who profited or expected to profit by this Western trade would be loath to have a measure taken which might injure that trade and destroy the prospects of future benefits from it. Disunionists sought to overcome the objections of those who yet expected much of Western trade in the way of promoting Southern prosperity. To meet the demands of New Orleans and preserve peace with the West, they generally agreed that, in case of separation, it would be necessary to guarantee free navigation of the Mississippi; it was frequently suggested that Western products be admitted free of duty.[18] Some Southerners professed

[15] *DeBow's Review*, XXIII, 471-474 (Nov., 1857). Cf. *ibid.*, XXI, 177-186.
[16] *Ibid.*, XXIX, 463.
[17] New York *Herald*, October 23, 1860.
[18] *DeBow's Review*, XXX, 93 (Maj. W. H. Chase, of Florida).

to believe that, in case of a dissolution of the Union, the close commercial relations of the two sections and the absolute necessity to the West of the Mississippi river as an outlet for her commerce would induce the West to cast her lot with the South rather than with the East;[19] they were not averse to admitting free states into their slaveholding republic.

It is rather strange how tenaciously Southern men on the eve of secession clung to the belief that the old alliance of the South and West, based upon commercial relations and common opposition to the tariff and financial policies of the East, still continued. For example, Governor Wickliffe, of Louisiana, in his message of January, 1859, said: "The position of the Northwestern States of the Mississippi Valley, on this question [slavery] is of especial interest to us. These States are, by geographical position, commercially our allies, whether slave or free, while many of the States on the Atlantic side of the Alleghanies are necessarily hostile in commercial interest. . . . It is cheering to find our commercial allies of the Northwest sustaining our Southern policy."[20] This statement is accurate in no particular. The value of the trade between the West and East was several times greater than the value of the trade between the West and South. Not only did most of the foreign imports of the West come by way of the East; but by far the larger part of Western exports went that way. The travel between East and West was much greater than between South and West. Much Eastern capital was invested in the West. In politics, too, the West and East had been drawing closer together. The tariff no longer divided them as it did in the days of Calhoun. Both stood for a liberal policy in regard to improvement of rivers and harbors. The South had abandoned her old liberal attitude on the public lands question, and steadily opposed homestead bills and land grants to railroads; while in some quarters the old demand for distribution of the proceeds from the sale of public lands was revived. The East, on the other hand, was inclined to support the public lands policies of the West. On the immigration question, the West agreed with the East rather

[19]Senator Hammond, of South Carolina, Mar. 4, 1858, *Cong. Globe*, 35 Cong., 1 Sess., 961; "Barbarossa," *The Lost Principle*, 225; *DeBow's Review*, XXIII, 603, (Edmund Ruffin).

[20]New Orleans *Daily True Delta*, Jan. 19, 1859.

than with the South; the same was true of the Pacific railroad question. On the paramount issue of slavery, the people of the free states of the Northwest were rapidly losing their old indifferent attitude, and becoming more hostile to the institution.

Along with their pictures of the prosperity and progress which would follow the formation of an independent Southern confederacy, disunionists frequently advanced arguments to prove that it would be accompanied by no countervaling disadvantages. Secession would be peaceful, they said, because the interruption of Southern trade, in case the North should undertake coercion, would bring such prostration to Northern industry and commerce that she would not have the means to go to war. Furthermore, England and France would not permit a blockade, because a cutting off of the supply of cotton would bring ruin to important industries.[21] Thus the disunionists had an argument at every turn.

About the time of Lincoln's election there was published a volume by Edmund Ruffin entitled, *Anticipations of the Future to Serve as Lessons for the Present Time, in the Form of Extracts of Letters from an English Resident in the United States, to the London Times, from 1864 to 1870,* etc.[22] Ruffin was a man of considerable ability. He was known throughout the South, and his name carried great weight because of his long record of valuable services to Virginia and the South at large, chief of which were his contributions to improved methods of agriculture. He was a secessionist of long standing, and one of the leaders of the movement.[23] His book gives such a complete statement of the disunion arguments, colored perhaps by his Virginia viewpoint, that a summary of it is desirable.

Ruffin allowed Lincoln to serve one term and his more radical successor, Seward, to serve part of one without a dissolution of the Union. When, however, Seward proposed to stand for a

[21]*DeBow's Review,* XXIII, 596-601; XXIX, 457-463; XXX, 95 ff.

[22]The earliest notice I have seen of the book was in the *National Intelligencer,* Nov. 15, 1860, which said the work belonged to the "disunion literature of the current day." It was published anonymously, but the authorship was evident from the appendage of a series of essays on "The Causes of the Independence of the South" which had appeared in 1856 and of which Ruffin was known to be the author. Essays were in Richmond *Enquirer,* Dec. and Jan., 1856-1857; *DeBow's Review,* XXII, 583-93; XXIII, 266-72, 546-52, 596-607.

[23]For a brief biographical sketch, see *ibid.,* XI, 431-436.

second term, six cotton states seceded. Whereupon, after some attempts at settlement, the Federal government established a blockade of Southern ports, and war ensued, the northern slave states remaining neutral. By May, 1868, because of the loss of Southern trade and cotton, there were great suffering, threatening mobs, and sanguinary riots in the North. Northern merchants and manufacturers felt very severely the loss of $40,000,000 due them from the South and sequestered by the government of the new confederacy. The South suffered also from the blockade; but there were compensations in that it taught the Southern people to be independent of the North. Soon Virginia, North Carolina, and Maryland found it no longer possible to remain neutral, and entered the war on the side of the South. Another $50,000,000 of debts were sequestered. The North did not attempt to carry the war into the border states. In July, 1868, it was reported that the imports and revenues of the North had fallen off tremendously; for the "greater part of the former importations to Northern ports and in Northern ships, was for transhipment to and consumption in the Southern states."[24] In August outbreaks and violence were reported in the impoverished Northern cities; New York was sacked and burned—a rather bitter commentary on the supposed friendship of the South and New York City. Soon the North was unable to continue the war; and a truce was made.

By February, 1869, renewal of commercial intercourse and peaceful relations had given a wonderful impulse to trade and business in the South. But Southern merchants had entirely ceased going to the North to purchase goods of any kind: "For all Northern fabrics being now subject to high duties, would thereby be so much enhanced in price, that but few kinds can be sold in Southern markets, in competition with European articles subject to the same rates of duties only—or of Southern manufactures, now protected by the same tariff law which had formerly been enacted by the superior political power of the North, and to operate exclusively for the profit of Northern capital and industry."[25] Northern ship owners were transferring their ships to the South; Northern manufacturers were coming; and much Northern capital was seeking investment there. A month later it was reported that the "commercial prosperity of the South is growing with a force

[24] P. 283.
[25] P. 318.

and rapidity exceeding any previous anticipations of the most sanguine early advocates for the independence of the Southern states."[26]

The Western states had taken but little part in the war. The South had granted them free trade and free navigation of the Mississippi. Because of this indulgent and conciliatory treatment the people of the Northwest had not tried to open direct trade with Europe, but were content to trade principally with New Orleans. On April 7, 1869, it was reported that New England and the West were at loggerheads over the tariff.[27] The volume closes with a prediction that the North would soon split, the Western states, upon their own offer, going with the South. "And should New England be left alone, thenceforward its influence for evil on the Southern states will be of as little effect, and its political and economical position scarcely superior, to those conditions of the present republic of Hayti."[28]

By April 14, 1869, it was reported, commercial treaties had been made by the South with European powers. No duties were to be over 20 per cent. The treaties might be terminated after ten years. The tobacco growers, who had so often in the old Union requested the government to attempt to secure a relaxation of the heavy duties imposed upon their product by France and England, now had their wishes gratified.[29]

Ruffin's book was written during a political campaign when it was well understood that, in case of Lincoln's election, the cotton states would in all probability secede; but its content was only an amplification of a series of letters published in the Richmond *Enquirer* in December, 1856, and January, 1857. And the arguments for secession which he used were typical of the secessionist *per se* propaganda to which the people of the South had been accustomed for at least a decade.

Southern people were strengthened in their expectations of beneficial economic effects to follow secession by a class of politicians, writers, and newspaper editors representing those Northern commercial and mercantile interests whose business was largely with the South, and those Northern manufacturing inter-

[26] P. 323.
[27] P. 328.
[28] P. 338.
[29] P. 329. Cf. "Barbarossa," *The Lost Principle*, 176 ff.

ests who either sold their products in the South or purchased their raw material there, or both. The best known and most trustworthy individual of this class was Thomas Prentice Kettell, mentioned before in connection with the secession movement of 1850. He was, in 1860, the editor of *Hunt's Merchants' Magazine.* His views carried considerable weight, especially in the South, where his free trade principles, his sympathetic attitude on the slavery question, and his interest in Southern economic development had long been known. Early in the presidential campaign of 1860 there was published a book by him entitled, *Southern Wealth and Northern Profits, As Exhibited in Statistical Facts and Official Figures; Showing the Necessity of Union to the Future Prosperity and Welfare of the Republic.* The book showed an excellent understanding of the commercial and financial relations of the North and South; the conclusions were supported by tables of statistics, largely drawn from official sources. The burden of the book was, as the title indicates, that the South produced wealth, but that this wealth accumulated in the North: Capital, said Kettell, accumulates slowly in all agricultural countries and rapidly in commercial and manufacturing countries.[30] He described the resources of the South, her enormous production of cotton and numerous other products, and her immense exports to the North as well as to Europe. He further showed the extent of Southern purchases in the North, the value of the commerce carried for the South by the North, the Northern tonnage so employed—in short he discussed every form of profit derived by the North from her relations with the South. The total profits the North derived annually from Southern wealth he summarized in the following table:[31]

[30]P. 126.
[31]P. 127. There is no way to check these items with any accuracy, were it worth while to do so. The fishing bounties were paid from the general revenues, and, therefore, by both North and South in proportions of their respective contributions. The second is undoubtedly greatly exaggerated. The average yearly receipts from customs, 1856-1860 inclusive, was $54,487,600. Assuming that the people of the South paid as much *per capita* as the people of the North, which they probably did not (See ante p. 103.), the South paid about $21,440,000 annually. A part of this at least was disbursed in the South. The sixth item is probably much too large. So, also, is the last. Northern investments in the South and loans and extensions of credit greatly exceeded in amount Southern invest-

```
Bounties to fisheries, per annum................$ 1,500,000
Customs, per annum, disbursed at the North.... 40,000,000
Profits to Manufacturers...................... 30,000,000
Profits to Importers.......................... 16,000,000
Profits to Shipping, imports and exports........ 40,000,000
Profits on Travelers.......................... 60,000,000
Profits of Teachers, and others, at the South,
    sent North................................  5,000,000
Profits of Agents, brokers, commissions, etc...... 10,000,000
Profits of Capital drawn from the South........ 30,000,000
    Total from these sources................$232,500,000
```

In sixty years, according to Kettell's estimate, $2,770,000,000 had been transferred from the South to the North in these ways. Such heavy drains had prevented the accumulation of capital in the South.[32]

Kettell's arguments were addressed to the Northern people; he urged them not to endanger their prosperity by the unnecessary agitation of the slavery question. The South and West were portrayed as having great natural resources, whereas the East had few; the prosperity of the latter depended upon manufacturing and shipping for others.[33] He described the efforts which had been made in the South to make the section independent of the North, and the progress already made toward that goal; these he attributed to the anti-slavery agitation. He considered the possibility of a dissolution of the Union. In that case, "it is quite apparent that the North, as distinguished from the South and West, would be alone permanently injured." As for the South, "in the long run it would lose—after recovering from first disasters—nothing by separation."[34]

Disunionists saw in Kettell's book an argument for secession. John Townsend, of South Carolina, cut Kettell's estimate of Northern profits from Southern industry to less than half—$105,000,000 annually or $2,100,000,000 in twenty years. What would not this sum have accomplished for the South in twenty years? he asked. Direct trade and flourishing cities. *"Domestic*

---

ments in the North and deposits of Southern funds in Northern banks. The item should read, "interest on Southern debts to Northern citizens;" at any rate such an item, and it would not be a small one, should be included in the table.
   [32]P. 127.
   [33]P. 75.
   [34]P. 75.

manufactures would have occupied every water power, and the whole South,—wealthy and equipped, and armed at every point, —would have been able to defend herself against the world."[35] DeBow, another disunionist, in his review of *Southern Wealth and Northern Profits,* said: "The author deserves, by his labors, not only on this occasion, but during a long and active career, the most substantial recognition, as one of the noblest and truest patriots, the most profound economists, and ablest statistical philosophers of the age."[36]

Of Northern newspapers which encouraged the Southern people to believe that disunion would be followed by unprecedented prosperity, none was more widely read and quoted or wielded greater influence in the South than the New York *Herald.* It kept close watch of events and the state of public opinion in the South, and should have known, perhaps did know, the temper of the people. It constantly advocated a policy of meeting Southern demands and avoidance of wounding Southern sensibilities in order that the South might not be compelled to resort to measures which would work injury to the navigating, mercantile, and financial interests of New York, which the *Herald* represented. In case of disunion, according to the *Herald,* the imports of the Northern confederation would so fall off that it would have to resort to direct taxation, while the South would have ample revenue. Manufactures would be established in the South with Northern capital. Northern shipping would rot at its docks. Part of the Northern population would migrate to the South, so the disproportion in numbers would cease to exist. The value of real estate in the North would be greatly reduced.[37]

The views which disunionists, and others both South and North, held in regard to the economic benefits to follow the formation of a Southern confederacy did not go uncontroverted in the South. Conservative journals, such as the New Orleans *Picayune,* perhaps the best newspaper in the South, the Montgomery *Daily Confederation,* the *Republican Banner and Nashville Whig,* and the Savannah *Daily Republican,* did not consider that the Union

[35]*The South Alone Should Govern the South. And African Slavery Should Be Controlled by Those Only Who Are Friendly to It* (pamphlet), 3rd edition, p. 51.
[36]*DeBow's Review,* XXIX, 213.
[37]October 30, 1860, editorial, for example.

injuriously affected the economic interests of the Southern states.
Said the *Picayune,* 1858: "One of the most erroneous ideas,
strangely obtaining considerable currency at the South, is that
which attributes apparent decay of the older, and comparative slow
growth of the younger Southern States, to a fixed policy of the
General Government, assumed to be partial to sections in which
slavery does not exist."[38] The Montgomery *Daily Confederation*
said, 1859: "Nor are we wanting in a proper appreciation of the
value of the Union. . . . We sing no anthems to its glories, at
the same time we cannot forget that under it, we have grown to be
a great, prosperous, and after all, a happy people."[39] Occasionally
DeBow's Review contained an article which refuted the views
presented by the majority of its contributors.[40] Conservative
statesmen often described the South as prosperous, and attributed
that prosperity to the Union. Such a one was Alexander H.
Stephens.[41] Senator Bell, of Tennessee, in his speech on the
Lecompton bill, 1858, described the disunionists *per se* of the South,
and expressed his dissent from their doctrines.[42]

Disunionists were forced to admit on the eve of the war that
the South was enjoying a comparative degree of prosperity; and
they expressed concern lest a feeling of content with their economic condition would make the Southern people incapable of
maintaining their rights.[43] The Charleston *Mercury* found it
necessary to protest against an editorial of the New Orleans *Bee,*
"an inveterate old Whig paper," for intimating "that the Southern
people are so cankered by prosperity as to be incapable of resist-
ing the sectional domination of the North, and that the Union will

---

[38]May 22, 1858.

[39]May 19, 1859. A year earlier it had said: "We scout the position so often
assumed that we are inferior—that we are degraded in this Union . . . That the
North does our trading and manufacturing mostly is true, and we are willing that
they should. If we thought as some seem to think on the subject, we should
boldly raise the standard of secession, and never cease the strife until the Union
were dissolved." May 19, 1858.

[40]XXIV, 431-39, e.g.

[41]Letter to J. J. Crittenden, Jan. 2, 1860; address to his constituents, Aug.
14, 1857, *Toombs, Stephens, Cobb Correspondence,* 415 ff.

[42]*Cong. Globe,* 35 Cong., 1 Sess., Appx., 139-40.

[43]Speech of R. B. Rhett, July 4, 1859, in Charleston *Mercury,* July 7; address of Col. A. P. Aldrich at the fair of the South Carolina Institute, Nov. 17,
1859, *ibid.,* Nov. 19.

be continued because of this prosperity."[44] Disunionists found it necessary, also, to allay the fears of those engaged in industry and commerce who, while desirous of Southern industrial and commercial independence, believed that the sudden disruption of established relationships which disunion might cause would prostrate their business.[45] Much of the disunion argument seems to have been designed to win over this class of men.

Some of the leaders in the various efforts made to effect an industrial and commercial revolution in the South were not convinced by the arguments of the unconditional disunionists. James Robb, to whom more than to any other individual belongs the credit for the successful building of the New Orleans, Jackson, and Great Northern railroad, undertook to expose the fallacies of the secession arguments. It would be suicide for the South to abandon the Union. The pursuits of the people of the South were incompatible with any considerable progress in manufacturing and commerce. The remedy for dependence upon the North was not secession but a change of habits. The South had better be dependent upon the North than upon Europe. "The Southern mind is deluded in the belief that England and France will give to a separate Southern Confederacy, founded on Slavery, Free Trade, and Cotton, their entire sympathies." If self-interest did not appeal to New England, would it appeal to England and France? The belief that the withdrawal of Southern trade would ruin the East was too absurd to merit notice. "Where," he asked, "is the evidence of the prosperity of the Southern States being seriously endangered by a continued fellowship with New England? Our material progress for the last fifteen years is without example, . . . "[46]

William Gregg, one of the ablest and sanest thinkers in the South upon questions affecting the economic interests of the section, was not a secessionist *per se*.[47] The South was not ready

[44] April 30, 1859.

[45] See, for example, A. J. Roane in *DeBow's Review*, XXIX, 462.

[46] Letter to Alexander H. Stephens, Nov. 25, 1860, in a pamphlet, *A Southern Confederacy. Letters by James Robb, late a citizen of New Orleans, to an American in Paris and Hon. Alexander H. Stephens, of Georgia*, pp. 11-24.

[47] The statements relative to Gregg's position are based upon a series of essays on "Southern Patronage to Southern Imports and Domestic Industry" which appeared in *DeBow's Review*, July, 1860, to February, 1861, but all of

for independence, he said. The Southern people should make themselves commercially and industrially independent of the North before going out of the Union. There would be no advantage in turning from the Yankees and relying upon Europe.[48] Free trade among the states he considered the greatest bond of Union; and at the time he wrote, 1860, still thought it, "if properly poised and equalized throughout our common country, will dispel the dark cloud which hangs over truth and justice . . ."[49] Yet Gregg was not oblivious to some of the possible advantages of disunion. If a line were drawn which would be a barrier to the importation of Northern locomotives, for example, two years would not elapse before the South would manufacture them herself. Disunion would stop the practice followed by Southern banks and money lenders of employing their money in New York rather than at home, which was a "monstrous barrier to Southern enterprise."[50]

Yet, after giving due weight to such Union arguments as we have just analyzed, it remains that the disunionist arguments in regard to the material benefits of their project were not adequately refuted in the South. Unionists more frequently took the course of appealing to the common history of the American people, their common republican institutions, the greatness of the Union, its prestige among the nations of the earth, its vast military strength, the weakness and insignificance the South would have as an independent nation, her inability to protect an institution condemned by the opinion of the world, and the danger of plunging the country into fratricidal war. They also found it effective to cast aspersions upon the motives of the secessionist leaders, to represent them as restless spirits, broken down politicians, disappointed in their political ambitions.

Northern men contributed but little to a true understanding of the causes of the disparity of the sections in prosperity and progress, and of the effect which a division of the Union might have upon the great material interests of the country; such an

---

which were written before Lincoln's election. But see Victor S. Clark in *The South in the Building of the Nation*, V, 323.

[48]*DeBow's Review*, XXIX, 78, 79, 773, 778.

[49]*Ibid.*, XXX, 217.

[50]*Ibid.*, XXIX, 79, 495.

understanding, it is believed, would have tended to allay disunion sentiment. Northern men were not as well informed as they should have been of the number of disunionists *per se* in the South, nor of the arguments they advanced. Practically all of the discussions dealing with disunion were colored by partisan bias. As we have seen, representatives of those business interests of the East which were closely allied with the cotton power exaggerated the value of the Southern connection and the injurious effects of disunion upon the North. They sought to fix the guilt for endangering the Union upon the Northern "fanatics" who were agitating the slavery question. Republican and anti-slavery writers and oraters, who, it must be remembered, were not trying to win converts in the South but to build up a great party in the North, dealt with disunionism in a variety of ways. They denounced as mercenary those who would calculate the value of the Union in dollars. They commonly charged that threats of disunion were mere gasconade for the purpose of frightening Northern men into voting for Southern measures. They often, also, as did William H. Seward in his great speeches during the campaign of 1860, protrayed the magnitude of Northern productions and Northern internal commerce as compared with the products exchanged between the sections, and minimized the value of the Southern trade and Southern raw materials to the North and the injury which would be inflicted upon Northern interests by disunion.[51] Senator Wilson, of Massachusetts, said cotton was not king; cotton made but one-seventeenth part of the manufactures of the North.[52] The Republicans, and anti-slavery men generally, attributed the "decline" of the South and its dependence upon the North chiefly to the blighting effects of slavery; they saw no hope of remedy so long as slavery continued to exist.[53]

---

[51]In a speech at Palace Garden, New York City, Nov. 2, 1860, he said: "New York is not a province of Virginia or Carolina, any more than it is a province of New York or Connecticut. New York must be the metropolis of the Continent." New York *Herald*, Nov. 3.

[52]*Cong. Globe*, 35 Cong., 1 Sess., Appx., 169, speech of Mar. 20, 1858, in reply to J. H. Hammond's "Mud-sill" speech of Mar. 4.

[53]The speech of Senator Wilson just quoted is a good example. Another is Hannibal Hamlin's reply to Hammond, Mar. 8, 11, 1858, *Cong. Globe*, 35 Cong., 1 Sess., 1002-1006, 1025-1029.

Perhaps the ablest and most philosophical exposition of moderate Republicanism made between 1854 and 1861 is George M. Weston's *Progress of Slavery*,[54] a work which it would have been well worth the while of Southern thinkers to study. We are here concerned only with those of the propositions he sought to establish which relate to disunion. He told of nullification in South Carolina and of its partisans and sympathizers in other slave states. "The real cause of this Southern predisposition to listen to the appeals of the Palmetto nullifiers, was Southern discontent at the prosperity of the North. . . . Refusing to see the true cause of their own misfortunes, and eager to attribute them to every cause but the right one, they insisted that they alone were the real producers of wealth, and that the North was thriving at their expense." This doctrine of the nullifiers had been steadily insisted upon during the following quarter of a century. "It has, without doubt, become the settled conviction of large numbers of persons in the slave States, that in some way or other, either through the fiscal regulations of the Government, or through the legerdemain of trade, the North has been built up at the expense of the South."[55] These were the views which prompted disunion. He illustrated the reasons for wanting to dissolve the Union by an extract from a public address of John Forsyth, of Mobile:

I have no more doubt that the effect of separation would be to transfer the energies of industry, population, commerce, and wealth, from the North to the South, than I have that it is to the Union with us, the wealth-producing States, that the North owes its great progress in material prosperity. . . . The Union broken, we should have what has been so long the dream of the South— direct trade and commercial independence. Then, our Southern cities, that have so long languished in the shade, while the grand emporia of the North have fattened upon favoring navigation laws, partial legislation by Congress, and the monopoly of the public expenditure, will spring into life and energy, and become the entrepots of a great commerce.[56]

The slavery agitation was not the cause of disunion feeling but the pretext, according to Weston. The disunionists had been chiefly instrumental in getting it up: "It is quite notorious that it

[54] Published in 1858.
[55] P. 68.
[56] P. 69.

is not the slaveholding class at the South which particularly favors nullification."

The impoverished condition of the South, which Weston considered the source of the disunion feeling, he thought attributable in part to slavery and in part to, "that unnatural diffusion of their population over new territories," which the Republican party was opposing.[57] There were no internal elements of change in slave society. The slaves were held to their condition by force. The masters were confined to planting by the want of flexibility and adaptibility in the character of the labor which they controlled and upon the proceeds of which they subsisted. The non-slaveholding whites were degraded by slavery with no hope of escape from their abject poverty.[58] There was no hope from any elements of such a population of the growth of towns, of the mechanic arts, or of manufacturing and commercial interests. "Throughout the South, towns are built up only by Northern and European immigration, and without it there would be scarcely any manifestation of civilization. Mills, railroads, cotton presses, sugar boilers, and steamboats, are mainly indebted for their existence in the Southern States to intelligence and muscle trained in free communities."[59] The redemption of the South would come only with the gradual encroachment of the free-labor system of the North and Europe and the non-slaveholding regions of the South upon the slave belts. That encroachment had begun, or soon would begin. As the slave area should be contracted, the discontented area would also be diminished, and the Union would be strengthened. "If the course of events in the immediate future be such as may reasonably be anticipated, no separate Southern Confederacy could possibly embrace more than a few States in the southeast corner of the existing Union; and the scheme of such a Confederacy would be put down by the good sense of the people in that quarter, if, indeed, their patriotism would allow it to be even entertained."[60]

[57]P. 58.
[58]P. 13.
[59]P. 15.
[60]P. 70.

6

The Pacific Railway Issue in Politics Prior to the Civil War

The following essay originally appeared in the *Mississippi Valley Historical Review,* XII (September 1925), 187–201. It is reprinted here by permission of the Organization of American Historians. The original pagination appears in brackets.

O NE OF THE great national issues or problems of the period from about 1840 to 1860 which have not received their just deserts from historians, was that of communication and transportation between the settled portions of the United States east of the Rockies and the possessions on the Pacific. It is the object of this article to deal with some aspects of this question, particularly with the extent of public interest in it, why so much interest was manifested, and why such great public interest did not earlier result in the establishment of a Pacific railroad or other satisfactory means of communication.

The question of communication with the Pacific was one of considerable interest from the time of our first claim to Oregon, but it began to arouse something like general interest in the later 1830's and early 1840's. Such an interest may be accounted for by the growth of our whaling industry in the northern Pacific, the extension of the fur trade to the Oregon country, the discovery of new routes, the diplomatic contest with Great Britain over the ownership of Oregon, and a growing interest in the possibilities of trade with China and other Asiatic countries, evoked by the actual increase in that trade and by British efforts to open Chinese ports to the commerce of the world.

As early as 1835 the United States Senate requested President Jackson to consider opening negotiations relative to a canal across New Granada or Central America.[1] Senator Benton, of Missouri, early took an interest in establishing means of overland transportation. From time to time after about 1836 (when very few railroads existed anywhere in the United States) various individuals suggested building a railroad to

---

[1] James D. Richardson, *A Compilation of the Messages and Papers of the Presidents* . . . (Washington, 1895-99), IV, 512.

Oregon[2] but it was Asa Whitney, New York merchant, who popularized the idea. In 1845 he proposed to build a railroad along a vaguely defined route from Lake Michigan to Puget Sound if the government would sell him for ten cents an acre a strip of land sixty miles wide the length of the road. According to Whitney and other advocates of the plan the road would bind Oregon to us, settle our western lands, thus solving our immigration problem, and, finally and most important, become the great artery of a magnificent trade between Asia and the United States and between Asia and Europe across our territory. It was to be the ultimate solution of the problem that had excited the imagination of Columbus and so many others, to find a short route to the Indies.[3] Whitney memorialized Congress and gained many friends for his plan there. During several years he toured the country addressing mass meetings, railroad conventions, chambers of commerce, and state legislatures, and inducing them to pass resolutions indorsing his project. He wrote voluminously. A majority of the newspaper press of the country at one time or another lent him support. His plan was kept prominently before the country for about seven years before it was definitely rejected.

But Whitney's bold scheme soon raised up numerous advocates of other routes and plans. For example, Senator Benton championed a national road, built by the government, from St. Louis as the eastern terminus. As long as Oregon was the only territory on the Pacific to which we had a claim, the Whitney road found considerable support even as far south as the Gulf states; but even then several Southerners suggested a southern route for a Pacific railway terminating in Mexican territory.[4] No direct evidence has been found to prove that they advocated war upon Mexico to secure such a route. There is plenty of evidence, however, to show that the government sought to acquire California from Mexico because, among other reasons, the fine harbor of San Francisco might become the "depot of the vast commerce which must exist on the Pacific."[5] And once the Mexican War was begun

---

[2] These early suggestions are discussed in some detail in E. V. Smalley, *History of the Northern Pacific Railroad* (New York, 1883); J. P. Davis, *The Union Pacific Railway* . . . . (Chicago, 1894); and H. H. Bancroft, *History of California* (San Francisco, 1884-90), VII, chap. xix.

[3] See especially Whitney's third memorial to Congress in 30 Cong., 1 Sess., *House Report* No. 733.

[4] *DeBow's Review*, I, 22-23; III, 328-39, 475-83. Cf. Edward Mayes, "Origin of the Pacific Railroads, and Especially of the Southern Pacific," in *Publications of the Mississippi Historical Society*, VI, 313-14.

[5] E. g., J. K. Polk, *Diary* . . . (Chicago, 1910), I, 71-72; M. W. Willi-

there were numerous suggestions that the government seize the territory over which ran specified, prospective railroad routes.6 During the negotiations for peace a large sum was offered Mexico for the right of way across the Isthmus of Tehuantepec but was refused.7 The treaty of Guadalupe Hidalgo contained an article relative to a railroad which might be built along the Gila River, designated as a part of the boundary.

The acquisition of the Mexican cession, the discovery of gold in California, the great migration thither, and the phenomenal development of that region gave the establishment of means of communication with the Pacific an importance and interest it had not possessed before. The government must be able to dispatch troops to the new possessions to defend them against foreign enemies, along the emigrant trails to protect the emigrants against the Indians, or to the Mexican border to prevent Indian depredations across the frontier (as required by treaty). Means were required to transport troops for these several purposes speedily and cheaply and along with them the necessary military stores. The mails must be carried to and from the new possessions. Better means of transportation were needed for the convenience and safety of the thousands of emigrants. It was represented that, unless there could be a constant and speedy interchange of intelligence and goods between the people on the east side of the Rockies and those on the other, estrangement would arise and eventually political separation might occur.8 Transcontinental railroads and other means of communication and transportation would promote the settlement of the intervening territory along the routes and the development of the resources of the vast interior. A railroad near Canada might help to draw her into our system;9 one along the Mexican frontier might hasten the absorption of the northern tier of Mexican states.10 The control of transit routes across the Isthmus might in the fullness of time bring the regions traversed under the Stars and Stripes.11 To the rapidly growing popula-

---

ams, *Anglo-American Isthmian Diplomacy, 1815-1915* (Washington, 1916), 53; Richardson, *op. cit.,* IV, 536-47, 635; *DeBow's Review,* I, 64-66.

6 *DeBow's Review,* III, 147-48, 475-83, 495; *American Railroad Journal,* XIX, 761-62.

7 Richardson, *op. cit.,* V, 16-17.

8 The best statements of the above mentioned considerations are to be found in [*Annual*] *Report of the Secretary of War* (*Jefferson Davis*), Dec. 3, 1855, and in his letter to Rep. J. M. Sandidge, Jan. 29, 1856, in Dunbar Rowland (ed.), *Jefferson Davis, Constitutionalist,* II, 588-90.

9 *Cong. Globe,* 35 Cong., 1 Sess., App., 430.
10 *Idem,* 33 Cong., 1 Sess., 882; *DeBow's Review,* XXI, 469-90, *passim.*

11 Richardson, *op. cit.,* V, 447-48.

tion of the Pacific Coast, satisfactory means of communication with and transportation to the rest of the Union was a matter of urgent importance and almost of necessity. The establishment of such facilities there became the public policy of paramount interest and the highest object of statesmanship.

Weighty as were the political and military considerations which counselled the construction of a railroad or canal connecting with the Pacific, it must be said that the great interest in the subject shown by the people of the Mississippi Valley and farther east grew chiefly out of the expectation that, with the provision of proper transportation facilities, a great tide of trade and travel would set in, not only with the Pacific Coast and the settlements which would accompany the road but also between Europe and Asia by way of the United States. The people of every city or town of any pretensions whatever near our Mississippi Valley frontier or on the Gulf believed that, if they could make their city the terminus of a railroad, or of *the* railroad, to the Pacific, or of an isthmian route, so that it might exact tribute from the enormous trade to develop, it would become a great metropolis. Said a citizen of New Orleans: ". . . we shall have all the commerce and travel of the Northern Atlantic States, and all the commerce and travel of Europe that is destined for the Pacific Ocean, for India and China, passing through our city; portions of their products will be left for sale here, or exchanged for our own, or those of the great West, and the thousand products of our artistical and manufacturing skill. Is not every State in the West and South interested in securing such a mart as New Orleans will then be for their productions? It will then be the market of the world . . ."[12] Even people of cities on the Atlantic Coast entertained glowing expectations of the nourishing qualities of that stream of trade and travel even after it should have been divided and subdivided.[13]

By about 1850 the main outlines of the railroad system of the United States were rapidly taking form either in the shape of roads actually built or building or in well-defined projects for which charters had been or were about to be secured. Cities and states were contending in

---

[12] *American Railroad Journal,* XXV, 502.

[13] For example, "The subject of connecting the cities of Savannah, Mobile, and New Orleans by a railroad, has already been much agitated in the South. This will, undoubtedly, be soon undertaken; and, together with the New Orleans and Opelousas road, now under contract, would form the eastern half of the great connection between the Atlantic and Pacific. If the El Paso route is the one adopted by the government, Savannah would become the great Atlantic Depot, and San Diego the Pacific." *DeBow's Review,* XV, 641.

"mighty rivalry" with each other for these arteries of commerce which would assure their future greatness. Every railroad company with a project pointing westwardly anywhere near a possible starting point for a Pacific railroad or a possible direct continuation of one to the Atlantic, the Gulf, or the Lakes, was determined to make its road a link in, or at least a branch of, a great chain of railroads stretching to the Pacific. The possibility that a road might occupy such a favorable position was used to win the favor of investors and the public. It would seem that the locations of several roads projected in the Mississippi Valley during this period were determined very largely by the possibility of making them links in, or continuations of, a Pacific railway. Said the agent of the New Orleans, Opelousas, and Great Western: "The hundreds of millions of gold produced by California; the rapid development of our possessions in Oregon; the great increase in the whale trade in the north Pacific; an increased trade with Mexico and South America; the absolute certainty of finally crushing the Chinese walls and overthrowing Japanese nonintercourse; and the opening of commercial relations with 700,000,000 people who inhabit Asia, and the millions of the islands of the Pacific; . . . will furnish to this road and its St. Louis branch a transportation and business unknown to the annals of railroad prosperity on this globe."[14]

The question of communication with the Pacific had its sectional aspects also. About this time the people of the South were becoming keenly aware of what they pleased to call "Southern decline." Their section was not keeping pace with the North in various lines of economic progress. There was much analyzing of causes and searching for remedies. Commercial conventions were held to consult over the matter.[15] A railroad to the Pacific by a southern route was among the most prominent measures considered for the regeneration of the section. Said the New Orleans *Delta,* commenting on the deep interest shown in a Pacific railway by the Southern Commercial Convention meeting in Memphis, 1853: "This was the Aaron's rod that swallowed up all others. This was the great panacea, which is to release the South from its bondage to the North, which is to pour untold wealth into our lap; which is to build up cities, steamships, manufactories, educate our children, and draw into our control what Mr. Bell calls 'the untold wealth of the gorgeous East.' "[16]

---

14 *American Railroad Journal,* XXV, 517.
15 See R. R. Russel, *Economic Aspects of Southern Sectionalism, 1840-1861,* (University of Illinois Studies in the Social Sciences, Vol. XI, Nos. 1-2, Urbana, 1923), especially chap. v.
16 Quoted in Richmond *Enquirer,* June 24, 1853.

In the North there was not the same disposition to look upon a Pacific railroad as an instrument for sectional economic aggrandizement. There was a sectional aspect of the question, however, which the leaders of neither section overlooked. If, for example, the first railroad to the Pacific, and probably the only one for a generation, should follow a southern route, California and the intervening territory would be settled most largely by Southern people, would in all probability be slaveholding, would be economically allied to the South, and thus the South would gain an advantage in the sectional struggles of the time. If, however, the first railroad should follow a northern or central route, the North would, in a similar manner, gain the political advantage. If an isthmian route or a railroad route near the Mexican border were adopted, it might result in the annexation of territory, which would be allied to the South in interests. In 1849 a distinguished Southerner wrote: ". . . I can tell you that the accursed question of slavery is already mixing itself up with the road, and the free States, who are removed from it, will not go for it if it is to go through slave territory."17 The Southern Commercial Convention of January, 1855, resolved, "That the construction of a railroad to the Pacific Ocean, from proper points on the Mississippi river, within the slave-holding States of the Union, is not only important to those States, but indispensable to their welfare and prosperity, and even to their continued existence as equal and independent members of the confederacy."18

After about 1846 no one suggested improved wagon and stage roads to the Pacific as more than a temporary, makeshift solution of the problem; although many believed such roads would have to precede and blaze the trails for railroads. Telegraph lines would be valuable but would solve the problem only in part, and that a minor one. A canal across one of the isthmian routes was considered desirable by many, but its construction would be a long and costly undertaking. Railroads across the Isthmus, connecting with steamship lines in both oceans, could be provided quickly and at comparatively small cost. But isthmian projects in general would require the consent of foreign governments to their construction. In case of war with a stronger naval power, they might be closed to our commerce, mails, troops, and military supplies, and our Pacific coast rendered defenseless. Because of

---

17 *DeBow's Review,* VII, 37.

18 *Idem,* XVIII, 520. Cf. speech of J. A. McDougal of Cal., Aug. 24, 1852, in *Western Journal and Civilian,* IX, 97; and article by W. W. Burwell on "The True Policy of the South," in *DeBow's Review,* XXI, 469-90.

the greater distances to be traversed, they, especially railroads, were not expected to bring to our ports the great Asia trade. And, more, they could be of no direct commercial benefit to the vast interior of the country.19 Such projects, therefore, found their chief support in the Gulf ports like New Orleans and Mobile, whose interests would be best served by a canal or railroad across the Isthmus of Tehuantepec, and from the private companies which gained control of transportation across Panama and Nicaragua, namely, the Pacific Mail Company, the Atlantic and Pacific Ship Canal Company, and their subsidiaries. The country at large regarded means of transit across the Isthmus with no great favor except as a temporary convenience until transcontinental railroads could be constructed.

For providing the latter, plans and projects multiplied amazingly in the years immediately following the War with Mexico. Almost all of them agreed in demanding aid of the federal government; for no private corporation in that day would, or could, undertake such a gigantic task unaided. But the plans differed widely as to the kind and extent of the aid they demanded. They differed more widely still as to route and terminus. By about 1850 it was apparent from reports of explorers, travelers, and military reconnaissances that each of about five routes through the Rockies might prove practicable, namely, the extreme northern route between the 47th and the 49th parallels of latitude, the 42nd degree routes by way of South Pass and Great Salt Lake, Benton's or the central route by a pass at the head of the Arkansas River between the 38th and 39th parallels, the 35th degree route by way of the Canadian Valley and Albuquerque, and the extreme southern or 32nd degree route via El Paso and the Gila Valley. Each one had its staunch advocates, before as well as after the government surveys were made. On the Pacific end two of these routes (the 42nd degree route and Benton's route) naturally terminated at San Francisco and the others could be made to do so; and after that city had had a year or two of its phenomenal growth, it was generally agreed that San Francisco must be one of the western termini if not the only Western terminus. Memphis, St. Louis, and some point on the Mississippi or Missouri in line with Chicago were most frequently advocated for the eastern terminus, but there were at least a dozen other towns and cities which had their champions, ranging from Galveston, on the Gulf, to Superior, Wisconsin, at the head of lake navigation.

---

19 *Cong. Globe*, 33 Cong., 2 Sess., 225; App., 74; 35 Cong., 2 Sess., 458-59; *American Railroad Journal*, XXII, 723; *Hunt's Merchant's Magazine*, XXII, 153-54; Rowland, *op. cit.*, III, 364-65, 397, 418.

It was difficult to unite the people and interests of any state near the frontier in support of any single route, terminus, or plan of financing the road. The people of states farther removed were less divided as to route and terminus. Sectional agreement in support of a single project was out of the question. A partial analysis of the alignment on the issue of terminus and route will be sufficient to substantiate these statements.

In Missouri in 1849, a railroad, rather suggestively called the Pacific, was chartered and soon begun, to run from St. Louis to the western border of the state at the mouth of the Kansas River. A southwest branch was shortly provided for to run via Springfield to the southwest corner of the state. Another railroad, the Hannibal and St. Joseph, was to cross the northern part of the state from east to west. A north and south road was to connect the Hannibal and St. Joseph with St. Louis. People of St. Louis generally demanded that the Pacific railway be built from the mouth of the Kansas by the central route, but if that could not be secured they were prepared to go for a continuation of the southwest branch of their Missouri Pacific by the 35th degree, or Albuquerque, route. But people along the line of the southwest branch, including Congressman Phelps of the Springfield District, would support no route except that of the 35th degree.[20] People living near or interested in the Hannibal and St. Joseph Railroad believed that St. Joseph should be the eastern terminus of the Pacific railway, as did, to a diminishing degree, people interested in any one of a prospective chain of roads continuing the Hannibal and St. Joseph eastward via Quincy and Springfield, Illinois. People financially interested in or living near any of the chain of roads leading from St. Louis to Cincinnati and thence to Baltimore or Pittsburgh were favorable to St. Louis for a terminus and a central route. A chain of railroads connecting Terre Haute, Indianapolis, Columbus, Pittsburgh, and Philadelphia could connect about equally well with the Hannibal and St. Joseph or the Missouri Pacific, and, consequently, Pennsylvania, and central Ohio and Indiana were for either a St. Louis or a St. Joseph terminus with little choice between them.

Iowa by about 1853 had developed projects for three main east and west roads across the state, the Dubuque and Pacific, the Mississippi and Missouri, to run from Davenport to Council Bluffs, and the Burlington and Missouri River. Each road was urged as a link in the road to the Pacific, and each connected with various roads or chains

---

20 *Cong. Globe*, 35 Cong., 1 Sess., App., 424; 36 Cong., 1 Sess., 2331, 2408-11, 2439-40.

of roads to the east across Illinois or beyond. The people of Chicago and that city's eastern connections wanted the Pacific railroad to connect with one of Chicago's several western railroad radii, preferably the Chicago and Rock Island, which was continued by the Davenport and Council Bluffs and pointed toward South Pass and San Francisco.

The people of New York could, and did, profit by either the Panama or Nicaragua transportation route. Of transcontinental routes, they preferred a northern one connecting with the Great Lakes, but they did not oppose a central route from St. Louis or St. Joseph. Senator Seward more than once made the proud boast that, no matter what route might be chosen, its eastern terminus would be New York City.[21] Michigan and New England could gain no special benefit from a road terminating south of Chicago, and, therefore, preferred the extreme northern route.

The settlers and speculators of Superior, Wisconsin, and vicinity were convinced that no Pacific railway which did not connect with that magnificent inland waterway system, the Great Lakes, at its western-most point could be expected to attract any of the China trade. The population of far away Oregon Territory or, a little later, the State of Oregon and Washington Territory inclined strongly to the same view.

Arkansas citizens were divided three ways as to where they wanted the Pacific railroad to cross their state. They could not agree even in their choice between the 35th degree and the 32nd degree route.[22] Tennessee people were united in support of a Memphis terminus and had little choice between the two southern routes. Because of the Virginia and Tennessee and the Memphis and Charleston railroad projects, most of the people of Virginia east of the Alleghenies, of South Carolina, and of northern Georgia and Alabama who wanted a Pacific railroad at all, supported the pretensions of Memphis. However, interested persons in Savannah, the central parts of Georgia, Alabama, and Mississippi, and northern Louisiana inclined to favor a connection by way of Vicksburg, Shreveport, El Paso, and the valley of the Gila. The hopes of the city builders of New Orleans centered chiefly in a project for a railroad across the Isthmus of Tehuantepec, but when that project encountered unexpected difficulties and the New Orleans, Opelousas, and Western Railroad made a promising start, they bent

---

21 *Idem,* 33 Cong., 2 Sess., 750; 35 Cong., 1 Sess., 1584.

22 Some of them wanted a route from Memphis via Little Rock to Fort Smith; others, one from Memphis via Little Rock to Fulton in the southwest corner of the state; still others wanted it to run from Cairo, Illinois, via Little Rock to Fulton. Fort Smith was on the 35th degree route; Fulton was on a proposed connection with the 32nd degree route.

their efforts toward making the latter the first link in a road to the Pacific.

Numerous railroad conventions were held for the purpose of crystalizing or creating public sentiment ,in favor of particular plans or locations. The most notable of these were the St. Louis and Memphis Pacific railroad conventions of October, 1849, and the Philadelphia convention of April, 1850.23 At least three of the sessions of the Southern Commercial Convention devoted more time to the subject than to any other.24 Several Pacific railroad companies were formed, and waited in a receptive mood for federal aid. Western governors frequently discussed the subject in their messages, and legislatures resolved and petitioned in regard to it. Both the Democratic and Republican parties declared in favor of a Pacific railroad in their platforms of 1856, the Republicans going so far as to say that it should be built by the "most central and practicable route." In 1860 the Republicans and both wings of the Democrats declared for the immediate construction of the railroad. But because federal aid was demanded by almost all of them, the struggle among the various rival interests and projects had to be fought out very largely in Congress, and, in spite of the fact that the nation as a whole after about 1849 approved the extension of considerable aid to one or more transcontinental railroads, it was impossible until 1862 and 1864 to get legislation that would insure the building of a road.

The difficulties were enormous. Pacific railway legislation had to contend for the time of Congress with the exciting sectional quarrels over slavery. The isthmian projects could command no governmental financial aid beyond liberal contracts for carrying the mails, yet they used their influence to defeat legislation which might bring rivals into the field. Democrats from the old South, especially, had constitutional scruples against federal aid to internal improvements and a disinclination to increase government expenditures which could not be overcome. Whigs and Democrats were inclined to divide along party lines over such questions as whether or not the federal government could charter a railroad company; if so, whether it could authorize it to operate in the states or only in the territories, and whether money appropriations in aid of a Pacific railroad must be confined to sections in the territories

-----

23 Proceedings in *American Railroad Journal,* XXII, 663-64, 690-93, 708-11, 721-23; XXIII, 228-31; *Western Journal and Civilian,* III, 71-75 (St. Louis).

24 Memphis, 1853, Charleston, 1854, and New Orleans, 1855. See Russel, *op. cit.,* chap. v.

or might also be extended to sections within the states. Yet neither party was able to unite upon a Pacific railroad bill and force it through as a party measure.

The Pacific railway question also became involved with other issues over which much division had arisen. Advocates of land grants in aid of railways on the alternate sections principles insisted upon applying that principle to Pacific railway bills. Many congressmen who favored giving away the lands to actual settlers for homesteads objected to grants to railways. Many congressmen from landless states objected to large grants to Pacific railroads because they wanted the lands divided among the several states. Tariff men insisted that only American iron be used in the construction of railroads to the Pacific.

But the greatest obstacle in the way of Pacific railway legislation lay in the inability to agree upon a route or routes. If a bill were framed for a central route the advocates of northern and southern routes would unite with the small, compact minority altogether opposed to government aid and defeat it. If the bill provided for two roads, or for three roads, or for one main trunk with several branches to take care of the chief contenders for the terminus, the votes gained by such log-rolling process were always offset by votes lost on the ground that the project was too costly for the country to bear. On more than one occasion the old guard which opposed government aid in any form or amount united with the friends of some particular plan or route to amend a bill in such a way as to make it unsatisfactory to other friends of a Pacific railway, and then united with the latter to defeat the bill upon its final passage. Even bills to establish overland mail service by stage were bitterly fought over because it was believed that the choice of the stage routes might have an influence on the selection of the route of a Pacific railway.[25] Representatives from the Pacific Coast were about the only ones who would support almost any bill to further the

[25] *Cong. Globe,* 35 Cong., 1 Sess., App., 25-28; 35 Cong., 2 Sess., 239, 261-63, 305; 36 Cong., 1 Sess., 1061, 1131-33, 1647-49, 2338-39, 2457-60. Prof. F. H. Hodder has shown that the organization of Kansas and Nebraska as territories, 1854, was in large part an incident in the struggle over the terminus and route of a Pacific railway. "The Genesis of the Kansas-Nebraska Bill," in *Proceedings of the State Historical Society of Wisconsin, 1912.* Prof. Hodder further developed this thesis in his presidential address before the meeting of the Mississippi Valley Historical Association, Detroit, May 1, 1925, (printed in *Mississippi Valley Hist. Rev.,* XII, 3-22). Dr. James C. Malin has described how our Indian policy in the West in the period before the Civil War was greatly influenced by the sectional and local struggle over the route of a Pacific railway. *Indian Policy and Westward Expansion* (Bulletin of the University of Kansas, Humanistic Studies, Vol. II, No. 3, Lawrence, 1921), especially pp. 44-52.

establishment of means of communication with the Pacific, and even they did not always coöperate effectively among themselves.26

The limits of this article will not permit even a summary account of the chapters or episodes in the struggle of the several contending interests over the terminus and route of a Pacific communication, with their varying hopes and fortunes. New factors constantly entering or being interjected into the struggle modified its charter somewhat, but none altered it essentially until the secession of eleven Southern states in 1860 and 1861 left the location of the route to the North alone.

An adequate account of the struggle would require a retelling of the story of American isthmian and Mexican diplomacy prior to the Civil War with particular reference to, and greater, but not undue, emphasis upon, the attempt to get transit rights and privileges and the right to protect the same, and somewhat less emphasis upon attempted extension of slave territory.27 It would include also the story of the politico-economic activities and intrigues of the several American companies which secured or tried to secure the privilege of providing and operating transportation facilities across the Isthmus. The account would tell also how a bill giving aid in money and lands to a Pacific railroad and leaving the route to be selected by the President, Pierce being the president-elect, was about to pass the Senate in the second session of the Thirty-Second Congress, but was defeated at the last minute because Southern men found it was loaded against the choice of a southern route.28 Another chapter would show how Southern men had the stage all set and the public mind largely prepared for government aid for a railroad by the route of the thirty-second degree early in Pierce's administration but were frustrated in the House of Representatives by the advocates of a central route.29 Many Southerners then in desperation lent encouragement to a plan fathered by Albert Pike, of Arkansas, to have the road built by a combination of southern states, cities, and railroad companies without the aid of the federal govern-

---

26 For example, Gwin and Broderick in the Senate. *Cong. Globe,* 35 Cong., 1 Sess., 1298, 1537, 1641-42; 35 Cong., 2 Sess., 357-59.

27 Williams, *op. cit.,* and J. M. Callahan, "The Mexican Policy of Southern Leaders under Buchanan's Administration" (in American Historical Association, *Annual Report, 1910,* pp. 135-51), are authoritative, but do not entirely cover the subject.

28 The statement is based upon an unpublished study by the author of this article. Davis, *op. cit.,* 44-53 gives the same explanation, but does not try to determine whether or not the bill was loaded. I believe it was.

29 Thomas H. Benton partially analyzed the southern plans in a speech in the House of Representatives, Jan. 16, 1855, *Cong. Globe,* 33 Cong., 2 Sess., App., 73-82. See also *ibid., 335.*

ment.30 The account would further relate how the Buchanan administration did its utmost to further the projects of the Southerners, particularly by sending the great overland mail by the extreme southern route, from St. Louis and Memphis, and by lending energetic aid in behalf of the Tehuantepec speculators.31 But it would also show how Southern political and diplomatic finesse was more than offset by such great factors as capital and commerce, growth of population, and extension of settlements, working for the north or center. Most of the California mail was northern in origin or destination. The same was true of commerce. Settlements extended into Kansas, Nebraska, and Minnesota, and sprang up along the central route with the discovery of gold in the Pike's Peak region, and at Carson City, 1858, and the Mormon colony in Utah increased in numbers. Most of the population in California was in the northern part, and Oregon had sufficient poulation to be admitted to statehood in 1859. By 1860 the railroad system was more fully developed north of the Ohio than south of it, and connecting links for a Pacific railway were pushed farther to the west across Missouri and Iowa than across Arkansas and Louisiana. Finally, while the organization of the sectional Republican Party did not insure the building of a railroad to the Pacific by a northern or a central route, it rendered the building of one by a southern route well-nigh hopeless.

---

30 *DeBow's Review,* XVI, 636-37; XVII, 205-13, 408-10, 492-506, 593-99; XVIII, 520-28, 632-35; XXI, 469-90; XXII, 81-105, *passim.*

31 See especially the report of Postmaster General Aaron V. Brown in Cong. *Globe,* 35 Cong., 1 Sess., App., 25-28; speech of Sen. Wilson of Mass., Jan. 11, 1859, in *idem,* 2 Sess., 304-15; letter of Robert Toombs to W. W. Burwell, Nov. 30, 1857, in "The Correspondence of Robert Toombs, Alexander H. Stevens, and Howell Cobb" (American Historical Association, *Annual Report, 1911,* Pt. II).

7

Removing an Obstacle from Northern Routes: The Kansas–Nebraska Bill

The following essay originally appeared in *Improvement of Communication with the Pacific Coast as an Issue in American Politics, 1783–1864* (Cedar Rapids, 1948), 150–167. The original pagination appears in brackets.

THE organization of Kansas and Nebraska territories, 1854, involving as it did the repeal of the Missouri Compromise, was another incident in the struggle over the location and construction of a railway to the Pacific. Those people who in 1854 wanted to have the Nebraska country opened to white settlement and territorial governments organized therein were animated by several motives and considerations; by no means the least of these was a desire to remove a serious obstacle to the construction of a transcontinental railroad by a central or northern route.[1] The opposition to opening the Indian Country to whites was likewise animated by various motives, but one was the disinclination on the part of the partisans of a southern route to contribute to the removal of such an obstacle. The fact that the repeal of the Missouri Compromise came to overshadow the Pacific railroad issue in popular interest and historical importance should not be allowed to obscure the logical relation.

Back in the administrations of Monroe, J. Q. Adams, and Jackson, the policy had been adopted of removing Indian tribes from the organized states and territories and relocating them in unorganized territory. In pursuance of this policy, numerous tribes from farther east were settled along the western borders of Arkansas, Missouri, and Iowa. These re-

[1] This thesis has been fully developed by the late Professor F. H. Hodder, of the University of Kansas, in two able articles, "The Railroad Background of the Kansas-Nebraska Act," *Miss. Val. Hist. Rev.*, XII, 3-22 (Je., 1925), and "The Genesis of the Kansas-Nebraska Bill," *Proceedings of the State Hist. Soc. of Wis.*, for 1912; and by Professor James C. Malin, of the University of Kansas, in his *Indian Policy and Westward Expansion (Bul. of the Univ. of Kans., Humanistic Studies*, II, No. 3). The writer is greatly indebted to both Professor Hodder and Professor Malin. The approach in this chapter is different from that of Professor Malin and the interpretation differs considerably from that of Professor Hodder.

located tribes in every case were guaranteed their new lands in perpetuity, and in a few cases they were further guaranteed that they should never again be included in any organized state or territory.[2] By the Indian Intercourse act, of 1834, all the unorganized territory of the United States was designated the "Indian Country," and white persons were forbidden to settle there or even trade with the Indians therein without a license issued by the proper federal agent.[3] Thus an immense block of territory, one thousand miles long and six hundred miles wide, extending from Texas on the south to the national boundary on the north and from Arkansas, Missouri, Iowa, and Minnesota Territory on the east to New Mexico, Utah, and Oregon on the west was closed to occupation by white people.

Western people considered the policy of the permanent Indian frontier a mistaken one from the start.[4] They knew the lands beyond the line were habitable and were confident that they would sooner or later be wanted by our advancing population.

The first proposals by responsible persons for opening portions of the Indian Country to white settlement were made with the object of affording protection to emigrants to Oregon. That seems to have been the object of Senator Atchison in introducing a bill, December 1844, for organizing all of the Indian Country and Oregon; of Douglas, then in the House, in the same session of Congress in proposing to organize as Nebraska territory the region between the thirty-eighth and forty-third parallels from the Missouri to the Rockies; and of Secretary of War Wilkins in recommending a similar measure in his annual report for 1844.[5] It was felt that a few thousand settlers scattered along the emigrant routes would afford protection to the emigrants and obviate the necessity of establishing military posts.

When the building of a railroad to the Pacific came to be a matter of public discussion, it was generally understood that

[2] Collection of extracts from the treaties, *Cong. Globe,* 32 Cong., 2 Sess., 556.
[3] *U. S. Statutes at Large,* IV, 729-35.
[4] J. C. Malin, *op. cit.,* 26-29, 78.
[5] *Cong. Globe,* 28 Cong., 2 Sess., 41, App., 44; *H. Exec. Docs.,* 28 Cong., 2 Sess., I (463), No. 2, p. 124.

construction would have to be preceded or accompanied by the settlement of land along the route. It was evident that, as long as the great Indian Country remained closed to white settlement, it would be extremely difficult to build and operate a railroad across it. All supplies for construction gangs and maintenance crews would have to be brought in from the outside, it would be difficult to protect the road from the wild Indians of the Plains, and, still more serious, there could be no prospect of any considerable way traffic in the region to contribute to the road's support. The southern route for a railroad ran all the way through lands open to settlement and partially settled and under organized governments.

Accordingly all the plans proposed prior to 1854 for building the Pacific railroad by a route north of Texas involved the opening of at least portions of the Indian Country to settlers. Asa Whitney would get funds to prosecute the work by selling the lands in a strip sixty miles wide the full length of the road. In the plan which Stephen A. Douglas published in 1845 as a rival to Whitney's, he proposed the organization of a Nebraska Territory "with land enough on both sides of the Platte for a good state." Both the St. Louis and Memphis Pacific railroad conventions, of the fall of 1849, recommended as a measure preliminary to building the road the establishment of a line of military posts along the route which might be selected and the encouragement of settlements about the posts by liberal grants of lands to settlers. Thomas Hart Benton's bill, introduced December, 1849, called for the extinguishment of the Indian title in a strip one hundred miles wide from Missouri to California and the opening of the lands to whites.[6]

There were of course other reasons why people in the West came to demand the opening of portions of the Indian Country to settlement and the organization of territorial governments there. People of a speculative turn, and all Westerners were, wanted to get land cheap which might some day bring a high price. City and commonwealth builders near the frontier wanted trade areas extended in their hinterlands. As Senator

---

[6] See above, 11-12, 46, 50, 51.

Borland put it, "We have now an outlet for our trade and travel only on one side; and so long as we remain in that condition, we will be unable to develop even the half of our resources. We want a market on both sides; we desire to see settlements made west as well as east of us." [7] Statesmen believed or professed to believe that the Pacific coast region could not be kept in the Union unless settlements were continuous across the continent. As Douglas once put it, "I have no faith that we can hold our settlements on the Pacific in connection with those on this side of the mountains, unless we have a line of settlements across the country." [8]

Officials of the Bureau of Indian Affairs, often Western men in touch with Western public opinion, read the signs early. In his annual report for 1848, Indian Commissioner Medill said that, if the policy of keeping the Indian wards segregated from the whites was to be maintained, some of the tribes would have to be moved "so as to leave an ample outlet for our white population to spread and pass towards and beyond the Rocky Mountains." He recommended the gradual removal of most of the border tribes between the Kansas and Platte rivers to the district south of the Kansas "as the convenience of our emigrants and the pressure of our white population may require." [9] Medill's successors, Orlando Brown and Luke Lea, repeated the recommendation.[10] In his report for 1851, Lea represented the removals to be an "imperious necessity, in view of the already imposing demonstrations of the public feeling in favor of the early organization of a territorial government on which these Indians reside." D. D. Mitchell, Superintendent of Indian Affairs for the St. Louis district, became convinced that the policy of trying to civilize the Indians by segregating them from whites, other than missionaries and Indian agents, was a failure. He proposed, 1851, organizing the territory without removing the Indians, permitting the whites to occupy lands to which the Indian title was extin-

[7] *Cong. Globe*, 32 Cong., 1 Sess., 1685.
[8] *Ibid.*, 1758.
[9] *Ibid.*, 30 Cong., 2 Sess., App., 32.
[10] *Ibid.*, 31 Cong., 1 Sess., App., 25-26; 31 Cong., 2 Sess., App., 27; *Sen. Exec. Docs.*, 32 Cong., 1 Sess. (613), No. 1, p. 286.

guished, and granting lands in severalty to the more civilized Indians.[11] Some of the Indians themselves were represented as being anxious to part with a portion of their lands in return for a larger annuity, and some, indeed, wished to become citizens of the United States.[12]

In September, 1851, commissioners of the United States government signed the Treaty of Fort Laramie with the chiefs of the wild tribes north of the Arkansas River. The chiefs consented to the establishment of roads and military posts in their country and promised to abstain from depredations upon the emigrants to the Pacific coast. The United States government agreed to pay the tribes annuities to the sum of $50,000 for a number of years to indemnify them for game destroyed by the emigrants and other losses.[13] This treaty was interpreted, and no doubt so intended when made, to cover railroads as well as wagon roads. In 1853 a similar treaty was made at Fort Atkinson with the wild tribes south of the Arkansas,[14] thus formally securing the right of way for emigrant trails or railroads by the thirty-fifth parallel route.

In the summer and autumn of 1852 there were so many manifestations of public sentiment in favor of the organization of Nebraska Territory, especially in Missouri, that the subject could no longer be sidetracked in Congress.

In September, 1852, some persons claiming to be residents of the Nebraska country organized a local government and elected one Abelard Guthrie territorial delegate to Congress. Guthrie agitated the cause in Missouri.[15] Then Thomas H. Benton, on the lookout for a popular issue, took up the Nebraska question.

Benton was engaged in a desperate attempt to return to the United States senate. Back in 1849 the Democratic party of Missouri had split into two wings, Benton and Anti-Benton, over aspects of the slavery question. This split had resulted

[11] *Ibid.*, 322-326.
[12] J. C. Malin, *op. cit.*, 71-75; *Daily Mo. Repub.*, Feb. 2, 1853.
[13] Supt. Mitchell's reports, *Sen. Exec. Docs.*, 32 Cong., 1 Sess. (613), No. 1, pp. 288-90; 32 Cong., 2 Sess. (658), No. 1, pp. 335-38.
[14] *Ibid.*, 33 Cong., 1 Sess. (690), No. 1, p. 363; *U. S. Statutes at Large*, X, 1013.
[15] *Daily Mo. Repub.*, Sept. 30, 1852, Feb. 2, 1853.

in 1851 in the election of a Whig, H. S. Geyer, to succeed Benton. The latter thereupon began a campaign for the seat of David R. Atchison, the leader of the Southern Rights Democrats; and, although Atchison's term would not expire until 1855, the campaign was already warm in 1852.[16]

In speeches about the state, Benton posed as the champion *par excellence* of a Pacific railroad with St. Louis as a terminus and vehemently called for the organization of "Nebraska," representing the two measures to be complementary and interdependent.[17] He whipped up a demand for the organization of the territory among Missouri farmers by advising them that the lands in the Indian Country to which Indian tribes did not hold specific title were already open to preëmption under the federal laws [18] — a clear misrepresentation of the laws. However deep and abiding Benton's interest in the Pacific Railroad and Nebraska may have been — and there were those who doubted his sincerity — he undoubtedly hoped to put his rival in an embarrassing position.

Atchison was indeed embarrassed. During the long struggle over the organization of the territory acquired by the Mexican War, he had taken strong ground against the exclusion of slavery from the territories. According to the Missouri Compromise, of 1820, that portion of the Indian Country which lay north of 36°30′ was to be forever "free." To Benton's claim of being the father of the Pacific railroad, Atchison replied, and truthfully, that he had done more of a practical character to insure its construction with a Missouri terminus than his rival for all the latter's grandiloquent speeches. As for route, he would await the results of the surveys before committing himself in favor of a particular one; he astutely remembered, as Benton did not, that Missouri offered three points of departure for the Pacific and that the people were divided three ways on the question of the route. As for the organization of Nebraska, Atchison and his friends tried for the time to stem the tide. They tried to persuade the farmers

[16] P. O. Ray, *The Repeal of the Missouri Compromise.*
[17] *Ibid.,* 75.
[18] *Letter . . . to the People of Missouri; Central National Highway from the Mississippi River to the Pacific* (Mar. 4, 1853).

that it was to their advantage to have the terriory remain un-settled so that they could continue without competition to supply the California- and Oregon-bound emigrants and the detachments of the United States army on the plains.[19] Atchison's arguments were of little avail. Nebraska sentiment grew.

The [St. Louis] *Western Journal and Civilian*, of November, 1852, expected the territory between Missouri and Utah to be organized at the approaching session of Congress. Upon the consummation of this event, it said, the Missouri Legislature could authorize the Pacific Railroad Company to extend its line to the Pacific provided the assent of the territories of "Kansas" and Utah and the State of California could be obtained.[20] In his message, December 28, 1852, Governor King, friendly to Benton, asked the Legislature to memorialize Congress on behalf of a Pacific railroad "and also press the necessity of taking the incipient steps to extinguish the Indian title to the territory west of us, and through which the road must run, and finally to bring about the organization of such territory. . . ." [21]

When Congress met, Hall, of Missouri, introduced another bill for the organization of a "Territory of the Platte." [22] February 2, 1853, Richardson, of Illinois, chairman of the Committee on Territories, reported a substitute providing for the organization of the territory between the parallels of 36°30′ and 42°30′ under the name Nebraska. One section appropriated $50,000 to enable the Executive to extinguish Indian titles.[23] The bill said nothing about slavery; presumably the new territory would be free under the Missouri Compromise. A few days later Hall and Richardson succeeded in getting their bill taken up in the Committee of the Whole. It was debated briefly but in a creditable manner.[24]

[19] *Address of Senator Atchison to the People of Missouri* (Jan. 5, 1854); *Cong. Globe*, 32 Cong., 2 Sess., 1113.
[20] IX, 88.
[21] *Mo. Repub.*, Jan. 1, 1853.
[22] *Cong. Globe*, 32 Cong., 2 Sess., 7, 47.
[23] *Ibid.*, 474, 475.
[24] Entire debate is in *ibid.*, 542-44, 556-65.

The sponsors of the bill were pressed to state their reasons for wanting the territory organized. They advanced the arguments which already have been recounted. They wanted to protect the emigrant trains against Indians. They would afford emigrants the protection of officers and courts of law against their lawless fellows. They wanted to satisfy the demands of prospective settlers. There were "today," said Richardson, five, ten, or fifteen thousand people waiting upon the borders of Missouri for permission to go in. They wanted the territory settled to consolidate the Union and attach the Pacific coast settlements. They wanted to facilitate the building of the Pacific railroad. "Why, everybody is talking about a railroad to the Pacific Ocean," said Hall. "In the name of God, how is the railroad to be made if you will never let people live on the lands through which the road passes? Are you going to construct a road through the Indian territory, at the expense of $200,000,000, and say that no one shall live upon the land through which it passes?" [25]

The opposition to the bill was ostensibly based upon two grounds. Sutherland, of New York, especially, voiced the old familiar Eastern opposition to measures designed to promote Western expansion. "I can understand this policy of gentlemen coming from the old States who are afraid that their people will go away and settle in the new Territory," said Richardson. The attack centered chiefly, however, upon the alleged injustice being done the Indians and upon the violation of solemn treaties, which the bill was said to involve. The proponents of the bill denied that its terms violated the Indian treaties, and they assailed the whole policy of the permanent Indian frontier. They quoted officials of the Indian Department as recommending the proposed changes. They refused to believe that the professed solicitude for the Indians was sincere; it was designed to cover other motives of opposition.

Representative V. E. Howard, of Texas, was especially solicitous for the Indians and intent upon preserving the old Indian policy. Hall refused to accept his professions. He had

[25] *Ibid.*, 560.

understood that "according to Texas politics, and according to Texas morals, the Indians had no rights whatever." There might be other considerations. "If the gentleman can convince this House that the Territory of Nebraska shall not be organized. . . ; if the people of Texas can prevail upon the Government of the United States to drive the Indians of Texas, the Camanches and other wild tribes, into the Territory of Nebraska, it may have the effect of rendering your overland routes from Missouri and Iowa to Oregon and California so dangerous that the tide of emigration will have to pass through Texas — an object which Texas has most zealously sought to accomplish for many years past. In addition to that, if in the course of time a great railroad should be found necessary from this part of the continent to the shores of the Pacific, and the doctrine prevail that all the territory west of the Missouri is to be a wilderness from this day henceforth and forever, Texas being settled, the people of this country will have no alternative but to make the Pacific road terminate at Galveston, or some point in Texas." [26]

Practically nothing was said about slavery during the debate on the bill. It is reasonable to suppose, however, in view of the recent excitement over the question of slavery in the territories, that considerations in regard to it affected the voting upon the bill. No party issues were involved as yet in the Nebraska question.

The Hall-Richardson Nebraska bill shortly passed the House, the test vote standing 107 to 49.[27] The representatives from the Northwest, who would, presumably, wish the territory opened and organized for all of the reasons advanced during the debate, and who had no objections to the exclusion of slavery therefrom, voted 38 to 2 in its favor. The representatives from Missouri and Kentucky, who would favor the organization for all the reasons mentioned except that they might object to the exclusion of slavery, gave 9 votes for the bill and none against. The members from the other Southwestern states, who, presumably, would be loath to organize

[26] *Ibid.*, 558.
[27] *Ibid.*, 565.

a territory from which slavery would be excluded and which would develop into a "free" state and who would be reluctant to vote for a measure to facilitate the building of a railroad to the Pacific by a central route, gave 7 votes for the bill and 9 against it, while several members, including the two from Arkansas, abstained from voting. The favorable votes can probably be accounted for in part by the feeling current in the West that Western men must stand together on Western measures if any were to be adopted and in part by the favor which all proposed legislation calculated to open new opportunities to small farmers met among such men as Andrew Johnson, of east Tennessee, a great champion of the Homestead bill. The delegations of the old Southern states cast 27 votes against the Nebraska bill and only 5 for it. Four of the five came from Maryland and Virginia, whose railroad interests largely supported a Missouri terminus for the Pacific railroad and whose westward migrants moved largely in the same belt. The Eastern States voted 47 to 10 in favor of the bill. The lone California representative, of course, voted aye.

In the Senate the Nebraska bill was reported favorably by Douglas, from the Committee on Territories, while the debate on the Rusk Pacific Railroad bill was at its height and just the day before the adoption of the Shields amendment, which, per Rusk, Borland, Bell, *et al*, killed that bill.[28] On March 2 and 3, Douglas made earnest efforts to have the Nebraska bill taken up for consideration.[29] Atchison reluctantly gave his support. He explained that when he came to Washington for the session he was strongly opposed to the organization of the territory unless the Missouri Compromise should be repealed and slaveowners be allowed to take their slaves with them into the region. He had found, however, that there was no prospect of repealing the compromise, and he would bow to the wishes of his constituents, "whose opinions I am bound to respect." Rusk and Houston, of Texas, Adams, of Mississippi, Borland, and Bell threatened to talk the bill to death if it were taken up. They assigned reasons for their opposition similar to those

[28] *Ibid.*, 658; above, 99ff.
[29] Senate debate is in *Cong. Globe*, 32 Cong., 2 Sess., 1020, 1111, 1113-17.

advanced in the House; and, just as in the House, the friends of the bill refused to accept the assigned reasons as the true ones. "I also know," said Douglas, "that there is a large number using the argument of sympathy for the Indians simply for the purpose of killing the bill."

The bill was laid on the table the last day of the session by a vote of 23 to 17.[30] Except for Atchison and Geyer, of Missouri, not a single senator from a Southern state voted for the bill. Gwin, of California, as usual voted with the Southerners. Of the five Eastern senators who voted to table, four were inveterate opponents of measures calculated to build up the West. The vote made it as clear as a pikestaff that a Nebraska bill could not be got through the Senate unless a few more votes could be gained.

In the House meanwhile, Phelps and Hall, both of Missouri, secured an amendment to the Indian Appropriation bill authorizing the president to extinguish Indian titles in the proposed territory and appropriating $50,000 to be used for the purpose.[31] This much was accepted by the Senate.

After Congress adjourned, the fight in Missouri between the Benton and Atchison factions waxed warmer. Benton issued a pamphlet letter to the people and made speeches.[32] He reported progress: He had persuaded Secretary of War Davis to survey his 38th parallel route. An appropriation had been made for extinguishing the Indian title to lands along the route. Nebraska was still to be organized; that must be attended to. Benton men accused Atchison of reneging in voting for a Nebraska bill which left the Missouri Compromise intact.[33] Atchison was forced to define his position anew. In speeches at Parkville, Platte City, and Weston he said he would vote to ratify the treaties with the Indians (surrendering lands). He would also vote to organize the territory if it were to be open to slaveholders and non-slaveholders alike. He would vote to *let the people of the territory decide whether slavery should*

[30] *Ibid.*, 32 Cong., 2 Sess., 1117.
[31] *Ibid.*, 825; *Mo. Repub.*, Mar. 30, Je. 7, 1853.
[32] [Weekly] *Jeffersonian Inquirer*, Aug. 4, 1855, republication of speeches made at Kansas, Westport, and Independence, May 6, 7, 1853.
[33] *Mo. Repub.*, Je. 16, 1853.

be permitted or not; but he would never vote to make Nebraska a free territory. He ridiculed Benton's route for the railroad. When the surveys should have been made, he would vote to appropriate both land and money in aid of a railroad, and, if it were not entirely incompatible with the public interest, he would vote for a Missouri terminus, either at St. Joseph, Kansas, or the southwest corner, depending upon the findings of the surveyors.[34]

When Congress met in December, 1853, the Nebraska question came up again. The chairmen of the committees on territories could not have sidetracked it had they been of a mind to do so;[35] and there is no evidence that they were. In fact, in view of the way conditions and events were rapidly shaping or being shaped to make the southern route the inevitable choice, the Northwestern men must have felt there was no time to lose. At the preceding session of Congress, lands had been granted to Arkansas to aid in building a railroad diagonally across the state from Cairo to Fulton with a connection from Little Rock to Memphis. Texas was on the point of bestowing a large grant of land upon the imposing New York Atlantic and Pacific Railroad Company to extend the road from Fulton to El Paso. James Gadsden had been sent to Mexico by President Pierce to secure, among other things, the strip of land south of the Gila which held the most eligible route in that quarter. Jefferson Davis, as Secretary of War, was in charge of the surveys of the several routes for a Pacific railroad. Davis seemed to have become the President's closest adviser. The chiefs of the Corps of Topographical Engineers were believed to prefer the southern route. The Pierce administration was certainly friendly to Southern interests in general.[36]

The task of Douglas, Richardson, and their associates was quite precisely defined by the logic of circumstances. They must frame a Nebraska bill which would *pass both houses* and

[34] *Ibid.*, Je. 13, 22, 1853; *Address of Senator Atchison to the People of Missouri*, Je. 5, 1854, extracts from addresses of the preceding year; N. Y. *Herald*, Dec. 18, 1854.

[35] *Daily Mo. Repub.*, Jan. 7, 1854, Washington correspondence for Dec. 31. *Cf.* F. H. Hodder, "The Railroad Background of the Kansas-Nebraska Act," *Miss. Val. Hist. Rev.*, XII, 3-22.

[36] See above, 118-22, 124-27, 138, and below, 168ff.

receive Pierce's signature. As prominent politicians of the Democratic party (and Douglas at least had presidential aspirations with good prospects of attaining them), they must frame a bill which would cause as little discord as possible in the party ranks. The vote in the Senate at the preceding session demonstrated that they needed at least a few Southern votes in that body. Considering Atchison's reversion in the summer and the confidence being shown by the Southern wing of the party, inspired by various marks of President Pierce's favor, there appeared to be no possibility of reconciling Southern senators to the Richardson bill that had been defeated in the Senate in March. To attempt to force it through was certain to raise the slavery question in a way calculated to split the party wide open. Shortly after the question had gone to the Senate Committee on Territories, a Washington correspondent put the matter as follows: "This is one of the most important questions of the session. It involves the Pacific railroad question, and the slavery question, and a number of local questions, and questions in relation to our Indian relations. . . . [The Committee] has a very delicate duty to perform in regard to the terms on which the territories are to come in. To revive the old Missouri controversy is not desirable. How to avoid it is the question." [37]

The committee attempted to solve its problem by adopting the principle of the Compromise of 1850 with regard to slavery in the territories, namely, leaving the decision to the territorial legislature with provision for the appeal of slave cases directly to the Supreme Court of the United States so that a decision might be had from that tribunal as to the constitutionality of restriction: Southern Democrats professed to believe that under the Constitution neither Congress nor the territorial legislature had the right to prohibit slavery in a territory. The Democratic Party had announced wholehearted acceptance of the Compromise of 1850 in its national platform of 1852 and had won an overwhelming victory. Southern men would have to vote for the territorial bill with

[37] *Mo. Repub.*, Jan. 4, 1854, quoting the N. Y. *Journal*, of Dec. 26.

the Compromise provision or run the risk of being considered unfaithful to the South's peculiar institution; for a vote against the bill would be equivalent to voting to retain the existing law excluding slavery as an unfit institution. Northern senators and representatives might be persuaded that the territories would actually become "free" by virtue of their soil and climate and that it was unwise to continue to exclude slavery by federal law just as "a taunt and a reproach to our Southern brethren." [38]

The Committee on Territories proposed to divide the territory to be organized into two, Kansas to extend from the 37th to the 40th parallel and Nebraska from the 40th parallel to the Canadian boundary. This division was made, as Professors Allen Johnson and F. H. Hodder have clearly shown, at the request of the Iowa delegation in Congress and of local interests in or near the portion of the Indian Country lying west of Iowa.[39] They feared that with only one territory, the valley of the Kansas, being somewhat more accessible than the valley of the Platte, would be somewhat earlier settled, would get the seat of government, and would, therefore, get a link in the Pacific railroad several years before the valley of the Platte. Douglas himself explained that the division had been made after consultation with the Iowa delegation and a part of the Missouri delegation.[40] Dodge, of Iowa, said: "Originally I favored the organization of one territory, but representations from our constituents, and a more critical examination of the subject — having an eye to the systems of internal improvement which must be adopted by the people of Nebraska and Kansas to develop their resources — satisfied my colleague [Jones], who was a member of the committee who reported this bill, and myself that the great interests of the whole country and especially of our State demanded two territories, otherwise the seat of government and leading thoroughfares must have fallen south of Iowa." [41]

[38] For a similar interpretation see Geo. F. Milton, *The Eve of Conflict*, 108 ff.
[39] Johnson, *Stephen A. Douglas*, 239; Hodder, *op. cit.*, 16-17.
[40] *Cong. Globe*, 33 Cong., 1 Sess., 221.
[41] *Ibid.*, App., 382.

There are reasons for believing that the committee seriously considered creating a third territory west of Arkansas, in what is now Oklahoma, but gave up the plan because "certain parties of influence" could not be reconciled to the ejection of the civilized tribes there. [42] As it was the southern boundary of Kansas was moved northward from the parallel of 36°30', as provided in the Richardson bill of the preceding session, to the 37th parallel so as not to disturb the Cherokees in one half of their lands.[43] A territory west of Arkansas might have facilitated the extension of the "systems of internal improvement" of Arkansas and the Southwest Branch of the Missouri Pacific along the 35th-parallel route.

The northern boundary of Nebraska also was moved up to the Canadian boundary. No public explanation of this seems to have been made. The reason which most readily occurs is that it was as easy to put the boundary at one line as another and the slavery question might as well be settled for all the organizable territory at once. It should not be forgotten, however, that the northern route to the Pacific was being surveyed and had influential champions. Douglas himself had probably switched his personal interest to this route. He, Bright, of Indiana, Breckinridge, of Kentucky, and several other prominent Democratic politicians had acquired an extensive tract of land at the western end of Lake Superior, which was expected to be a terminus of a Northern Pacific railroad. Douglas had taken great interest in the survey of the northern route. Colonel Isaac I. Stevens, who was in charge of it, conferred with him as to route and reported his success.[44] In the same session of Congress that passed the Kansas-Nebraska bill, Douglas introduced a measure providing for three railroads

[42] Washington correspondence of the *Mo. Repub.*, Jan. 4, 13, 17, 1854; Washington correspondence of the N. Y. *Jour. of Commerce*, Dec. 30, 1853, cited in G. F. Milton, *op. cit.*, 109.

[43] *Cong. Globe*, 33 Cong., 1 Sess., 221.

[44] *Correspondence of R. M. T. Hunter* (Am. Hist. Asso., *Rept.*, 1916, II), 158, 168, 262; Geo. F. Milton, *op. cit.*, 104-06. Professor Hodder thought Douglas was interested only in the Platte Valley route (*op. cit.*); and Milton thinks he exerted his public influence only in behalf of the "central" route (p. 106). Different sections and interests in Illinois preferred different routes. Douglas was too shrewd to openly espouse only one of them while representing Illinois as senator.

to the Pacific, one by a northern route, one by a central, and one by a southern.

The details of the great debate over the repeal of the Missouri Compromise are not germane here. The extreme violence of the opposition had not been anticipated. It came mostly from the Free-Soilers and Northern Whigs, but not only. Had the Kansas-Nebraska bill not contained the provision repealing the Missouri Compromise, the debate would have been still more violent with Northern Democrats and Southern Democrats strongly arrayed against each other, and the bill would not have passed the Senate. As it was, few of those who voted for the bill did so with enthusiasm, but *the bill passed.*[45] As had been anticipated, Southern representatives mostly felt constrained to vote for the bill because of the concession as to slavery, but, considering the objects for which the Northwest wanted the territory organized and the strong probability that neither territory would become slaveholding,[46] it is not surprising that they could muster little fervor for the measure. It is noteworthy that both Senators Bell and Houston, members of the Committee on Territories, opposed the bill on the same grounds they had opposed the Richardson bill at the preceding session.[47]

The immediate purpose and larger implications of the Kansas-Nebraska bill certainly did not escape alert Southerners outside Congress. Albert Pike, of Arkansas, stated them in his speeches and addresses in behalf of his plan for building a Southern Pacific railway. "Not content," he wrote, "with the natural and regular growth towards manly stature of the great country lying in the North-west, they have resorted to the system of forcing, as men use hotbeds in horticulture; and we see new territories of vast size and comparatively unpeopled, organized and established on the line of a Northern Pacific Railroad — Oregon and Washington standing on the shores of the Pacific, and Nebraska and Kansas on those of

---

[45] In the Senate the Democrats voted 28 for, 5 against, the Whigs, 9 for, 7 against; in the House the Democrats voted 101 to 44 and the Whigs 12 to 52. *Cong. Globe,* 32 Cong., 1 Sess., 532, 1254.

[46] *Ibid.,* 279, App., 149; Geo. F. Milton, *op. cit.,* 149.

[47] *Tex. State Gaz.,* Dec. 1, 1855 (Houston's speech).

the Mississippi — each clasping hands with the other on the slopes of the rocky mountains. It needs no prophetic eye to see in the future a cordon of free States carved in succession off from these territories, extending with a continuous and swarming population across the continent, giving such power to the Northern vote in Congress as has hitherto been only dreamed of, and securing to their road, the Nile of this new Egypt, aid from the National Treasury, and countenance and encouragement from the general government." [48]

After the Kansas-Nebraska bill had become law, the people of Missouri and elsewhere in the Northwest remembered its original objects. An anti-Benton meeting in St. Louis condemned Benton for opposing a measure "whereby the Great West, and especially St. Louis and Missouri, were to be largely benefited" [49] — Benton had opposed the bill because of its repeal of the Missouri Compromise. Senator Atchison rightfully regarded the passage of the bill in the form it took as a great victory for himself over Benton. In an *Address . . . to the People of Missouri*, dated June 5, 1854, he vindicated his record on the territories, the railroad, and other questions of interest to his state. [50] "The Douglas bill was a Western measure," he said. "It was designed to add to the power and wealth of the West. . . . All of the railroad interests are largely interested, for a terminus on the Western frontier, blocked by an Indian wall, is very different from an indefinite extension westward through new and rapidly opening settlements. Every interest of St. Louis was connected with the territorial question, and there can be no plausible excuse for the envenomed hostility which the St. Louis representative [Benton] has manifested since the Senate first commenced to act on the subject during the present session of Congress." He hoped Congress would grant lands to the territories to extend the Hannibal and St. Joseph up the Platte, the Missouri Pacific up the Kansas, and the Springfield road (the Southwest Branch) across the Neosho and Arkansas rivers in the direc-

[48] *DeBow's Rev.*, XVII, 595.
[49] *Mo. Repub.*, May 29, 1854.
[50] *Ibid.*, Je. 21, 1854; also as a pamphlet.

tion of Albuquerque. Let all the roads be constructed to the foot of the Rockies and the one on the most practicable route extended to the Pacific. The roads would prove profitable even if they should never go beyond the mountains.

Opening the territories to settlement and organizing territorial governments therein did remove an obstacle to the building of a railroad to the Pacific by central and northern routes. The congregation of population along the Kansas and the Platte furnished arguments for selecting a route in the vicinity of one or the other. The territories promptly developed projects for "links" in the Pacific railroad and for other railroads and petitioned Congress for land grants in aid. On December 26, 1854, Mr. Whitfield, delegate from Kansas territory, introduced a bill for a land grant in aid of a road in Kansas.[51] In the next session of Congress grants were requested for Kansas, Nebraska, and Minnesota, and the following year for New Mexico as well.[52] Thereafter the territories had almost as many requests for land grants in aid of railroad projects as full-fledged states.

In an indirect way, however, the organization of the territories contributed strongly to delaying the great project its friends had hoped to advance. The bitter debate over the repeal of the Missouri Compromise and the subsequent struggle over whether Kansas should become a slave or a free state greatly exacerbated the sectional feeling of the time, which, in turn, rendered the federal government well-nigh impotent to take a national measure for a national purpose.

[51] *Cong. Globe*, 33 Cong., 2 Sess., 130.
[52] *Ibid.*, 34 Cong., 1 Sess., 1325, 1944; 34 Cong., 2 Sess., 341, 352, 357, 920, 1000, 1069.

8

The Economic History of Negro Slavery in the United States

The following essay originally appeared in *Agricultural History*, XI (October 1937), 308–321. It appears here by permission of the Agricultural History Society. The original pagination appears in brackets.

A NY DESCRIPTION of the economic characteristics of Negro slavery must be tested by the economic history of the institution. In turn the economic history of Negro slavery, to be truthful, must be written with the inherent characteristics of slavery and the native traits of Negroes in mind. It also should be written whole, and it should be written with the general economic history of the entire country as a background. Thus, it is at least possible to avoid attributing conditions in one period of history or in one portion of the Union to slavery while attributing the same conditions in another period or in another region to entirely different causes. It is believed that many misjudgments have been commonly pronounced upon slavery in its economic aspects and that such misinterpretations have been due principally to a too exclusive concern with slavery in only one section of the Union during only one period, namely about 1830 to 1865, and to using the approach of political rather than economic history.

Slavery was first introduced into the Continental English Colonies in response to the demands of the tobacco-growing industry. It was early found that the soil and climate of Virginia and Maryland, particularly, were suitable for growing tobacco. Tobacco was not bulky in proportion to its value, it was not perishable, and the small ships of the day could collect it from the wharves of individual planters on the numerous rivers and creeks of the Tidewater region; consequently, it would stand the long shipment to Europe. The English Government imposed discriminatory taxes on tobacco not grown in English colonies and forbade its growth in the British Isles. The English and European appetite for the weed grew. Thus an adequate market was established. Enterprising tobacco growers in the Colonies naturally looked about to see how they might enlarge the scale of their operations.

Land and labor were the chief requisites for growing tobacco on a large scale. Land was easily obtained, but labor was not. Men would not work for wages when it was so easy to become independent farmers. Planters first had recourse to white indentured servants, and the plantations in Virginia and Maryland in the seventeenth century were built up chiefly with that kind of labor, but it was not entirely satisfactory. To secure such servants the planters had to pay their passage to America,—a considerable sum. The supply was limited and many were "jail birds" or poor quality.[1] A large proportion died before they had become acclimated. At best they served only the period of indenture— about four years on the average—and then they were free and their children with them.

The use of Negro slaves elsewhere suggested their use in the English Colonies. The English Government encouraged it, prompted largely by the desire of various influential people at home to profit by the African slave trade. The tobacco planters were hesitant; they had to overcome racial prejudice and gain experience in handling slaves. Although Negroes fresh from Africa or from a few years' sojourn in the West Indies were not as effective laborers as their descendants came to be a few generations later, they could be taught the comparatively simple operations involved in colonial agriculture, the supply was adequate, and they were comparatively cheap. In the tobacco and corn fields the slaves could be worked in gangs and readily supervised. They could be advantageously employed on the plantations the year around, and the women and children could be used as well as the men. Perhaps most decisive of all, they throve and multiplied, and they served for life and their children after them, thus giving planters reasonable assurance that their labor forces would not melt away. Restraints, therefore, were gradually broken down, and slavery eventually came to be firmly established in the tobacco belt.

For similar reasons, and without the preliminary indentured-servant stage, rice and indigo plantations with Negro slave labor developed in the eighteenth century in the Carolinas and Georgia. In the case of rice growing, an added inducement to employ slaves was that they stood the fevers of the swamps better than whites.

The New England Colonies were unable to utilize slave labor in their agriculture to any considerable extent. It was not because Puritan consciences would not permit; they did not gag at the African slave

---

[1] There is a difference of opinion among students as to the quality of these transported prisoners. See, for example, C. M. Andrews, *Colonial Folkways*, 190-194 (New Haven, 1919), and T. J. Wertenbaker, *The First Americans, 1607-1690*, p. 25 (New York, 1929).

trade nor at selling captive Indians into slavery. Nor was it that more intelligent labor was required to grow wheat, corn, beans, and pumpkins in New England than corn, tobacco, rice, and indigo in the South; the Southern staples certainly required the greater care and skill. The fundamental reason was that, except in a few localities, New England farmers found no product for which there was a ready market. They had, perforce, to produce only for home consumption and for the very limited local markets. There was, therefore, little incentive for the New England farmer to enlarge the scale of his operations to what can be called plantation size. The members of the family, with extra help at the harvest season drawn from the fisherfolk and from the artisans of the towns and countryside, constituted an adequate labor force on the small farm. Producing little that was salable and, therefore, having little with which to buy, New England farm families were constrained to do much household manufacturing, and Negro slaves were not so well adapted to that.

If they had been tempted to use it, New England farmers would have found Negro slave labor rather expensive, considering its low efficiency, because of the cost of shelter, fuel, and clothing during the winter months. The policies of land disposition initially adopted and long continued in the New England Colonies were less conducive to the accumulation of large holdings than were those of the Southern Colonies; but it is not unreasonable to suppose that this handicap would have been overcome if there had been strong inducements for individuals to acquire large holdings for farming purposes.

In connection with the reasons why New England farmers did not employ many slaves, it is an illuminating fact that neither did they use many white indentured servants. It is very illuminating also that the back-country districts of the South, being debarred from growing staples by inaccessibility to markets, had a rural economy quite similar to that of New England—with few plantations, little bound labor, and much household manufacturing.

The chief New England industries which produced for commercial markets and in which, therefore, there was an incentive to large-scale operations, were fishing, lumbering, and ship building; shipping also employed many men. It is almost obvious why Negro slaves could not be used advantageously in such occupations. They required chiefly strong men, and therefore complications concerning ownership of the women and children would have arisen. They were largely seasonal; and masters would have had difficulty in finding employment for their slaves in off seasons. The risks to life and limb were great; and slaves, unlike wage laborers, were capital and would have to be replaced by purchase. A large proportion of the workmen must be skilled and intelligent, as in fishing, at least, men could not be worked in gangs and closely supervised. Rude Africans could hardly be made into skilled artisans to work at the numerous handicrafts of prefactory days. So the chief employment of Negro slaves in New England was as menials: and the rich or well-to-do who could and would afford such servants were not numerous enough to utilize a large number.

The economy of the Middle Colonies was more like that of New England than that of the South, but there were districts which produced wheat or livestock for export, generally in the forms of flour or biscuit and salted meats. In such districts plantations developed, and a considerable number of slaves appeared, although not nearly so many as were to be found farther south. Quakers were numerous in Pennsylvania and New Jersey, and they had scruples, sometimes overcome, against holding slaves. These colonies were fortunate also in getting a large number of high-grade indentured servants from Germany. For these reasons and perhaps others, indentured servants continued to be more numerous than slaves in the Middle Colonies throughout the eighteenth century.

The American Revolution, with its philosophy of equality and inalienable rights of life, liberty, and pursuit of happiness, brought a reaction against slavery. This reaction, together with the hostility of a growing class of wage earners to slave competition, was sufficient to bring about, within two decades, provision for either immediate or gradual emancipation of the slaves in all the Northern States and to dedicate the Old Northwest to freedom.[2]

It was one of the accidents with which history abounds that, after slavery had been abolished in the North, after a strong antislavery sentiment had developed, and after the likelihood that the institution should ever be reestablished was *nil,* industries developed there in which slaves could have been employed to advantage had they been available. They probably could have been used in the textile mills, which sprang up in great numbers as the industrial revolution came on. Such mills employed men, women, and children, and the operations did not require skill beyond the capacity of Negroes to acquire. The work was easily supervised, and the chances of loss by death or serious injury were not great. Whether slaves would have been used in textile factories is a different question. White free-labor was available and the

---

[2] In 1795, John Adams said: "Arguments might have some weight in the abolition of slavery in Massachusetts, but the real cause was the multiplication of labouring white people, who would no longer suffer the rich to employ these sable rivals as much to their injury."

choice between the two classes would have been determined by a variety of factors impossible to evaluate at this distance in time.3

As means of transportation improved and the growth of an industrial population expanded the home market for foodstuffs, Northern agriculture became more commercialized and specialized along the trade routes. Wheat came to be the chief market crop in extensive areas; corn and hogs were stables in other localities. Slave labor might not have proved to be as well adapted to the production of such commodities as to the production of Southern staples.4 For example, swinging cradles in the wheat harvest might have been pretty strenuous exercise for prime field hands, and apparently there would have been difficulty in finding suitable employment for slave women and children at some seasons of the year. But good soil, large yields, and fair prices might easily have offset such minor defects in adaptability. As it was, there was not a sufficient number of whites who would work for the wages which farmers could offer, and Negro slaves were not available at all; the plantation system was not developed, and the small farm prevailed. But there is no good reason to doubt that, if slaves had been available, they would have been utilized and plantations would have developed.

In the South the sentimental reaction against slavery caused by the Revolutionary philosophy coincided in time with a severe depression in the tobacco industry and the decline of indigo. Under the double impact, thousands of slaves were freed by their masters in Virginia and Maryland, and in spite of the social dangers involved in freeing so many still primitive people, these states might have followed the example of their Northern sisters had not the spectacular development of the cotton-growing industry and the slightly less spectacular development of sugar-growing intervened.

The causes for the rise of the cotton-growing industry have often been well told. The development of labor-saving machinery for spinning and weaving in England and elsewhere lowered the prices of cotton goods and thus stimulated the demand for them. Futher improvements made it practicable to utilize short-staple cotton as well as long in manufacturing cloth. Eli Whitney's famous invention made it possible to gin short-staple cotton at a small fraction of the cost of ginning by hand and thus to grow such cotton in America profitably at a price manufacturers could afford to pay. Reduction in the cost of the raw

---

3 See p. 316-318 for suggestions.

4 See F. L. Olmsted, *A Journey in the Back Country,* 2:103 ff. (New York, 1907) for interesting contemporary speculations on this point.

material still further reduced the prices of cotton goods, stimulating the demand for them and, therefore, in turn, for raw cotton. Only a few localities in the South were adapted to long-staple cotton, but vast areas were as well adapted to the short-staple variety as any regions on the globe. Land, the section's resources yet untaxed, remained cheap. Cotton had a high value in proportion to bulk, and the South had numerous navigable rivers on which it could be floated to the sea; so the staple could stand the cost of transportation to distant markets even before railroads penetrated the interior. As production increased prices fell, but they were seldom so low that people forsook cotton for other crops. Thanks to improved gins and plows and to the substitution of the mule and the horse for the slow-moving ox, production costs fell somewhat also. Prices and production fluctuated widely, making the industry highly speculative; but this feature perhaps repelled few. Finally cotton growing could utilize slave labor.

If ever any industry was made to order for Negro slavery, cotton growing was. It occupied the slaves a large portion of the year as well, if not better, than tobacco culture, and on farms and plantations the interstices could easily be filled in with other necessary and not unprofitable tasks. Cotton growing could utilize men, women, and children of all abilities and skills, the dullest and slowest as well as the quickest and most intelligent. Although it lent itself well to the gang system and to supervision, a large force was not essential. The cotton belt, except for a few localities, was about as healthy as any other part of the Lower South; and cotton growing could not be termed a dangerous occupation.

The sugar industry developed rapidly after Etienne de Boré had demonstrated on his Louisiana plantation during 1794-95 that sugar could be grown profitably in that region. On account of the vagaries of the weather, production fluctuated widely from season to season, making the industry even more speculative than cotton growing, but frequently the profits were large. The industry remained confined almost exclusively to lower Louisiana.

Sugar growing was not quite so well adapted to slavery as cotton. It required a larger proportion of grown men in the gangs. Health conditions were not as good in the sugar belt as in most parts of the cotton belt. For various reasons, especially the cost of sugar-making machinery and of leveeing, it was a large-scale industry; the small slaveholder could not engage in it. But it met most of the qualifications for the profitable use of slaves. And because it was a large-scale industry, sugar planters did not, as did cotton and tobacco planters, have any direct competition from small farmers.

The cotton-growing industry, reenforced by the sugar industry, eventually employed an absolute majority of all the slaves in the country and provided the chief market for slaves that were sold.

After the American Revolution the tobacco-growing industry, which had employed the bulk of the slaves in Colonial days, did not again enjoy real prosperity until the 1850's. Thousands of planters removed with their slaves from the tobacco to the cotton belt. Slave prices were always higher in the cotton and sugar areas than in the tobacco areas with the result that most of the slaves sold in the latter were bought up by traders who took them to the Lower South. This traffic, indeed, reached such proportions that the abolitionists charged Virginians and others with breeding slaves for sale. This charge, which was strongly resented, was not true in the literal sense, but, no doubt, the money received from the sale of surplus slaves enabled many a tobacco planter, who otherwise must have removed from the tobacco belt or given up slaveholding altogether, to go on year after year holding slaves and raising tobacco. In general, if all the natural increase of the slave population of the tobacco States had had to remain there, the tobacco industry could not have absorbed them, and, unless other commercialized industries which could utilize slaves in sufficient numbers had then sprung up, the surplus slaves would have been emancipated. It was, therefore, principally the prosperity of cotton growing which maintained slavery as a vigorous institution in the border slave States.

The rice industry grew steadily and utilized an increasing number of slaves, and hemp was a product of slave labor in various localities. Household service, in town and country, continued to absorb a considerable portion of the slave population.

As time went by there developed in the South other industries or occupations which demanded labor bond or free. Steamboats were operated, loaded, and unloaded, and railroads were built and operated. A number of cotton factories sprang up, especially in the Carolinas and Georgia, and there were saw mills, flour and grist mills, iron works, car shops, and tobacco factories. Nearly all of the handicrafts of the time were followed to a greater or less extent in the slaveholding States, where they competed for labor against agriculture and domestic service, and attracted some slave labor. Slaves were owned or hired in considerable numbers by artisans. Many a master hired out his slaves to railroad contractors or went in person with his gang to work at railway grading, and occasionally a railroad company would buy slaves for construction and maintenance work. The Virginia tobacco factories and iron works, and at least one cotton factory, the Saluda, in South Carolina, successfully employed Negro slaves for several years. There was a protracted debate in Southern journals as to whether they could be successfully utilized in factories and, if not, whether other labor could be found, that is, whether the section could have an industrial revolution or not.[5]

In general as time passed the class of white and, to a less extent, free-Negro wage-labor grew, by immigration, transfer from agriculture, and otherwise, and gradually took over a large proportion of such jobs, especially the ones requiring skill, while the slaves were more and more concentrated in staple agriculture and domestic service. During the 1850's the slave population of Baltimore, St. Louis, New Orleans, and Charleston actually declined although those cities, except Charleston, were growing rapidly, while in a number of other towns, including Richmond, Savannah, Augusta, Memphis, Nashville, and Mobile, the slave population declined relatively to the white.

The reasons for this partial displacement were various. Slaves could not be so advantageously employed in some of the occupations indicated as in agriculture. In some cases the character of the industry would practically necessitate hiring labor instead of owning it—because the work was seasonal or required quite unnatural proportions of men, women, or children—and slaveowners were loath to entrust their valuable slaves to the care of those whose interest would be to exploit them to the limit. Some trades demanded more skill than Negroes could readily acquire. The newly organized manufacturing and railroad companies had trouble enough in raising capital for construction and equipment without saddling themselves with debts incurred in buying hands. In some of the employments concerned, the risks of loss of slaves by accident or disease were great; free laborers usually bore their own risks. As towns grew and Negroes became more sophisticated, it became increasingly difficult to control slaves. White labor was becoming class conscious and demanding the exclusion of slaves from various employments in which whites commonly engaged.[6]

The chief reasons why slaves retained almost a monopoly of domestic service even in the towns were the disinclination of free-born whites to do menial tasks and the preference of employers for servants

---

[5] Kathleen Bruce, *Virginia Iron Manufacture in the Slave Era*, ch. 6 (New York and London, 1931); C. H. Wesley, *Negro Labor in the United States, 1850-1925*, ch. 1 (New York, 1927); U. B. Phillips, *Amercian Negro Slavery*, 375-378 (New York, 1918); Robert R. Russel, *Economic Aspects of Southern Sectionalism, 1840-1861*, ch. 2, "Movement for the Diversification of Industry, 1840-1852," p. 33-64 (Urbana, Ill., 1923).

[6] Wesley, *Negro Labor in the United States*, ch. 3; Bruce, *Virginia Iron Manufacture in the Slave Era*, 236-237; Russel, *Economic Aspects of Southern Sectionalism*, 53, 218-220.

who would remain in their service more permanently than the average hired domestic.

For various reasons a free-labor class did not develop as rapidly in agricultural as in nonagricultural pursuits. White free labor had greater relative advantages over Negro slave labor in the latter than in the former and, therefore, as long as there was not enough for both, naturally gravitated into the nonagricultural employments,—always excepting domestic service. The skill required was usually greater than in agriculture and consequently wages tended to be higher. The towns had social attractions. Immigration from the North and from Europe largely entered at the seaports and tended to stay there. In the towns the varied nature of industry made it more practicable to provide separate tasks or distinctions in task for whites and Negroes and thus enable the whites to avoid feeling that they were doing slaves' work.

In the towns, with their denser population and more varied industry, employers could employ free labor and be reasonably assured of constantly having a supply available. In the rural districts, however, with their sparser population, planters hesitated to dispose of slaves and engage wage labor because they did not feel assured of being able to fill vacancies that were certain to arise. In other words, until there should be a large free-labor class in the country, planters would fear to rely upon it, and this fear would, in turn, prevent the class from developing. The story is told of a sugar planter who, becoming disgusted with slave labor, sold all his slaves and hired German and Irish immigrants in their stead. During the first grinding season they struck for double wages, and the planter went back to slaves.[7]

In the rural South it was still too easy for freemen to become independent farmers for any large number to seek work for wages. During the last decade before the War between the States, Southern agriculture was so prosperous that, in spite of the shift of slaves from town to country, demand greatly outran supply. Prices of slaves soared to unheard of heights; smuggling from Africa was renewed; and agitation began for a repeal of the laws against the foreign slave trade (an agitation inspired in part by other than economic motives, to be sure). A large number of small white farmers increased their production of staples. Yet few whites, "poor" or otherwise, entered Southern agriculture as wage earners.

If slavery could have been maintained in the South until the growth of population and scarcity of land caused a large number of white people of good quality to work for wages on farms and planta-

7 Phillips, *American Negro Slavery*, 337.

tions, then, according to all the signs, employers would have preferred the white wage-labor. And if, in such a case, a surplus of labor had developed, slaves would have been set free, presumably, to shift for themselves.

But, as has been so often remarked, although still frequently overlooked, the displacement of Negro slaves by white wage earners in any branch of industry did not, or would not, prove that free labor in general was superior to slave labor; it only proved that white labor of a certain quality was superior to Negro slave labor of a certain quality in a particular branch of industry.

The statement has frequently been made that Southern slaveowners would have been well advised at some time before 1861 to free their slaves and hire the freedmen back for wages. The proposal is manifestly absurd if made applicable to a period before the Negroes had been in America long enough to acquire the white men's ways and want to live like them and not run off to the woods and swamps or join the Indians. But even for later periods, if considered only in its economic aspects, and if it is not assumed that the slaveholders should have foreseen that persistence in slavery would lead to war and a long train of consequences, the suggestion does not seem wise. In the country districts the freedmen, like the whites, would have desired to become independent farmers, and, unless land ownership or leaseholding had been denied them (something we have no right to assume), at least the more capable and enterprising would have succeeded. The masters would, therefore, have had a smaller labor force to exploit for their own advantage, and furthermore, those Negroes who had to earn their living by working for wages would in all probability have been less effective workers as freemen than they had ben as slaves.[8] The average Negro would have been content with a lower standard of living and, consequently, would not have worked as regularly. He would have been sick or ailing more frequently and would have lost considerable time during the intervals between quitting his old jobs and finding new ones.

These conclusions seem to have been borne out by experience after the slaves were actually freed. The planters tried to continue their plantations substituting wage labor for slave, but the experiment failed, and they were forced to divide their landholdings into small farms, which were rented out to white or Negro tenants, usually on a crop-

---

[8] M. B. Hammond, *The Cotton Industry; An Essay in American Economic History,* 186 (New York, 1897) ; U. B. Phillips, "The Economics of Slave Labor in the South," *The South in the Building of the Nation,* 5:121 (Richmond, Va., 1910).

share system. Only as time passed and land values increased, have the landowners been able to make better bargains with their tenants, and, in the case of Negro tenants especially, to exercise such a degree of supervision over them as to restore some of the advantages of the old plantation system. If the slaves had been freed in more propitious times, not in a country half-devasted by war and with ill feeling between the races augmented by the events of the reconstruction period, things might not have worked out in just the same way, but it is unlikely that the result would have been substantially different.

Negro slavery was introduced into this country to meet a demand for labor which could not be met as satisfactorily in any other manner. It was long maintained for various reasons but chiefly because it continued to satisfy the demand for labor, caused by the continued scarcity of free white wage-earners. The introduction and perpetuation of Negro slavery do not prove that free whites were less effective workers than Negro slaves.

It has often been asserted that, had it not been for the War between the States and consequent abolition, slavery would soon have died out anyway because of economic inadequacy. If the analysis presented in this article is at all sound, this common judgment requires much qualification. If the fate of Negro slavery had been left to be determined solely by the economic interest of the master class, it is not likely that it would have died a natural death for a long time.9 But the fate of the institution, even barring forces exercised from outside the slaveholding States, would not have been determined solely by the self-interest of the masters.

It is, of course, impossible to tell just what would have happened if something else had not occurred, but certain tendencies are reasonably clear. Southern society was not static. A free labor class was growing and was becoming increasingly class conscious and hostile to slave-labor competition in one trade after another. As means of transportation improved, a larger and larger part of the small-farmer class would have been drawn into commercialized agriculture, and, losing hope of acquiring slaves, would have become more antagonistic to the planters. As means of transportation and communication developed, the Negroes themselves would have grown more sophisticated, less satisfied with their status, and more difficult to control as slaves. As the slaves became more and more concentrated in the cotton and sugar belts, greater areas in the South would have become "abolitionized." All of these "internal"

---

9 *Cf.* L. C. Gray, *History of Agriculture in the Southern United States to 1860,* 476 (Washington, 1933).

dangers to the peculiar institution were recognized before the War by the master class and thoroughly canvassed. There are strong grounds for believing that one of the most impelling motives to secession was the desire of the slaveholding class to shake off the external threats against slavery in order to be better able to cope with internal dangers.

9

The Effects of Slavery upon Nonslaveholders in the Ante Bellum South

The following essay originally appeared in *Agricultural History*, XV (April 1941), 112–126. It appears here by permission of the Agricultural History Society. The original pagination appears in brackets.

PERHAPS no interpretation of the economic history of American Negro slavery is more generally accepted today than that the institution was detrimental to the nonslaveholding whites of the South. There have been frequent expressions of the view that the master class knew its own interest. Occasional admissions of doubt that emancipation conferred economic benefits upon the typical Negro are encountered, but it would be difficult to find any divergence from the opinion that the peculiar institution was a curse to the nonslaveholding whites. The fact that the latter did not become abolitionists is usually attributed to ignorance of their own interests, domination by the slaveholders, racial prejudice, or fond expectations of rising into the master class.[1] It is the purpose of this article to attempt to show that the commonly accepted interpretation requires great qualification to bring it into accord with the truth.

In 1860 approximately one-fourth of the white families of the South were slaveholding and three-fourths nonslaveholding; and of the slaveholding families a great many had only one or two slaves each. In earlier years of the period, the proportion of slaveholders was slightly larger.

The slaves and slaveholders were very largely concentrated in belts—the so-called black belts—which coincided with the areas devoted to the growing of staples, chiefly cotton, tobacco, sugar and rice.[2] There were also many slaves in the cities and towns in or near the

---

[1] See, for example, William E. Dodd, *The Cotton Kingdom*, 32 (New Haven, 1921).

[2] Ulrich B. Phillips, "The Origin and Growth of the Southern Black Belts," *American Historical Review*, 11:798-816 (July 1906).

staple-growing areas. These had been marked out by climate, the character of the soil, and, not least, by accessibility to market. Cotton, for example, for climatic reasons could not be grown to advantage north of an irregular line crossing North Carolina, Tennessee, and Arkansas. South of this line cotton was grown on the better lands which lay within reasonable distances of navigable rivers or of railroads. Some of the best of the present-day cotton lands were not utilized for that crop as late as 1860, because they were too far from navigable rivers while railroads had not yet penetrated into their vicinity.[3]

The great majority of the nonslaveholding whites lived outside the principal staple-growing districts in what is commonly called back, up, or hill country, or in mountainous regions. In these areas there were comparatively few slaves. The people were mostly small farmers and, because of lack of markets or inaccessibility to them, were engaged in a more or less self-sufficing agriculture with much household manufacturing.

It is difficult to see how people living in the back country could be injured by slavery in the black belts. Except possibly to a slight extent and in a most indirect way, it was not slavery which prevented them from producing staple crops for market; it was inaccessibility. Such markets as they had for their surplus bacon, lard, mules, whiskey, etc. were chiefly among the planters or in the towns which served the staple-producing districts. In so far as it was slavery which caused planters to concentrate on the growing of the great market crops while purchasing various supplies elsewhere, the institution created markets for back-country farmers and thus benefited them.

It is said that slavery had driven nonslaveholding whites out of the black belts and out of staple production and had thus worked them a great injury; that, had it not been for slavery, more of them would have lived in the staple-producing regions and raised the great market crops and would have had a higher standard of living on that account.

This time-honored indictment of the peculiar institution has such great plausibility that its validity has seldom been questioned. The black belts were a fact. Even nonslaveholding whites who lived in the staple-growing areas did not produce the staples in quantities proportionate to their numbers. Virtually all the sugar and rice and the bulk of the cotton and tobacco were produced by slave labor. In 1850, according to J. D. B. DeBow, there were about 800,000 slaves engaged in cotton

---

[3] Very illuminating on this point is Charles W. Ramsdell, "The Natural Limits of Slavery Expansion," *Misssssippi Valley Historical Review*, 16:151-171 (September 1929).

growing and only about 100,000 whites, and there is no reason to doubt the essential accuracy of his estimate.4 Much the greater part of the cash farm income of the South was received by a comparatively small number of planters, all of whom employed slave labor, of course. In the cotton States in 1850, according to William E. Dodd, "A thousand families received over $50,000,000 a year, while all the remaining 666,000 families received only about $60,000,000."5 This may also be accepted as approximately accurate. Yet, in spite of such prima facie evidence, the contention that slavery drove nonslaveholding whites out of staple production and thus did them a great injury contains considerably less than a half truth. Both the extent to which slavery excluded nonslaveholding whites from commercialized agriculture and the extent of the injury caused by such exclusion have been greatly exaggerated.

It is recognized at the outset that the problem involves not only the question of the comparative effectiveness of Negro slave labor and free white labor, but also that of the efficiency of the plantation as compared with the small farm as a unit of agricultural organization. The plantations of the ante bellum South were operated with slave labor almost exclusively. Almost all white agricultural workers were employed on small farms; very few served as wage earners on plantations. Moreover, the plantation system could not have existed extensively in the ante bellum South without slave labor, for the simple reason that, where land was cheap and plentiful and it was easy to become an independent farmer, free whites would not work for low enough wages, in large enough numbers, and with a sufficient degree of regularity to permit large-scale farming.6 White indentured servitude, with which the earliest plantations had been started, was an impossibility in the ante bellum period. Therefore, any competitive advantages which the plantation may have possessed over the small farm as a unit of farm organization must be accredited to the institution of slavery.

---

4 J. D. B. De Bow, *The Industrial Resources, etc., of the Southern and Western States*, 1:175 (New Orleans, 1852-1853). See also A. N. J. Den Hollander, "Tradition of 'Poor Whites'," in William T. Couch, ed., *Culture in the South*, 411 (Chapel Hill, 1934).

5 *Cotton Kingdom*, 24.

6 This point has been developed at greater length in Robert R. Russel, "The Economic History of Negro Slavery in the United States," *Agricultural History*, 11:308-321 (October 1937). Only whites of the poorest quality worked as farm laborers in the Old South—that is, when they worked at all. Often young men of a better sort worked for neighbors for hire (sometimes as overseers) until they could accumulate the little capital required to start farming on their own account. People who worked regularly at trades or other occupations oc-

In sugar and rice culture the plantation undoubtedly had great competitive advantages over the small farm.7 Sugar growers who owned sugar-making machinery had a great advantage over those who did not, and the machinery was so expensive that only large producers could afford it. The cost of building levees also was conducive to large-scale operations. The plantation had similar advantages over the small farm in rice growing. Since plantations would have been impossible without slavery, it is proper to conclude that slavery kept small farmers from growing sugar cane and rice or, at least and more probably, from growing other crops on lands which were actually devoted to sugar and rice.

In the growing of cotton and tobacco, however—and these staples employed about eight slaves to every one in sugar and rice—it is very doubtful that the plantation was superior to the small farm as a unit of agricultural production.8 The planter might buy supplies, sell his produce, and obtain credit—a very doubtful advantage—on somewhat better terms than the small farmer. Joseph C. Robert has described the marketing of tobacco in ante bellum Virginia in great detail. The buyers were very numerous, widely distributed, and quite competitive. The planter seems to have had little advantage over the small farmer in selling his product.9 In a newer community where marketing facilities were not so well developed, the advantage of the large-scale farmer in buying and selling may have been considerable. In a district where the large planters bought and sold through nonresident merchants or agents and the small farmers were too few and too poor to support competitive buyers and retail merchants adequately, the small

---

casionally worked for farmers at harvest or other special seasons when wages were temporarily high. Plantations obviously could not be run with such labor.

7 There is a well-reasoned statement of this fact in Edward C. Kirkland, *A History of American Economic Life*, 181-182 (New York, 1932). See also Lewis Cecil Gray, *History of Agriculture in the Southern United States to 1860*, p. 479-480 (Washington, 1933).

8 U. S. Census Office, Seventh Census, 1850, *Statistical View of the United States. . . Being a Compendium of the Seventh Census . . .* , by J. D. B. De Bow, 178. Cf. Ulrich Bonnell Phillips, *American Negro Slavery*, 309-330 (New York, 1918); M. B. Hammond, *The Cotton Industry: An Essay in American Economic History*, 98-110 (New York, 1897); Gray, *History of Agriculture in the Southern United States*, 478-480; Kirkland, *History of American Economic Life*, 182-183; Rosser H. Taylor, *Slaveholding in North Carolina: An Economic View*, 81, 86-91 (Chapel Hill, 1926); Frederick L. Olmsted, *A Journey in the Back Country in the Winter of 1853-4*, 1:73, 131, 141, 167; 2:65-70, 119 (Putnam's Sons edition, New York, 1907).

9 *The Tobacco Kingdom: Plantation, Market, and Factory in Virginia and North Carolina, 1800-1860* p. 94-117 (Durham, 1938). The facts are given by Robert. The conclusion has been drawn therefrom by the writer.

farmers would receive considerably less than the planters for what they might sell and pay considerably more for what they might buy.[10]

The planter was able to effect a division of labor among his hands that was not possible on a small farm, but the operations and the machinery required in farming in those days were too simple to permit any considerable advantage to be gained from that. In fact the division of labor on a large plantation tended to become fixed and, by its inflexibility, may have impaired rather than promoted efficiency. For example, there would have been a moral difficulty about sending a dignified coachman to the field to plow or "chop." A farm worker of a reasonable degree of competence probably increases his efficiency by making the frequent changes from one sort of common task to another which are necessary on the farm.

The slaveholder had no compunctions about putting female slaves in the field gangs. White women and girls of small-farm families also worked in the fields to a considerable extent. Frederick Law Olmstead reported: "I have, in fact, seen more white native American women at work in the hottest sunshine in a single month, and that near midsummer, in Mississippi and Alabama than in all my life in the Free States, not on account of an emergency, as in harvesting, either, but in the regular cultivation of cotton and of corn, chiefly of cotton."[11] However, white farm women and girls certainly did not go into the fields as regularly as slave women and girls. The planter had an advantage here as far as production of fields crops was concerned.

The cotton planter usually had his own gin and press while his small-farm neighbor had to pay toll. Whether the planter had a competitive advantage in his ownership depended upon the tolls paid by the farmer. The advantage may have been the other way. Other implements and tools used in cotton production and the implements and tools used in tobacco farming were too simple and cheap to give any advantage to the large-scale farmer in their use; it would be a poor farmer indeed who could not afford a plow and a mule.

These competitive advantages of the plantation over the farm, to the extent that they existed, were at least partially offset by certain disadvantages. The overhead expenses of the large planter were proportionally greater than those of the small farmer. The large planter had to hire an overseer or overseers and often had various other functionaries such as manager, foreman, drivers, and yard boy. The pro-

---

10 Olmsted, *Journey in the Back Country,* 2:65-67.

11 *Ibid.,* 56. Cf. Gray, *History of Agriculture in the Southern United States,* 362-363, 471.

duction and curing of tobacco required especially close supervision because care in handling greatly affected the quality, which was an
important factor in determining price. The number of slaves which
could be supervised efficiently by one overseer was, therefore, small.12
The planter himself, the mistress, and the sons and daughters did not
ordinarily engage in physical labor, as did members of the small-farm
family. The plantation house was often literally overrun with domestic
servants.

If large-scale farming had possessed any considerable competitive
advantages over small-scale farming in producing cotton and tobacco,
there would not have been so many small farms and small plantations
devoted to their production. Perhaps one-half the cotton was grown
on farms where there were either no slaves at all or fewer than ten or
a dozen.13 Such farms were too small to possess in any material degree
the alleged advantages of large-scale production. Probably an even
larger percentage of Southern tobacco was produced on small farms
or small plantations. Robert has shown that even in Charlotte County,
Virginia, where, in 1850, the average size of the tobacco farms was
greater than in any other county of the State, about 53 percent of the
crop was produced on plantations employing not more than ten or
twelve hands. Robert presents a frequency table showing for seven
Virginia counties the number of farms which produced tobacco in
1859 in quantities falling within each of several sets of limits. This
table seems to show that, except that farms with two hands were more
numerous than those with one—probably because large families were
more numerous than small—the numbers of tobacco farms employing
the several respective numbers of hands varied in regular fashion
inversely with the numbers of hands employed.14 If the plantation had
possessed any appreciable advantages over the smaller farm this inverse
variation would not have been so regular.

The laborers employed on the typical small farm, that is the members of the white farm family, were almost certainly as efficient as the
slaves on the plantations, if and when the whites chose to exert themselves to a reasonable extent. The qualification is essential, for many
whites did not choose to exert themselves very much. In the days of
the great slavery debate, Southern controversialists often enthusiastically

---

12 Robert, *Tobacco Kingdom*, 18; Taylor, *Slaveholding in North Carolina,*
89; Gray, *History of Agriculture in the Southern States,* 545.

13 Phillips, *American Negro Slavery*, 226.

14 These references are based on Robert, *Tobacco Kingdom*, 245-247, 249-
250.

asserted that their slaves constituted the best trained and most efficient labor force in the world. An occasional modern writer has placed a high estimate on the effectiveness of the slaves.[15] The typical slave was certainly a more effective worker than the free Negro after emancipation,[16] but the great weight of the evidence is that slaves were not as efficient as white workers of good quality. Ulrich B. Phillips seems to have aptly characterized slave efficiency: "The generality of planters, it would seem, considered it hopeless to make their field hands into thorough workmen or full-fledged men, and contented themselves with very moderate achievement. Tiring of endless correction and unfruitful exhortation, they relied somewhat supinely upon authority with a tone of kindly patronage and a baffled acquiescence in slack service."[17] The fathers of the Constitution expressed the prevailing estimate of their time regarding the relative productiveness of whites and slaves in the famous three-fifths clause.[18] Olmsted, in the 1850s, thought slaves were not nearly so effective as white farm workers in New York State.[19]

It has been quite common for writers, in trying to determine the relative efficiency of Negro slave labor and free white labor, to compare the slaves with the white wage labor of the plantation regions, but this method is unsound. The plantation slaves were of average quality. The wage earners were usually the poorest quality of whites, who worked

---

15 For example, Gray, *History of Agriculture in the Southern United States,* 361-364, 464-471.

16 Hammond, *Cotton Industry,* 186; Alfred Holt Stone, *Studies in the American Race Problem,* 125-208 (New York, 1908) ; U. B. Phillips, "The Economics of Slave Labor in the South," in *The South in the Building of the Nation,* 5:121 (Richmond, 1909) ; Edward Bryon Reuter, *The American Race Problem: A Study of the Negro,* 227-256 (ed. 2, New York, 1938).

17 *Life and Labor in the Old South,* 200 (Boston, 1929).

18 Max Farrand, ed., *The Records of the Federal Convention of 1787,* 1: 580-588; 3:253, 255, 342, 400, 428-430 (ed. 2, New Haven, 1937). C. C. Pinckney, when reporting to the South Carolina House of Representatives put it thus: "As we have found it necessary to give very extensive powers to the federal government both over the persons and estates of the citizens, we thought it right to draw one branch of the legislature immediately from the people, and that both wealth and numbers should be considered in the representation. We were at a loss, for some time, for a rule to ascertain the proportionate wealth of the states. At last we thought that the productive labor of the inhabitants was the best rule for ascertaining their wealth. In conformity to this rule, joined to a spirit of concession, we determined that representatives should be apportioned among the several states, by adding to the whole number of free persons three fifths of the slaves."—p. 253.

19 *Journey in the Back Country,* 1:64, 83, 90; 2:51, 106, 115, and *A Journey in the Seaboard Slave States,* 185, 203, 717 (New York, 1856). See also Charles H. Wesley, *Negro Labor in the United States, 1850-1925; A Study in American Economic History,* 3-6 (New York, 1927).

neither very hard nor very regularly.20 Whites of any competence either got land and farmed on their own account or found other employment which was more remunerative than farm labor for hire.

Slave labor was efficient enough, if employed at tasks for which it was adapted, to produce for the masters, taking one year with another, an appropriable surplus over the cost of maintenance. However, the appropriable surplus of the individual slave was normally so small that a master could not enjoy a large income unless he had a large number of slaves.21 A farmer with a few slaves worked along with them and made a somewhat better living than his neighbor who had no slaves. A farmer with a larger number of slaves might escape physical toil and enjoy a still higher standard of living. Only the great planters could live in a liberal style. The evidence seems conclusive that planters with fewer than about fifteen slaves did not live well.22

Except, then, in special cases like sugar and rice where much capital other than slaves was required for effective production, the much touted advantage of the plantation with slave labor over the small farm with white labor reduces to about this: The plantation could not produce more in proportion to land and equipment or to the number of hands employed; if large enough it could produce more goods and leisure for the white family. That, in all common sense, was why people acquired slaves and ran plantations. The small farm with reasonably good management and reasonable industry on the part of members of the farm family afforded at least as high a standard of living as the plantation afforded the planter family and the slaves averaged together.

Why, then, if Negro slave labor was not inherently superior to free white labor, and if the plantation possessed little, if any, competitive advantage over the small farm as a unit of agricultural organization, did nonslaveholding whites fail to produce a larger share of the cotton and tobacco? There were several reasons.

First and foremost come the major matters of enterprise and managerial ability. Nowadays, the more competent and industrious

---

20 Taylor, *Slaveholding in North Carolina,* 80, Gray, *History of Agriculture in the Southern United States,* 468; Frederick Law Olmsted, *Journeys and Explorations in the Cotton Kingdom* 1:82 (London, 1861), and *Journey in the Back Country,* 1:255; 2:12-13, 29.

21 Gray, *History of Agriculture in the Southern United States,* 474.

22 Olmsted made this point over and over again with much illustrative detail. For examples, see his *Journey in the Seaboard Slave States,* 329, 384-386, 393, 559-563, and *Journey in the Back Country,* 1:174-196, 230-231, 261-266; 2:22, 88, 167-174.

farmers in any community generally get the better land and larger acreages. In slavery days in the South, the better farmers got the more desirable lands, larger holdings, and also the slaves to work them and grew more cotton and tobacco. If a small farmer in the cotton or tobacco belt prospered by growing the staple of his region or otherwise, the natural and attractive thing to do was to buy land and slaves as he could. If he continued to thrive, he would eventually become a planter. Thus a small farmer would have been "driven out" by a planter. Of course the man who inherited land and slaves had a better chance of remaining in the planter class than one who had inherited nothing had of entering it. However, many a young man who inherited wealth in slavery days mismanaged his patrimony, lost it in whole or in part, and ended his days in "reduced" circumstances, while many a young man who started with neither land or slaves became a prosperous planter. Thomas J. Wertenbaker has shown that the planter class originated in this latter fashion in colonial times.23 Olmsted admitted that small farmers were not debarred from becoming planters in the ante bellum period.24 One suspects that most farmers who prospered did so not because they had come by land and slaves but because they attended to business and managed well, while most of those who failed did so because they took life too easy and managed badly. Credit has too often been given to slavery or the farm organization which rightfully belongs to the master.

Secondly, even in the staple-growing districts, the small farmers did not have as strong incentives to grow the staples for market as the planters had. They found it to their advantage to do a more general type of farming with more household manufacturing. In contrast, planters almost of necessity produced for the market. There would have been few planters if it had not been possible to grow market crops profitably on plantations. As a rule, a master will not employ a large force in a self-sufficing economy, because, after a certain volume of production has been reached, an additional application of labor can contribute but little to satisfy the wants of the farmer and his family but only to raise the standard of living of the laborers, something in which an employer is only mildly interested.25 In a self-sufficing economy in America a family with a considerable number of slaves would have enjoyed a rude plenty and have been freed from grinding toil but would have had the various cares and worries involved in slave-

23 *The First Americans, 1607-1690,* 22-48 (New York, 1929).

24 *Journey in the Back Country,* 1:141, 177; 2:66, 121-124.

25 Gray, *History of Agriculture in the Southern United States,* 475.

holding. A family without slaves would have enjoyed the same rude plenty, and although it must have engaged in hard labor, would not have had the cares and worries of the slaveholding family. A planter in the ante bellum South produced the various necessary and desirable articles for home consumption which could be produced cheaper on the plantation than they could be bought in the market. However, the wants of the slaves were simple, perforce, and easily satisfied, and the demand of the planter's family for such articles was limited. These wants having been satisfied, the planter sought to produce as large a salable surplus as possible in order that he might command for his slaves certain things from outside the community which might be necessary for their continued efficiency and for himself and family the various articles of necessity, comfort, and luxury which could not, or at least not advantageously, be produced on the plantation. The small nonslaveholding farmer, on the contrary, found it desirable to devote a larger share of his labor to the production of the numerous articles for consumption which could be produced advantageously at home, because, in proportion to numbers, the farmer family consumed larger quantities of such things than did the planter family and the slaves together.

The small farmer of the nineteenth century had a further reason for carrying on more self-sufficing activities than the planter. This was the feeling, already mentioned, that white women and girls, although allowed to work at various household industries which were just as useful and productive as plowing and hoeing, nevertheless, should not be expected to labor in the fields. The planter was under no moral pressure not to send his female slaves into the fields.

The planter had a further reason to concentrate his efforts on the growing of cotton or other staples in the fact that Negro slave labor was relatively more efficient therein than in the production of the various other things commonly produced on Southern farms in slavery days, for examples, fruit, poultry, dairy products, bacon, lard, soap, candles, whiskey, coarse textiles, clothing, and axe and hoe handles. The planter, on this account, sometimes found it to his advantage to grow more cotton or tobacco and buy other things. The small farmer and his family, on the other hand, could produce the varied articles of the general farm more effectively than could the slaves and, therefore, more often found it advantageous to produce them at home instead of buying them at the store.26 The fact that in a given community

---

26 Cf. Walter L. Fleming, "The Slave-Labor System in the Ante-Bellum South," in *The South in the Building of the Nation,* 5:16. A planter told the

planters specialized more in producing the great Southern staples while small farmers went in more for general farming does not of itself prove that white labor was less efficient than slave labor in cotton and tobacco, as has so often been assumed; it can just as well prove that white labor was more efficient than slave labor in general farming.

In comparisons of slave-labor plantations with small white-labor farms this simple fact has been too frequently overlooked! Even if the former had competitive advantages over the latter in the production of a crop, say cotton, the small farmers nevertheless would have grown that crop for a living if thereby they could have made a better or easier living than by producing something else. Nowadays small farmers in large areas of the South find it advisable to devote their major efforts to producing cotton, tobacco, or some other crop or crops for market while buying at the store a great variety of articles formerly produced at home; but the fact that they do so now does not prove that they would have done so in the 1830s or 1850s if it had not been for slavery. The abolition of slavery almost certainly made the Negroes of the South less effective as producers of farm products. It is certainly wrong to assume that it was the abolition of slavery only, or even principally, which gave the small farmers their "opportunity." The same general factors have operated to further commercialize agriculture in the South that have operated elsewhere, namely, cheap transportation, which has enabled people to get more for what they sell and to pay less for what they buy; the industrial revolution, which has made it possible to manufacture more and better goods in the mills and factories in towns and cities at incomparably lower costs than they can be made on farms; and the agricultural revolution, particularly the introduction of improved farm machinery, which has encouraged specialization and commercialization by making it too expensive to own machinery applicable to more than one or two crops and too great a handicap in competition not to adopt some of it.[27]

Since planters had such strong incentives to produce staple crops for market, they must remain where there was access to markets. Small farmers, who did relatively more subsistence farming regardless of location, were not under such pressure to remain in the commercialized farming districts. Therefore, if planter neighbors made attractive

---

English geographer, Robert Russell, that the reason more planters did not raise hogs and make their own bacon was that the Negroes would steal the little pigs and roast them. *North America, Its Agriculture and Climate,* 265 (Edinburgh, 1857).

27 Cf. Den Hollander, "The Tradition of 'Poor Whites'," 422-425.

offers for the land, the farmers might find it to their advantage to sell and move to a more remote region where land was cheaper but about as well adapted to their type of farming.

The American people during the slavery period were already a race of land speculators. Large numbers moved to the frontier and submitted for the time to frontier living conditions with the hope that the "progress of the country" and especially the development of means of transportation would soon catch up with them and give their lands a value far in excess of the original cost. Masters with numerous slaves would not or could not be frontiersmen unless the frontier had natural facilities for transportation to market and could almost at once be reduced to cultivation. If they had debts, as most masters did, they were under strong economic compulsion to get cash incomes every year. It follows, therefore, that the proportion of small farmers in the commercialized-farming districts would tend to be reduced by this movement toward the frontier. If a few years later the planter followed the small farmer to the erstwhile frontier and bought up his farm, the farmer was not injured; at least he had done what he had hoped to do and could move on to a new frontier to repeat the process.28

Once a given district became rather thickly settled with masters and slaves, small farmers moved out to get away from the "niggers" and live in a neighborhood where there were more of their own kind. Repelling them from good neighborhoods was probably the principal way in which slavery worked to the economic detriment of nonslaveholding whites. Some of the best lands in the South today are being cultivated by Negroes, who are in general less efficient farmers than whites, because once the Negroes were there in great numbers, the whites would not move in.29

It is true, of course, that if slavery had never been established in the United States and, therefore, the plantation system had not developed extensively, the lands held by planters would have been held by small farmers who, in many instances no doubt, would have been the same persons who were planters. In that hypothetical case, being located near transportation facilities and finding prices, at least of cotton, somewhat higher than they actually were by reason of the smaller production which would have occurred, small farmers would have grown greater quantities of cotton and tobacco, but considerably less

28 Olmsted, *Journey in the Seaboard Slave States,* 576-577; Frederick Jackson Turner, *Rise of the New West,* 90-92 (New York and London, 1906); Fleming, "The Slave-Labor System in the Ante-Bellum South," 107, 113-114.

29 Phillips, *American Negro Slavery,* 396.

than actually were grown in the South by planters and farmers combined. In this sense, then, slavery may be said to have "driven" nonslaveholding farmers out of staple production and deprived them of an economic opportunity. This is far different from the usual implication, namely, that plantations produced a great quantity of cotton and tobacco very cheaply and thereby depressed prices so greatly that, while planters continued to make money, small white farmers could not make a living by growing the staples. Futhermore, even this concession requires qualification. It may well be that, if slavery had never been established in the South or, although established, had been abolished later, the direct benefits conferred upon small farmers by the absence or removal of competition from plantations and slaves would have been more than offset by the possible injury to the prosperity of the section as a whole.[30]

The farmer folk of the South who received the most meager rewards were the "poor whites." Slavery has so often been blamed for the condition and even the existence of the poor whites that their relation to the institution seems to require special mention.

The poor whites were the ne'er-do-wells of the Southern countryside. They were poor, ignorant, shiftless, and almost utterly lacking in pride and the desire to improve their lot. They lived on the poorer lands interspersed among the plantations and better farms or in the pine barrens, sand hills, or other undesirable locations. In some cases they owned the land they occupied, in others they were merely squatters. They lived from hand to mouth. They farmed in a feeble sort of way, raising a little corn and garden truck and keeping a few hogs. Sometimes they raised a little cotton or tobacco. They hunted and fished a little. Some of them made corn whiskey and sold it to the planters and the slaves. They did odd jobs now and then for neighboring planters or farmers but shunned steady employment. They were often suspected of doing a lot of petty stealing from their more provident neighbors. Occasionally the terms "low whites" and "mean whites" were used to denote them.[31]

The abolitionists were fond of denominating all the nonslaveholding whites of the Southern countryside as poor whites. This was a libel

---

[30] Robert R. Russel, "The General Effects of Slavery upon Southern Economic Progress," *Journal of Southern History,* 4:34-54 (February 1938).

[31] Good descriptions are Paul H. Buck, "The Poor Whites of the Ante-Bellum South," *American Historical Review,* 31:41-54 (October 1925); and Den Hollander, "The Tradition of 'Poor Whites'," 403-431. Frank L. and Harriet C. Owsley almost reason the poor whites away.—"The Economic Basis of Society in the Late Ante-Bellum South," *Journal of Southern History,* 6:24-45 (February 1940).

on the great majority of the small farmers of the section, who were reasonably industrious and self respecting and, in general, made a fairly comfortable living. There were, however, thousands of poor whites. William Gregg, a public-spirited cotton manufacturer of South Carolina, once estimated that one-third of the white population of his State belonged to that class.[32] However accurate his estimate may have been, they were found in all the Southern States and the proportion was too high in all.

There seem to have been several causes for the development of the poor-white class. The poor quality of a large proportion of the indentured servants, so numerous in the South in colonial days, may explain it in part. The comparative ease of getting a living of a sort in a country where land, at least poor land, was so cheap, where corn, vegetables, and fruits grew without much care, where game, fish, and edible wild plants abounded, and where winters were short and mild, contributed to easy-going ways. Because of various historical factors, which will readily occur to anyone familiar with American colonial history, there had not been the feeling of community responsibility in the South that there had been in Puritan New England to insist that individuals conform to community standards of industry, thrift, and morality. Perhaps the principal cause was hookworm and repeated attacks of malaria, which sapped people's vitality and robbed them of hope and ambition, although it is not entirely clear whether people became poor whites because they had contracted hookworm or got hookworm because they were poor whites. The class of poor whites in all probability would have developed if slavery had never been introduced. There are poor whites now two generations after emancipation, and in spite of a greater density of population, better health services, more varied industry, public schools, and the many inducements to exertion offered by modern civilization. Similiar classes, under different names, although perhaps not so great in numbers, are to be found in other parts of the country; and, for that matter, the same general type may be found in varying proportions in every country on the globe.

However, in at least two ways slavery seems to have contributed to the formation of the poor-white class of the South. Contrary to the usual rule, many of the poorer whites might have been better off as farm laborers under supervision than as independent farmers, but slavery retarded the development of a wage-earning class in the plantation districts. Originally planters had resorted to the use of bound

---

32 *DeBow's Review,* August 1851, p. 133. Cf. Gray, *History of Agriculture in the Southern United States,* 487.

servants because competent free laborers were scarce in a country where it was so easy for people of any competence at all to become independent farmers on land of their own. Once slavery was firmly established in a district, it in turn discouraged the development of a free-labor class.[33] Planters preferred slaves to the poorer sort of whites. They also hesitated to attempt to use wage laborers instead of slaves, because, until a large wage-earning class should have developed, they could feel no assurance of being able to fill the vacancies that were certain to occur. Whites would not work in field gangs along with slaves under overseers. If it had not been for slavery, people with managerial ability might have made greater efforts to get the poor whites to work for wages or to rent the better lands and might have succeeded, as they did, in a measure, other things contributing, after the War for Southern Independence. By creating the black belts in ways described in preceding paragraphs, slavery created a social condition conducive to the development of such a class of poor whites. The more enterprising and intelligent of the small farmers either got out of the staple belts or graduated into the planter class leaving the less enterprising and less intelligent behind on poor lands which the planters could not use. Planters, having their own social life, took little interest in and felt little responsibility for their poor-white neighbors, except, perhaps, at election time. If the small-farmer population had remained larger, there might have been more churches, more schools, and a more wholesome community life in general, which would have given some stimulus, encouragement, and aid to the weaker and less fortunate members of society.[34]

Slavery was certainly no more detrimental to nonslaveholding whites engaged in nonagricultural occupations than it was to small farmers. There seems to have been no dearth of employment in the Southern countryside for such white artisans as there were. It is true that planters often had slaves trained in various skilled crafts, and they often became excellent workmen. They were, indeed, frequently hired out by their masters to neighbors who needed their services.[35] In

---

33 This point is developed more fully in Robert R. Russel, "The Economic History of Negro Slavery in the United States," 317-319.

34 Fleming, "The Slave-Labor System in the Ante-Bellum South," 113; Phillips, *American Negro Slavery,* 396; Olmsted, *Journey in the Back Country,* 2:61-70.

35 Wesley, *Negro Labor in the United States,* 6-7; Stone, *Studies in the American Race Problem,* 149-208; Reuter, *American Race Problem,* 227-256; Gray, *History of Agriculture in the Southern United States,* 500, 566; Ulrich B. Phillips, ed., *Plantation and Frontier (A Documentary History of American Industrial Society,* v. 1-2), 1:172, 253, 334 (Cleveland, 1910).

general, however, the Negro artisans were not as competent as the white, and the latter were preferred. It was the scarcity of the white artisans which caused planters to resort to training slaves in the trades. This scarcity, in turn, was due to the strong inducement there was all through this period for people of good quality to get land and live on it.

In the cities and towns of the slaveholding States, white wage earners had to compete with free Negroes and with Negro slaves, who were either employed in their masters' businesses, hired out by their masters to other employers, or allowed to hire their own time. Such free Negroes and slaves worked at practically every sort of task.36 They had a monopoly of domestic service. Either because of its character, or because Negroes had so long predominated in it, or both, the whites had come to look upon such service as menial and degrading, and employers preferred the Negroes because they were more obsequious. In other occupations the whites and Negroes, sometimes of both sexes, worked side by side, usually, but not always, with some distinction in tasks in favor of the whites. For example, in the Tredegar Iron Works at Richmond, Virginia, each white master workman was given a Negro "assistant."37

The white workers frequently resented the presence of the blacks, either because of race prejudice, or dislike of their competition, or both, and sought to have them excluded from the pursuits concerned. There was, for example, a strike of the white workers in the Tredegar works having this object, but it was unsuccessful, as were all other efforts to exclude Negroes. Employers could not afford to allow such a principle to be established, as white workers were not sufficiently numerous and permanent in most localities to permit reliance on them alone. The use of slaves, if they belonged to the owners of the business, gave the employers assurance that operations would not be interrupted or wages forced to too high levels by strikes and withdrawals; and, even if the slaves were hired from others, the assurance was nearly as great, for still there could be no strikes, and labor contracts were usually made for a year at a time.38

36 Phillips, *American Negro Slavery,* 402-424; Wesley, *Negro Labor in the United States,* 1-28; Gray, *History of Agriculture in the Southern United States,* 467, 566; Kathleen Bruce, *Virginia Iron Manufacture in the Slave Era,* ch. 6 (New York and London, 1931); A. H. Stone, "Free Contract Labor in the Ante-Bellum South," in *The South in the Building of the Nation,* 5:142.

37 For reasons not entirely clear, the hands in Virginia tobacco factories were nearly all Negroes,—Bruce, *Virginia Iron Manufacture,* 238-240; Robert, *The Tobacco Kingdom,* 197-208.

38 Wesley, *Negro Labor in the United States,* 69-86; Phillips, *American*

In the skilled trades the white workingmen were more efficient and were, therefore, preferred. Negro competition was not keen.[39] In unskilled and semiskilled labor the superiority of white workers to slaves was not so great, if, indeed any existed, but in general white workers had no difficulty in getting jobs, excepting, of course, that they sought none in domestic service. As the middle period wore on and the demand for labor in the cotton and sugar belts grew, there was a tendency for slave labor to be drawn from the towns to the farms where white labor was not available, leaving places in towns open to the whites. This tendency was reinforced by the increasing difficulty of handling slaves amid urban surroundings and by the better adaptability, generally speaking, of slaves to agriculture than to urban occupations.

Nonslaveowning employers of labor in the cities had no particular disadvantage in competition with slaveowning employers as they would have had in the country, for they were able to hire either whites, slaves, free Negroes, or all three. In fact, railroad companies, manufacturing concerns, etc. usually found it necessary or desirable to start with hired labor, free or slave, because with hired labor it was not necessary to raise so much capital at the outset. Employers sometimes preferred to hire their hands also, because this permitted a selection more in accord with existing needs and enabled the employers to expand or contract their labor forces and more readily adjust production to the state of business.[40]

In slavery days the cities and towns of the South, being neither numerous nor large, derived their support principally from plantation districts, where there were many slaves, rather than from small-farming regions, where there were few. It was chiefly the planters who bought, sold, borrowed, travelled, and sent their children to academies and colleges. It seems quite certain, therefore, that if it had not been for plantations and slavery, the cities and towns of the South would have been even fewer and smaller, resulting in even less opportunity for nonslaveholding whites.

In the days of the great slavery debate, the abolitionists, when

---

Negro Slavery, 413; Robert Royal Russel, *Economic Aspects of Southern Sectionalism, 1840-1861,* p. 53, 218-220 (Urbana, 1924) ; Olmsted, *Journey in the Back Country,* 1 : 199-200; 2 : 57; Bruce, *Virginia Iron Manufacture,* 234-237, 243-244.

39 Phillips, *American Negro Slavery,* 403, table.

40 Robert, *Tobacco Kingdom,* 199; Gray, *History of Agriculture in the Southern United States,* 566; Russel, *Economic Aspects of Southern Sectionalism,* 210-211, 219.

pressed closely to show how slavery injured the nonslaveholding whites, always replied that it did so by inspiring a contempt for manual labor among all whites who came in contact with it. This answer still finds favor in the textbooks. The writer has examined the contention at some length in another place and found that there was a grain of truth in it but little more than a grain.[41]

In conclusion, Negro slavery was in some respects to the economic advantage of many of the nonslaveholding whites of the slaveholding regions; in others it was to their disadvantage. To many nonslaveholding whites it was a matter of economic indifference. It is impossible to strike a balance in which confidence can be placed. It is certain that the net injury, if there was any, has commonly been grossly exaggerated. The fact that nonslaveholding whites did not seek to destroy the institution as injurious to their economic interests may only show that their common sense operating upon a familiar matter was sounder than the economics of abolitionists theorizing at a distance or of some modern historians theorizing after a long lapse of time.

---

[41] Robert R. Russel, "The General Effects of Slavery upon Southern Economic Progress," 37-40; See also Phillips, *American Negro Slavery*, 397-398.

10

The General Effects of Slavery upon Southern Economic Progress

The following essay originally appeared in *The Journal of Southern History,* IV (February 1938), 34–54, copyright © 1938 by the Southern Historical Association. It appears here by permission of the managing editor of *The Journal of Southern History.* The original pagination appears in brackets.

M ANY WRITERS have made sweeping generalizations as to the effects, allegedly injurious, of Negro slavery upon the economic progress of the South. It is believed that many time-honored generalizations about the subject are incorrect. The economics of slavery as expounded by the abolitionists, especially the English economist, J. E. Cairnes,[1] seemed to triumph on the battlefield. Such views have subsequently been accepted too implicitly not only in the North but even in the South.[2] It is proposed to examine anew several widely-accepted generalizations.

Slavery is still being blamed for the wasteful and unscientific methods of farming practiced in the South before the Civil War. The authors of two popular college textbooks in the economic history of the United States both quote a table of statistics found in Ezra C. Seaman's *Essays on the Progress of Nations*, published in 1868, which

---

[1] J. E. Cairnes, *The Slave Power: Its Character, Career, and Probable Designs* (New York, 1862).

[2] The writer's quarrel is principally with general histories and history textbooks, especially economic texts. Of the latter, Edward C. Kirkland, *A History of American Economic Life* (New York, 1932), is excepted, although it is believed that some of his conclusions require modification. Among the more detailed accounts which have greatly influenced recent textbooks are M. B. Hammond, *The Cotton Industry: An Essay in American Economic History* (New York, 1897), which is very critical of slavery, and the various works of Ulrich B. Phillips, especially *American Negro Slavery* (New York, 1918), and *Life and Labor in the Old South* (Boston, 1929). Those familiar with these works will readily recognize the differences between the conclusions reached in this article and the conclusions of the scholars named. The writer has great respect for the treatment of slavery in Lewis C. Gray, *History of Agriculture in the Southern United States to 1860*, 2 vols. (Washington, 1933), and agrees with most of it, but cannot accept his interpretation of several important matters.

compares the "free" and the "slave" states in respect to number of acres of improved and unimproved land in farms in 1860 and the total value and the average value per acre of farm lands. The comparison shows inferiority of the slave states in all respects; and the writers leave the impression that slavery was the cause.[3] One author says:

A second condition which made slavery possible and profitable was an abundance of new land . . . If land anywhere became scare and dear, slavery tended to disappear. Intensive and scientific methods of farming were seldom possible under the indifferent and wasteful slave system. Consequently, the colonial method was persisted in, of cropping a tract of land until it was exhausted and then moving on to a fresh piece.[4]

As a matter of fact, "skinning" the soil was practiced in all sections of the country. It was as common in most districts of the North as it was in the South. It was at least as common in the small-farm belts of the South as in the plantation districts. The preponderant reason was the same everywhere, namely, the cheapness of land. It was cheaper to acquire and clear a new farm of virgin soil than it was to restore, or even maintain, the fertility of the old. Contributory reasons were inertness and ignorance; but the want of initiative and knowledge was not as great among planters as among small farmers. The best farming in the South was done by planters,[5] many of whom took keen interest in agricultural reform and experimental methods[6] and farmed in an intensive manner.[7] In general, however, before the Civil War, it was only in the vicinity of cities where land became dear by reason of its demand for special purposes such as dairying and truck gardening, that much attention was given to manuring, fertilizing, and crop rotation. Speaking by and large, Southern soils—except rich bottom lands—wore out more rapidly than Northern. Cotton did not

---

[3] Ernest L. Bogart, *Economic History of the American People* (New York, 1935), 456; Harold U. Faulkner, *American Economic History* (New York, 1935), 391.

[4] Bogart, *Economic History of the American People*, 455.

[5] Avery O. Craven, *Soil Exhaustion as a Factor in the Agricultural History of Virginia and Maryland*, 1606-1860, in University of Illinois *Studies in the Social Sciences*, XIII, No. 1 (Urbana, 1925), 86-91, and *passim*. W. H. Russell told of a great sugar plantation which was "better tilled than the finest patch in all the Lothians." *My Diary North and South* (New York, 1863), 103.

[6] Craven, *Soil Exhaustion*, 86-121, 124-44; *id.*, "The Agricultural Reformers of the Ante-Bellum South," in *American Historical Review* (New York, 1895-   ), XXXIII (1926), 302-14; Gray, *History of Agriculture in the Southern United States*, II, 779-92.

[7] Gray, *History of Agriculture in the Southern United States*, I, 447, 449.

exhaust the soil as rapidly as grain crops; tobacco was hard on the soil.[8] But the land is nearly everywhere rolling or hilly, the soil is generally lighter than in the North, the greater part of the section lacks good native grasses, which would check erosion on lands retired from cultivation, and there are more heavy, dashing rains. Consequently there was much more soil erosion in the South.[9]

There was nothing inherent in slavery that prevented the adoption of more scientific methods of agriculture.[10] A planter could direct his slaves to spread manure, cotton seed, or marl, to plow horizontally on the hillsides, to avoid shallow tillage, and to pile brush in incipient gullies. The small farmer might do such things himself, but he was less likely to do them than the planter was to have them done.

Slavery may have retarded the adoption of improved agricultural machinery. At any rate, the proposition is true that employers will hesitate to entrust expensive and complicated machinery to careless, irresponsible, and incompetent workmen. On the other hand, large farmers, other things being equal, are abler and more likely to adopt improved machinery than small farmers. The small farmers of the South certainly made no better record in this regard than the planters. Cotton growers were not slow to adopt the cotton gin, one of the most revolutionary pieces of agricultural machinery in our history. Sugar-making machinery was complicated and expensive. Southern planters adopted the various improvements in the plow as the improved plows could be had. They rapidly substituted horses and mules for the slow-moving oxen when they were found to be better adapted to their pur-

---

[8] Hammond, *Cotton Industry,* 45, 79; Eugene W. Hilgard, *Report on the Geology and Agriculture of the State of Mississippi* (Jackson, 1860), 242; Craven, *Soil Exhaustion,* 32-33.

[9] R. O. E. Davis, *Soil Erosion in the South* (United States Department of Agriculture, *Bulletin No. 180* [Washington, 1915]), 8, 17-20; Craven, *Soil Exhaustion,* 27-39, 162.

[10] Cf. Craven, *Soil Exhaustion,* 162-64; and Gray, *History of Agriculture in the Southern United States,* I, 445-48; II, 940. Rosser H. Taylor, *Slaveholding in North Carolina: An Economic View* (Chapel Hill, 1926), 43, believes that slavery may have contributed to the clearing of new fields instead of improving old ones "as it was convenient to employ slaves in winter in clearing new fields." Phillips (ed.) *Plantation and Frontier, 1649-1863,* Vols. I and II in John R. Commons (ed.), *A Documentary History of American Industrial Society,* 10 vols. (Cleveland, 1910), I, 93, states that in the piedmont region the frequent need of clearing new fields disturbed the plantation routine and enabled small planters to hold their own against large. Taylor, *Slaveholding in North Carolina,* 81, states that the practice of paying overseers by allowing them a share of the crop "was criticized on the ground that it was rapidly producing deterioration of the soil." Craven, *Soil Exhaustion,* 38, believes the criticism valid, and so does Gray, *History of Agriculture in the Southern United States,* I, 448.

poses. In fact, the ox was displaced more slowly in New England than in other sections of the country, including the South.11

There is only a modicum of truth in the assertion, which still finds its way into print, that slavery inspired a contempt for physical labor among the white people of the South, and thereby rendered the section a great economic disservice. Slavery, or the presence of Negroes, which was the result of slavery, may properly be credited with responsibility for the idea universally prevalent in districts with considerable black population that whites must not perform *menial* services, that is, such personal services for others as cooking, washing, scrubbing, and attendance as maids or valets.12 Originally, perhaps, whites shunned the performance of such services simply because of their menial character. Because whites shunned them, they were the more readily assigned to Negroes; and the more the blacks were thus employed, the more odious to whites such tasks became. But, although slavery may have excluded whites from menial services, it does not follow that whites were deprived of productive employment on that account.

Slavery and Negroes may also have bred the idea in slaveholding regions that people who could afford to own or hire servants should not perform their own domestic tasks, much as generations of low wages for household servants in England have established the idea that no woman of the middle class or above may do her own housework, at least not without a servant or two about for the sake of appearances. It was indeed true that families in slaveholding regions began to employ domestic servants at a lower income level than was the case in nonslaveholding districts. In so far as slavery was responsible for this, the institution rendered the South an economic disservice to the extent that it caused a greater degree of idleness than existed among similiar classes in other sections—provided that such leisure is not to be considered economically desirable. But it should not be overlooked, in this

---

11 Perhaps the principal reason for delaying substitution in various localities was the lack of sufficient grain for feed, without which horses and mules could not do much hard work. There were other reasons for delay, however. See Percy W. Bidwell and J. L. Falconer, *History of Agriculture in the Northern United States, 1620-1860* (Washington, 1925), 111-13, 243, 403-405; Gray, *History of Agriculture in the Southern United States,* II, 851-52.

12 The line was often finely and strangely drawn. A Virginia farmer told Frederick L. Olmsted that he did not know that white farm laborers were particular about working with Negroes, but no white man would ever do certain kinds of work, such as taking care of cattle or getting water or wood for use in the house. If one should ask a white man to do such work, he would get mad and reply that he was no "nigger." Poor white girls never hired out to do servants' work, but they would help another white woman with her sewing and quilting and take wages for it. There were some "very respectable ladies" that would go out to sew. *The Cotton Kingdom,* 2 vols. (New York, 1861), I, 82.

connection, that mistresses on all but the largest plantations had heavy responsibilities in supervising servants in various household manufactures, in looking after the sick, in teaching the children, and in many other concerns.

There was no stigma attached in the South in slavery days to the performance of manual labor, as distinguished from menial, or of any other sort of labor not considered menial.13 There were *situations,* however, in which whites would not work with slaves, just as now there are situations in which whites will not work with Negroes. White wage earners, except perhaps immigrants who had not yet learned to draw the line, would not labor on a plantation under an overseer. They would, however, work with slaves if there was some evident distinction in tasks or status. A white farmer and his sons had no repugnance to working along with their own or hired slaves at any task required on the farm. White hired men, too, would work with the farmer and slaves. A farmer's wife and daughters might not work in the fields with slaves, but the women folk of nonslaveholding whites were about as likely to work in the fields as were Northern women similarly circumstanced. In both sections, as in England, women were withdrawn from the fields as standards of living rose. An overseer on a plantation was not supposed to do physical labor, even if so inclined; to do so, it was thought, and no doubt correctly, would be detrimental to discipline. A foreman who had charge of a small group of slaves on a farm or a small plantation—and there were many such—was expected to work along with the slaves. A large planter and his sons might not engage in physical labor; to do so would lower them in the esteem of their neighbors and slaves. It is difficult to say whether slavery was responsible for this pleasing fancy or only made it more possible to humor it. English country gentlemen and their sons likewise eschewed manual labor, and Northern millowners did not as a rule send their sons into the mills as hands. Furthermore, even planters who employed overseers usually had their time well-occupied with the management of their plantations, and their management was economically more productive than wielding the plow or hoe would have been.

The same situation obtained in the cities and towns of the South. In factories, mills, and shops, and about the wharves, white laborers, free Negroes, and slaves, sometimes of both sexes, worked side by side, usually, but not always, with some distinction of tasks. Frequently the

---

13 In the South considerable point was made of this distinction between menial and manual labor. In the North the word *menial* was not so commonly used, either as adjective or noun.

whites objected to working with Negroes and sought to have them excluded from certain employments, but never successfully. The opposition arose partly from race prejudice and partly from dislike of Negro competition. In the North, where Negro laborers were relatively few, the opposition of whites to Negro competition was more effective. It would seem unlikely that many whites were deprived of useful employment by their disinclination to work with Negroes or to labor at certain tasks commonly performed by slaves.[14]

Southern people in general were more inclined than those in the East and Northwest to dislike physical labor, especially heavy physical labor, and to seek "white-collar" jobs or to live by their wits. The evidence on this point is overwhelming. But it does not follow that slavery was the cause of this difference. A similar variance in other places and in other times has commonly been explained by differences in temperature, humidity, ease of making a living, eating and drinking habits, general health, cultural antecedents, and social organizations.[15] If such explanations are valid for other places and other times, they are equally valid for the United States in slavery times.

A more difficult question with regard to the general economic effects of slavery is whether or not the institution retarded the growth of population of the slaveholding states. If so, it was a grievous fault; for economic history shows that increase in population in a region has been conducive to the development of improved means of transportation, the commercialization of agriculture and manufactures, and the extension of the factory system—developments which, with all their evils, have contributed to economic progress.

At the close of the colonial period the six commonwealths which continued to permit slavery and to colonize new "slave" territory, that is, Delaware, Maryland, Virginia, the two Carolinas, and Georgia, together with Louisiana, Florida, and Texas, had a slightly greater

---

[14] The last four paragraphs are based upon numerous but widely scattered scraps of evidence gleaned from a variety of sources, especially *De Bow's Review* (New Orleans, 1846-1880); the various works of Olmsted dealing with the South; and Phillips (ed.), *Plantation and Frontier*, I, II. Considerable evidence is presented in an uncritical manner in Charles H. Wesley, *Negro Labor in the United States, 1850-1925: A Study in American Economic History* (New York, 1927), Chap. III. Particular statements made above are confirmed by Kathleen Bruce, *Virginia Iron Manufacture in the Slave Era* (New York, 1930), Chap. VI; Ivan E. McDougle, "Slavery in Kentucky, 1792-1865," in *Journal of Negro History* (Lancaster, Pa., 1932-   ), III (1934), 296; Alfred H. Stone, "Free Contract Labor in the Ante-Bellum South," in *The South in the Building of the Nation*, 12 vols. (Richmond, 1909), V, 142.

[15] The influence of such factors in the case of the poor whites is well described by Paul H. Buck, "The Poor Whites in the Ante-Bellum South," in *American Historical Review*, XXXI (1925), 41-55.

population than the seven states to the north which shortly became "free." In 1860 there were eighteen free and fifteen slave states. According to the census for that year the former had a population of 18,800,527, the latter, 12,315,374. Wherein lies the explanation? We can not now detect any differences in the birth and death rates of the two sections.

For one thing, the number of people of Southern birth who migrated to the North was much greater than the number of people of Northern birth who moved to the South. In 1850 there were 608,626 people of Southern birth living in free states and only 199,672 people born in free states residing in the South. The corresponding numbers for 1860 were 713,527 and 371,421.16 In 1860 there were, by careful estimate, about 800,000 more people of Southern birth and parentage living in free territory than there were people of Northern stock living in slaveholding regions. This accounts, then, for approximately 1,600,-000 of the 6,500,000 disparity in population between sections.

This large net loss to the South in intersectional migration, in turn, is to be explained almost wholly by the circumstances of the westward movement of population during the period and the various conditions and political maneuvers that determined which of the new states beyond the mountains should be free and which slave. The old story of thousands of small farmers from the South fleeing across the Ohio River to escape slavery is almost pure fiction.17 People from the older states moved west with various motives, the principal one being the acquisition of land. They usually followed the most available routes. Before the railroads were built, great numbers of people from Virginia and Maryland went up the Potomac Valley, crossed over to the Ohio River, using the Cumberland National Road after it had been built, floated down the Ohio, and eventually found homes in Kentucky and the southern parts of Ohio, Indiana, and Illinois, or beyond the Mississippi in Missouri, Arkansas, and Iowa. Many other people from Maryland, Virginia, and North Carolina crossed the Blue Ridge by various routes, picked up the trail in the Great Valley, and followed it down into Tennessee or turned off and went through Cumberland Gap into Kentucky. Thousands of Kentuckians and Tennesseeans in turn, of the first, second, or later generations, moved on west or northwest into southern Indiana, southern Illinois, Missouri, Arkansas, and, in less

---

16 *Compendium of the Seventh Census of the United States, 1850,* pp. 116 ff.; *Eighth Census of the United States, 1860, Population,* 616 ff. The District of Columbia is included with the South.

17 Taylor, *Slaveholding in North Carolina,* 56-58.

numbers, into Iowa and southwestern Wisconsin. Only slaveholders who wished to take their slaves with them were debarred from choosing a location north of the Ohio; scores of slaveholders, in fact, did take their slaves into Indiana and Illinois under life or other long-term indentures permitted by the early laws.18 Of the 608,626 natives of the South living in 1850 in free states, 505,096 resided in the four states of Ohio, Indiana, Illinois, and Iowa, and of the latter number 462,088 had been born in Virginia, Maryland, North Carolina, Kentucky, and Tennessee. The corresponding numbers for 1860 were 713,527, 530,843, and 481,322 respectively.

Many thousands of people from Pennsylvania and, to a less extent, from New York and New Jersey, crossed to the Ohio River, floated down that stream, and eventually settled on the left bank in Kentucky or crossed the Mississippi into Missouri. Other thousands settled first on the right bank of the Ohio, and then later, they or their children moved on into Kentucky or, especially, Missouri. Of the 371,421 people born in free states but living in 1860 in slave states, 208,059 were to be found in Missouri and Kentucky. Northerners certainly did not shun Missouri. In 1860 there were 166,620 people living there who had been born on free soil and 274,572 who had been born in other slave states. There was also a large interchange of population across the line between Pennsylvania and New Jersey on the one side and Virginia, Maryland, and Delaware on the other; 49,827 people born north of the line were living south of it in 1860, and 50,958 born south of it were living on the other side. There was much less exchange of population between New England and the Great Lakes region on the one hand and the Lower South on the other. But such exchange did occur. Thousands of Yankees undeterred by slavery went south to farm, work in mills, run steamboats, buy cotton, sell merchandise, teach school, and fill all manner of other jobs which became available. There were many more Northerners scattered about the Lower South than there were people from the latter region residing in the Upper North. In 1860 there were 12,549 natives of New England living in the seven cotton states and only 2,169 people from the cotton states to be found in New England.

The other important cause of the disparity of population between the North and the South in 1860 was the fact that the former had received much the greater share of the foreign immigration. In 1860 there were 3,582,999 people of foreign birth living in free states and the

18 John B. McMaster, *A History of the People of the United States from the Revolution to the Civil War,* 8 vols. (New York, 1883-1913), III, 526-28; V, 187.

territories and only 553,176 in the slave states. In 1850 the numbers had been 1,900,325 and 310,514. Why did not the slave states get a larger share of the immigrants? The blame has often been unjustly placed upon slavery.

Most of the immigrants in ante-bellum days, as since, landed at New York City, for that was the principal terminus of the trans-Atlantic packet lines and, after their advent, the steamship lines. Many remained in New York; the majority scattered to various parts of the country. Most numerous among the immigrants after 1845 (about the time the tide of immigration set in strongly) were the Irish. They were poor and sought work for wages. They found it chiefly in the cities and factory towns and in railroad and canal construction. The cities and mill towns were mainly in the East, and the railroads and canals were being built mostly there and in the Northwest. A considerable number of Irishmen found work building Southern railroads and many were employed at the wharves of New Orleans and other Southern towns. They showed no great prejudice against slavery or against Negroes.

Next most numerous among immigrants were Germans. They usually had more means than the Irish, and a larger proportion of them went to the growing Northwest, acquired land, and grew grain and raised livestock. They undoubtedly disliked slavery. But they would have preferred the Northwest even if slavery had not been in the picture. There they could get excellent land at the minimum government price located in districts which were being rapidly opened to markets by the building of railroads. They could practice a type of farming more like that of the old country. And acclimation was less difficult than in the South. Thousands of Germans went to the quasi-slave state of Missouri where land and farming were quite like those of states of the Northwest. And a considerable number were lured to the rich, cheap lands of Texas to grow cotton and grain.[19] Few of them acquired slaves, partly because they disliked slavery and partly because they could not afford to purchase them.

It would seem, then, to be a safe conclusion that neither slavery nor the presence of Negroes was in any direct sense responsible for the failure of the slaveholding states as a whole to grow as rapidly in population as the free states as a whole between 1790 and 1860. No doubt thousands of individuals were deterred from going South by race prejudice, dislike of slavery, or a disinclination to compete with slaves for jobs. But, since so many others were undeterred by such motives

---

[19] Albert B. Faust, *The German Element in the United States,* 2 vols. (Boston, 1909), I, 490-501; Olmsted, *Cotton Kingdom,* II, 96, 262-66.

and considerations, it is reasonable to suppose that, if economic opportunities had been great enough, people would have come in greater numbers from the North and from Europe to seize upon them.20

This conclusion is further justified by events which have occurred since slavery was abolished. The percentage of immigrants locating in the South has been even less than it was in slavery days. For example, in 1890 only 8.3 per cent of the foreign born of this country lived in the South whereas 13.4 per cent had lived there in 1860. Now it is possible that it has been the presence of the Negro, a resultant of slavery, which has repelled. But it is highly probable that it has been the comparative lack of economic opportunities in the South, still suffering from the ravages of war for much of the period.21 Many whites and blacks have gone North to get jobs, especially during the great boom prior to 1929. Moreover, the presence of Negroes has not kept Northerners out of particular localities or particular occupations in the South where oppotunities have called.

The conclusion just stated brings up another question which has caused historians much trouble, namely, to what extent, if at all, was slavery responsible for the comparative dearth of economic opportunities in the South which, in turn, kept the population from growing more rapidly? In agriculture slavery reduced opportunities somewhat for nonslaveholding whites but not for the population as a whole. Because of it the white farm population was probably less than it would otherwise have been, but the total farm population was greater. And, be it noted, when writers say that slavery retarded the growth of the population of the South, they mean total population, not white population only.

The story is briefly this: The staple crops of the South gave the incentive for men of enterprise to engage in large-scale agriculture. Land was plentiful and cheap. The labor problem was more difficult. People of good-enough quality would not work for low-enough wages, in large-enough numbers, and with sufficient regularity in a country where it was so easy to get land and farm independently. The solution was first found in indentured servants, and the earliest plantations were developed with that class of labor. As time passed Negro slaves were preferred, great numbers were imported, they throve and multiplied, and many farmers developed into planters.22

---

20 *Cf.* Emory Q. Hawk, *Economic History of the South* (New York, 1934), 220-21.

21 Gray, *History of Agriculture in the Southern United States,* II, 940.

22 The subject of this paragraph has been amplified and more thoroughly

Although a time did not arrive when more than about one third of the agricultural population of the South, including the Negroes, lived on plantations as distinguished from small farms,23 the great bulk of the staple crops came to be produced on plantations—all the sugar and rice, most of the tobacco, and at least three fourths of the cotton. There were several reasons for this.24 In the production of sugar and rice, which required considerable capital, small farmers could not compete with planters and were crowded out. The competitive advantages of the plantation in the growing of cotton and tobacco were not so great, if, indeed, there were any. But planters held slaves for the primary purpose of producing staples for market; they would not have kept slaves had it not been for this motive. Small farmers, on the contrary, were under no particular urge to engage in commercialized agriculture. They might make a better living by doing general or subsistence farming. Slaves were better adapted to the routine of the plantation than they were to the more varied tasks of general farming with considerable household manufacturing. Also, as a class, the planters were more enterprising and they were better managers than the small farmers; the more ambitious and capable of the small farmers were likely to graduate into the planter class. So planters got the better lands, near enough to transportation facilities to justify staple agriculture, while small farmers had cheaper, but not necessarily poorer, lands more remote from the routes of commerce and followed a more self-sufficing economy or, if they remained in the plantation belts, lived on the poorer lands and practiced a more general agriculture than their planter neighbors.

If slavery had not existed in the South and, consequently, there had been few or no plantations, it is reasonable to presume that the lands which were in fact in plantations would have been held by the more capable small farmers, who would have raised staples although in somewhat smaller quantities than they were actually produced. In this case the white farm population of the South would have been greater than it actually was, but not as great as the actual farm population, both white and black.

---

reasoned in Robert R. Russel, "The Economic History of Negro Slavery in the United States," in *Agricultural History* (Chicago, Baltimore, 1927-), XI (1937), 308-21.

23 The percentage depends upon where the line is drawn between the plantation and the farm. If the minimum number of slaves on a plantation be arbitrarily set at ten, about 30 per cent of the farm population resided on plantations in 1850. Cf. Gray, *History of Agriculture in the Southern United States,* I, 482, 529.

24 These reasons are developed at greater length in an unpublished paper by the writer on "The Effects of Slavery upon Non-Slaveholders in the Ante-Bellum South."

But immigrants into the North after 1790 went largely into non-agricultural occupations. To what extent, if at all, was slavery responsible for the backwardness of the South in other lines of economic development than agriculture? Manufacturing may be selected for consideration since, next to agriculture, it is the most fundamental industry.

Even in colonial times the Southern commonwealths did less manufacturing in proportion to population than did the Northern. In the middle period, as the industrial revolution proceeded, the South did a smaller and smaller percentage of the nation's manufacturing. In 1860 the capital invested in manufacturing in the South was only 9.5 per cent of the capital so invested in the entire country; and the number of hands employed was only 8.4 per cent of the nation's total. Moreover, nearly one half of Southern manufactures consisted of flour and grist, lumber, and turpentine, products of simple operations.

A number of reasons may be advanced to account for the industrial backwardness of the South, few of which have much relevance to slavery. In colonial times in the tidewater region, the continued and anticipated profits of staple agriculture, together with the superior adaptability of slaves thereto, made it unnecessary and unprofitable to do much household and shop manufacturing. In the Northern colonies and the back country of the South, the lack of markets for agricultural products constrained the people to do more manufacturing. A combination of factors—the abundance of white pine, water power near the sea, the demand for ships and boats for the fisheries and the carrying trade, markets for lumber in the same regions where the fish were marketed—caused lumbering and shipbuilding to be concentrated largely along the New England coast. In a similar fashion other special factors caused various other branches of manufacturing to be more or less concentrated in the North.

When the Industrial Revolution reached the United States, population was comparatively sparse in the South, distances were great, and means of transportation poor. The poorer whites afforded little demand for manufactured goods. Neither did the slaves, but the masters, who exploited their labor, presumably compensated for them in this regard. So markets were too dispersed and inadequate to encourage large-scale manufacturing. The population of the East was more compact and, therefore, transportation facilities could be provided at lower cost. The purchasing power of the people was greater.

The streams of the South were less manageable for power than were those of the East. Southern power sites were relatively inaccessible to natural avenues of transportation; in New England, especially, considerable power was available very near the sea.

The principal Southern raw material, cotton, was not at all bulky and would stand transportation to distant markets. The humid atmosphere of the New England seaboard was advantageous to cotton mills. For lumbering the North possessed much the same advantages over the South in the middle period that it had possessed in the colonial. Even before coal came to be used in smelting, parts of Pennsylvania had an advantage over other regions of the country in ironmaking by reason of the juxtaposition of wood, ore, and limestone in localities near navigable rivers or other means of transportation. When coal superseded charcoal the advantage of Pennsylvania was enhanced. To illustrate, in the days of charcoal furnaces a considerable secondary iron industry was developed in Richmond, Virginia, which used pig iron smelted in the back country and brought down the James River. After smelting with anthracite was well developed in eastern Pennsylvania, about 1850, the Richmond iron works procured their pig iron there and the back country furnaces died out.25 The principal iron ore field of the South, near present Birmingham, Alabama, was in ante-bellum days all but inaccessible. The Pittsburgh field, by way of contrast, lay at the head of a magnificent system of inland waterways transportation. After railroads penetrated northern Georgia, northern Alabama, and eastern Tennessee, during the fifties, numbers of small furnaces and foundries sprang up, but they could not compete with those of Pennsylvania except in the local markets.

In the East, where there had been more household and shop industry, and much manufacturing done under the "putting out" system, there were more laborers to be diverted to mills and factories when they came in. The opening of improved means of communication with the fine farming regions of western New York and the Northwest brought destructive competition to Eastern agriculture, released still more men, women, and children to become mill hands, and supplied them with food and raw materials. In the South the continued profitableness of staple agriculture prevented slaveowners from turning to manufacturing or diverting their slaves thereto. Although slaves were frequently used successfully in mills, factories, and shops, in fact in practically every mechanical pursuit, they were certainly not as well adapted to mechanical employments as to agriculture.26 It was difficult

---

25 Bruce, *Virginia Iron Manufacture in the Slave Era*, 275-78.

26 There was much discussion of this point in the South about 1845-1852. The concensus was about as stated here. *Ibid.*, Chap. VI; Wesley, *Negro Labor in the United States*, Ch. I; Phillips, *American Negro Slavery*, 375-78; Robert R. Russel, *Economic Aspects of Southern Sectionalism, 1840-1861*, University of Illinois *Studies in the Social Sciences*, XI, No. 1, Pts. I, II (1923), 41, 54.

to transform the small, independent, self-sufficing farmers of the South into urban wage earners.

Capital for industry in the East had come from the profits of merchandising and shipping as well as from the profits of industry. In the South there was no considerable source of capital outside manufacturing itself. The profits of agriculture, such as they were, were absorbed in expanding agriculture and providing facilities for transportation. If the section had offered exceptional opportunities, capital and labor would have been diverted from agriculture or would have flowed in from the outside, but such was not the case. Once the North had gained a good start upon the South in manufacturing, it became harder for the latter to make progress. For then infant industries in the South would have to get started in the face of unrestricted competition from firmly established industries in the North.[27]

Of the various reasons enumerated for the backwardness of the South in manufacturing, only one relates directly to slavery, namely, slave labor was not so well adapted to manufacturing as to agriculture, and, therefore, other things being equal, slaveowners preferred to keep their slaves engaged in the latter. A second reason for which slavery has frequently been blamed may relate indirectly to the institution, namely, a dearth of capital for investment. It becomes necessary, therefore, to ascertain what effects, if any, slavery had upon saving and investment in the South.

Slavery, as we have seen, made possible the development of large-scale farming. By all the rules of economic history the planters should have saved much for investment in further productive enterprises; it is the people with the larger incomes who do most of the saving for investment. The planters did save. They saved more than their small-farmer neighbors did. They saved enough to keep expanding their agricultural operations. They provided much of the capital for internal improvements and other productive undertakings. But the fact remains that they did not save as much for investment as might logically be expected of them.

Many of the planters, especially those of old families, did not have steady habits and frugal instincts. They often had visions of grandeur inherited from spacious colonial days and reinforced by real or fancied

---

27 The reasons for the backwardness of the South in manufacturing are described in greater detail in Victor S. Clark, "Manufactures," in *The South in the Building of the Nation,* V, 299-335; Russel, *Economic Aspects of Southern Sectionalism,* 54-64; Gray, *History of Agriculture in the Southern United States,* II, 931-36.

descent from English aristocracy.28 At any rate, planters who were making money, and often those who were losing it,29 lived well. They built big houses. Their habitations were literally overrun by domestic servants. They bought luxuries. Those with the largest incomes frequently spent their substance at Northern watering places or in European travel. How slavery could have been responsible for these enlarged views it is impossible to see, except, of course, that it was slavery that made it possible to indulge them.

Again planters' savings were diminished by the almost universal practice of living and operating not upon the income from the preceding crop but upon the anticipated income from the next crop; that is, they lived largely upon advances received from their factors upon contemplated or growing crops as security. These advances cost dearly. They cost not only interest but also the reduced prices which they occasioned, for the markets were frequently glutted and prices depressed because so many planters were under the necessity of selling their crops as soon as harvested in order to pay their debts. This practice of obtaining advances upon anticipated crops would not have prevented, it might even have facilitated, the accumulation of capital in the South, if the advances had been made by Southern men. But they were not. They were made in last analysis by Northern or British firms.30 Even if the planter eschewed advances from his cotton factor, the result was much the same, for in that case he bought supplies on long credit from his merchant who in turn had bought them on long credit from Northern jobbers or wholesalers. It would be difficult to name anything more efficacious in preventing the accumulation of capital than eight, ten, or fifteen per cent interest, often compounded.

This system of advances was caused partly by the lack of habits of thrift, already bemoaned. Its principal cause was the speculative character of a commercialized agriculture with distant markets. A farmer who produces for market is always under strong temptation to borrow money, get more land and hands, and put out a larger acreage, because there is always the possibility of raising a bumper crop and selling it at top prices. Nature is not consistent. There is always the prospect in any community of having a big crop while there is a total or partial failure

---

28 Thomas J. Wertenbaker has thoroughly discredited the old idea that Virginia was largely settled by cavaliers. *Patrician and Plebeian in Virginia, or the Origin and Development of Colonial Virginia* (Princeton, 1922).

29 Taylor, *Slaveholding in North Carolina*, 95-96.

30 Alfred H. Stone, "The Cotton Factorage System of the Southern States," in *American Historical Review*, XX (1915), 557-65; Hammond, *Cotton Industry*, 108 ff; Russel, *Economic Aspects of Southern Sectionalism*, 100-107.

elsewhere, with consequent high prices and big income for those who dwell in the favored community. Farmers gamble on the big year.31 Such speculation has by no means been confined to slaveowners and cotton growers. It has been as evident in nonslaveholding regions as in slaveholding—the wheat belt for instance. Slavery only made it possible for some farmers to gamble on a bigger scale.

Another thing, closely related to the factor just mentioned, which militated against the accumulation of capital in the South was the occasional overproduction of the staples. Within a few decades after the invention of the gin, the cotton states were producing over three fourths of the cotton sold in the world's markets. A big crop in the South sent the price down, a small crop sent it up. It happened more than once that a smaller crop of cotton at a high price brought in a larger aggregate amount to the growers than a large crop at a low price. But constant pleas to grow less cotton and more corn fell on deaf ears. In the cases of tobacco, sugar, and rice, the American crop was such a small part of the world's total that its quantity had comparatively little effect on world prices, and, therefore, there could be overproduction in the South, considered alone, only in the sense that labor and capital might more profitably have been directed into other channels. A chief reason for the overproduction of staples, when it occurred, was the speculative character of commercialized agriculture just noted. Slavery did not supply the urge to speculate, but it made speculation possible on a larger scale and thus contributed to overproduction. In general, of course, it was to the advantage of the South to produce great crops of cotton and other staples. Occasional overproduction was preferable to consistent underproduction. And without slavery there probably would have been consistent underproduction during the period under consideration.

It has frequently been stated that slavery "absorbed" capital in the South which otherwise might have been used in productive enterprises.32 Such a statement needs much qualification if it is not to be misleading. While foreign slave trade lasted, part of the profits of Southern industry went to Yankee skippers, English lords, Dahomey chiefs, etc., in exchange for slaves. Thus capital which might have been used to build sawmills or ships or for other productive purposes in the South was "fixed" in the form of slaves. Capital could not be taken out of the South by the internal or domestic slave trade, however. To

---

31 Cf. Hammond, *Cotton Industry,* 109; Olmsted, *Cotton Kingdom,* II, 49.

32 For example, Phillips seems to have said this. *American Negro Slavery,* 395-99; *id.,* "The Economic Cost of Slaveholding in the Cotton Belt," in *Political Science Quarterly* (New York, 1886-   ), XX (1905), 271-75.

illustrate, suppose Mississippi cotton planters, out of the profits of the industry, bought Virginia slaves. The slaves would still be in the South and presumably capable of paying for themselves and providing a reasonable profit on the investment. The saving of the planters would still be in the South also, although in Virginia instead of Mississippi, and, persumably, could be invested in factories, railroads, and other productive enterprises. They in turn might attract labor from the North or from Europe. Suppose, however, the Mississippi planters were able to hire free-born Virginians to come down and work the plantations and, instead of buying slaves, invested their savings in sawmills in their own state, employing workers attracted from the North or from Europe to operate the sawmills. The South as a whole would lose no laborers and no savings in this case, but Virginia would have been to the trouble and expense of rearing workers until they had reached maturity only to see them go away to contribute to the prosperity of another state. Thus slavery did not absorb Southern capital in any direct sense; it affected the distribution of capital within the section. The mere capitalization of the anticipated labor of a particular class did not destroy or diminish any other kind of property.[33]

But in an indirect way slavery may have had the effect of absorbing capital nevertheless. Take the case of the Virginia tobacco planters and the Mississippi cotton planters again. The Virginians probably received considerably more for their slaves than they had invested in rearing them, for the supply of slaves was not adjusted to demand and prices were normally considerably in excess of costs of production. And probably, instead of investing their profits in productive enterprises, the Virginians used them for living expenses, not having produced enough on their worn-out tobacco plantations to maintain their accustomed style of living. Thus as a consequence of slavery the profitable cotton industry of Mississippi might be carrying along .the incubus of an unprofitable tobacco industry in Virginia or at least enabling tobacco planters there to live in a style not justified by their earned incomes.[34] Under a free-labor system this would hardly have been possible. But, on the other hand, if it had not been for slavery, cotton growers of Mississippi might not have had any savings to invest.

---

[33] Gray, *History of Agriculture in the Southern United States,* I, 460, has put this point very clearly.

[34] For similar views of contemporaries of slavery, see Frederick L. Olmsted, *A Journey in the Back Country* (New York, 1861), 325; Cairnes, *Slave Power,* 72-76. See, also, Taylor, *Slaveholding in North Carolina,* 66. Edmund Ruffin of Virginia, another contemporary, held a contrary view. See "The Effects of High Prices on Slaves," in *De Bow's Review,* XXVI (1859), 647-57.

In conclusion, the importance of Negro slavery as a factor determining the character and extent of the economic development of the South has been greatly overestimated. It brought a racial element into the population which would not otherwise have been represented in any considerable numbers. The importation of slaves and the increase of the Negro population gave the South a larger total population, at any date, than it otherwise would have had, but no doubt retarded the growth of the white population. Slavery made possible the widespread development of the plantation system of farming and, thereby, gave a great impetus to the growing of the various Southern staples. This was beneficial to the South on the whole, although there was occasional overproduction, to which slavery contributed. Slavery may have retarded the diversification of Southern industry. It was conducive to the accumulation of capital on the whole, although it had the serious disadvantage of permitting more productive districts to contribute to the livelihood of the people of less productive regions. But compared with such great economic factors as climate, topography, natural resources, location with respect to the North and to Europe, means of transportation, and character of the white population, Negro slavery was of lesser consequence in determining the general course of Southern economic development.

11

A Revaluation of the Period before the Civil War: Railroads

The following essay originally appeared in the *Mississippi Valley Historical Review,* XV (December 1928), 341–354. It appears here by permission of the Organization of American Historians. The original pagination appears in brackets.

THERE HAS been a growing realization of late that the building and improvement of railroads constituted an important factor in the history of the period before the Civil War. We are coming to realize that we must take them more into account both in explaining the rapid transformation American society was undergoing and in interpreting the politics of that time. And it is a far cry from the treatment accorded railroads in one of the older political histories to that found in Beard's *Rise of American Civilization,* for example.[1]

Our comparative neglect of the railroad factor in the past has evidently been chiefly due to our preoccupation with the slavery question. To a great degree, however, this neglect may be attributed, it would seem, to the unusually voluminous, varied, and rather inaccessible character of the sources. These sources are gradually being mastered, by a policy of attrition, and we have at length accumulated a considerable mass of monographic and other secondary literature on railroads, some of it definitively done. In a short paper one cannot attempt a description of this literature.[2] Its existence makes a revaluation of the period a simpler matter and our failure to make such a revaluation less justifiable.

---

[1] Special mention should be made, also, of W. E. Dodd, *Expansion and Conflict* (Boston, 1915), chaps. x, xi, and of C. R. Fish, *The Rise of the Common Man* (New York, 1927). There are some good generalizations, although scattered and incomplete, in Edward Channing, *History of the United States* (New York, 1905-1925), V, VI.

[2] There is a rather full bibliography for the period in B. H. Meyer (ed.), *History of Transportation in the United States before 1860* (Washington, 1917). Another good bibliography is in F. A. Cleveland and F. W. Powell, *Railroad Promotion and Capitalization in the United States* (New York, 1909).

Granted, there are still great gaps in our secondary material. For example, we do not yet have a definitive railroad history of the Old Northwest for this period treating the section as a unit.[3] Such a study would reveal, better than any other, the complex factors which determined the location of railroads where physical contour was not fundamental. It should also give considerable light on the beginnings of consolidation and on the economic and social effects of the coming of railroads into more or less isolated communities. Someone should do for the Old Dominion what Professor Phillips has done for the eastern cotton belt.[4] Nowhere was there a more insistent, revealing, and significant public agitation conducted in behalf of railroads from the point of view of public policy and in behalf of state aid to railroad companies.[5] Perhaps no state illustrates better than Virginia the great obstacles to a reasonable state-aid program which lay in vested interests and in local rivalries, jealousies, and ambitions. Someone might well bring together and organize the scattered facts about railroad rates before the Civil War. We still await a definitive account of the Pacific railway issue in American politics during the period, showing, among other things, how it was interrelated with the slavery and other great domestic issues of the time and with our isthmian diplomacy. Perhaps more than anything else we need a much greater number of good economic and social histories of particular communities into which early railroads entered;[6] such histories would enable us to speak with authority about the economic and social effects of railroads—a subject on which it is too easy to generalize without data. These and other gaps in our secondary literature must be filled in before we can make anything like a final evaluation of the railroad factor in the history of the period. They do not excuse us, however, from making attempts at evaluation with the materials we have.

Now what can we do with our railroad material in its present state in the way of revaluing the period before the Civil War?[7] For one thing

---

[3] We have William F. Gephart, *Transportation and Industrial Development in the Middle West* (New York, 1909), and F. L. Paxson, "The Railroads of the 'Old Northwest' before the Civil War," Wisconsin Academy of Sciences, Arts and Letters, *Transactions,* XVII, 243-74.

[4] U. B. Phillips, *A History of Transportation in the Eastern Cotton Belt to 1860* (New York, 1908).

[5] A phase of this propaganda is described in C. H. Ambler, *Sectionalism in Virginia from 1776-1851* (Chicago, 1910), 311-19.

[6] An example of the sort of work we need is B. H. Hibbard, *History of Agriculture in Dane County, Wisconsin* (Madison, 1904).

[7] The writer has had occasion to read rather extensively in the sources. It

we should be able to give a more accurate and truthful description
and explanation of the great economic and social changes which
occurred. Railroads helped to take people west and to settle lands there
which otherwise must have remained unoccupied. They, with other
improved means of transportaion, obliterated old frontiers, revolution-
ized the character of the new frontier, and by 1860 bade fair to carry
it forward with seven-league boots. Improved means of transportation
caused self-sufficing rural economy to give way to commercial agriculture with distant markets.8 The railroads not only brought prosperity
to countless rural communities but they caused countless others, sometimes century old, to die out, unable to withstand the new competition
with more naturally favored districts far away. Even before the Civil
War, railroads were making some towns into cities and blasting the
prospects of others. Along with other improved means of transportation
and communication, they largely conditioned the progress of the
industrial revolution—by providing wide markets, by bringing together
raw materials and food supplies at manufacturing centers, and by
themselves utilizing and thus stimulating various manufactures.9 Improvements in transportation, at various stages, built up promising
home industries in many localities only for successive improvements to
destroy them to the advantage of more favorably located competitors
in other sections of the country. The building of railroads withdrew
thousands of laborers from other occupations thus forcing changes
therein and encouraging immigration. Railroads ruthlessly annihilated
vested interests in the form of canal and turnpike companies, stage
lines, and, later, steamboat lines. They contributed greatly to the
evolution of business organization.10 They were instrumental in greatly
increasing travel and the commingling of people, thus spreading ideas
and notions more rapidly and releasing social energies.11 They con-

---

would be impossible to cite all the material which has contributed to the various items in this evaluaton, and no attempt will be made to do so.

8 See especially R. M. Tryon, *Household Manufactures in the United States,
1640-1860* (Chicago, 1917) ; P. W. Bidwell, "The Agricultural Revolution in
New England," *American Historical Review*, XXVI, 683-702; and P. W. Bidwell and J. I. Falconer, *History of Agriculture in the Northern United States,
1620-1860* (Washington, 1925), chap. xxiv.

9 The best summary is in Victor S. Clark, *History of Manufactures in the
United States, 1607-1860* (Washington, 1916), chap. xiv.

10 For suggestions see Guy S. Callender, "The Early Transportation and
Banking Enterprises of the States in Relation to the Growth of Corporations,"
Quarterly Journal of Economics, XVII, 111-62.

11 C. R. Fish, in writing of early railway cars, contributes an illuminating
bit of interpretation: "This type, however, gave way to the long car, with two

tributed greatly to the growth of the United States mails. The telegraph enabled the daily newspaper to garner its crop of news, the railroads in part made possible the larger reading public necessary to the support of these news-gathering and news-mongering agencies.12 Improved means of communication and travel helped to establish the convention habit among the people of the forties and fifties, and conventions nourished all the "isms." Improved means of travel and communication greatly influenced our political methods and organization. This outline of changes caused or conditioned by improved means of transportation and communication might be extended. But some such outline as this, rounded out with accurate illustrative detail and animated with sympathy for and understanding of human beings of all classes and conditions, should find its way into our general histories.

A study of our railroad material will convince one that we have not been estimating highly enough the initiative, inventiveness, foresight, and boldness of intelligent Americans in the middle period. They grasped with astonishing quickness the utilities of the railroad and the possibilities of improving it. The remarkable fact is not that the railroads were first popularly considered as probably useful supplements to existing water transportation systems, but how quickly bolder spirits saw that they could become competitors and alter the course of trade and how promptly they acted upon their vision. Said a director of the Baltimore and Ohio Railroad Company, when construction on that line was begun, 1828: "We are about opening a channel through which the commerce of the mighty country beyond the Alleghany must seek the ocean . . ."13 For the writer of this paper, at least, it illuminates the character of the American people to know that a large proportion of the early railroad lines in this country, short as they were, were built as "links" in "chains" continental in their extent, some of them not connecting with established water routes except at their termini. Most of our present main lines east of the Mississippi existed on paper as chains of railroads years before more than the first links had been

---

double seats divided by an aisle. Just why this change was made it is difficult to say, but it is significant that when it was complete, the American traveled everywhere, whether by·canal boat, steamer or train, in a long narrow saloon, in close association with his fellow travelers, and with the opportunity for general conversation or for the expression of his opinion before an audience, willing or unwilling," *op. cit.*, 82.

12 I know of no work which attempts to show the correlation between railroads and newspaper circulation. There are so many factors making for an increased circulation that probably no such attempt would be of value.

13 Archer B. Hulbert, *The Paths of Inland Commerce* (New Haven, 1921), 149.

actually constructed. Not all early paper systems materialized, but most did; promoters read aright their physical geography and the signs of the times. The necessity of consolidating these chains under single companies, if railroads were to compete successfully with water routes for the carriage of heavy through freight, was not at once realized, to be sure, but consolidation in the form we know it had fairly begun before 1861. American inventive genius did not falter in the task of supplying the improvements necessary to make the railroad an efficient agency of transportation for heavy freight over vast distances; American engineers and builders eagerly watched developments on the other side of the water. The American public, once it had caught the spirit, constantly and confidently expected that the improvements would be forthcoming to meet the demands of a "new age." Our more philosophic citizens attempted to evaluate the railroad's economic, social, political, and moral significance for their time and for "generations yet unborn." Our railroad history contains ample material to illustrate the truth of Charles and Mary Beard's statement: "When at last the cloud lifts, when the fundamental course of American civilization is seen in a long, unbroken development, when the sharp curves of years are smoothed by the reckoning of centuries, then if all signs do not fail the middle period of American history will appear as the most changeful, most creative, most spirited epoch between the founding of the colonies and the end of the nineteenth century."[14]

Certainly in the past our general histories have dealt too largely, relatively speaking, with politics. As we work up our detailed knowledge of the history of transportation, manufactures, agriculture, public lands, immigration, education, culture, various reform movements, and other subjects, we shall be able to correct the emphasis. But much in our politics requires revaluation in the light of the facts about these other subjects.

Our state and local politics in the period concerned, have been treated too often as completely subordinated to and bound up with national politics. Complaints were indeed numerous in the ante-bellum period that state and local party contests turned altogether too largely on national issues. Such complaints were justified, but it is easy to exaggerate. There were all sorts of state and local issues which shared with national questions the interest and attention of politicians and people generally. Between 1845 and 1860 no questions figured more largely in state and local politics outside of New England, possibly, than railroad questions.

---

14 *The Rise of American Civilization* (New York, 1927), I, 632.

It could not be otherwise. The building of railroads was a matter of vital public interest. People were quick to grasp their economic and some of their social and political effects. They understood well enough that the outlines of a permanent transportation system were being laid down, and they realized accordingly that the determination of the location of railroads at the moment was fated with consequences for the future of their communities. In fact, they exaggerated the importance of the location of particular railroads, not foreseeing the great multiplication of lines in later years. From the point of state policy, a properly planned railroad system would settle the vacant lands, open mineral and other natural resources to exploitation, increase the taxable wealth, and build up cities within the commonweath with trade which otherwise might seek "commercial metropolises" in other states. If a city could secure a radiating system of these arteries of commerce, "its life blood," its future greatness seemed assured. And as Governor Bebb of Ohio said: "—wo to the commercial city that suffers these [artificial] rivers to be diverted from it."15 Farming communities realized no less well their interests in the routes railroads might take. "Every farmer along the line wants the road to run by his front door," said one harassed railroad president. In the South, where there was concern about southern decline, railroads were presented as an agency that might regenerate the economic life of the section, give it a varied industry, free it from galling dependence on the North, attract immigration, and enable it to contest more equally in the national councils.16

With such public interests involved, and I have not named all of them, all the agencies of social control were enlisted to assist in getting the roads properly located and built. The merits of rival routes were fought out in conventions, in newspaper columns, on the stump and platform, and in the pulpit, and the purchase of stocks and bonds was urged on grounds of civic pride and public spirit as well as of economic self-interest. Under the special-charter system, which generally prevailed, struggles over railroad routes were carried into the legislatures. Pressure was brought to bear upon legislatures to make railroad charters more and more liberal. The legislatures were requested to build railroads, or to grant state aid to private companies, or to permit municipal divisions to vote such aid, or, if constitutional provisions forbade state or local aid, to call constitutional conventions to alter the inconvenient

---

15 *DeBow's Review,* VIII, 444.

16 R. R. Russel, *Economic Aspects of Southern Sectionalism, 1840-61* (Urbana, 1924).

sections.17 Cities, counties, and townships were asked to vote bonds or subscribe stock, where constitutions and laws permitted. But such measures met opposition. The American people in the pre-Civil War period were individualistic. There was fear of corporations. There was the Jeffersonian tradition of non-interference. *Laissez faire* proclivities had been confirmed by experiences during the panic of 1837 and its aftermath. There was opposition to railroads from vested interests which would be injuriously affected—canal companies, turnpike companies, steamboat lines, stage lines. So railroad questions became campaign issues and led to spirited contests which we can not recount here. Even in years when the slavery controversy was most bitter, numerous state contests, to say nothing of local, turned primarily on the question of state aid to railroads or other railroad matters. It is doubtful whether any other subject occupied more of the time and interest of state legislatures in the period from 1848 to 1860 than did railroads. It is doubtful whether the average citizen in the West gave as much interest and attention to the slavery question, in the same period, as to railroad questions.

The general historian who would give a true picture of American life should insert paragraphs on the more or less corrupt influence of railroads upon politics years before the day of Oakes Ames and Credit Mobilier. Politico-railroad scandals were not as common before the Civil War as they afterwards became, to be sure, but the explanation for their comparative infrequency in the former period seems to lie chiefly in the deficiencies of the press of that time and a lack of tenderness in the public conscience with regard to business in politics. To illustrate, remarkably large numbers of railroad men were elected or appointed to offices in which they would be concerned with railroad matters; remarkably large numbers of state or locally prominent politicians became railroad presidents or financial agents without prejudice to their influence in party councils or their chances for political preferment.

Railroad issues figured in our national politics also. There was the Western demand for congressional grants of land in aid of railroads. This was one of the major western policies of the period. It lead to lengthy congressional debates and to all sorts of political combinations, log-rolling, lobbying, jobbery, and corruption. A land grant having been obtained from Congress, its history was only begun, both in the arena

---

17 In 1852 New Orleans was given a new charter largely to facilitate the giving of aid to railroad companies, and Louisiana adopted a new constitution of which the most important feature was the absence of the former prohibition of state aid to corporations.

of national and in that of state politics. There was the issue of the tariff on railroad iron—by no means an insignificant one. There was the difficult question of the remuneration to be paid the railroad companies for transporting mails, troops, and government freight. The building of railroads increased the number of cases concerning the bridging of navigable rivers.18

Accounts of the acquisition of Oregon, California, and New Mexico could be made more truthful and satisfying by putting them against a background of progress in means of transportation and communication. The process of acquisition was accompanied by interesting debates in Congress and out as to the ability of the United States to colonize, assimilate, and retain such distant possession with such a vast mountain barrier separating them from the settled eastern states.19 The proponents of acquisition expressed great confidence in the political properties of steam and electricity. "Manifest destiny" was manifest to men who were witnessing the wonders of a revolution in means of communication and travel.

The issue of better means of communication with the Pacific coast, whether by Pacific railroad or isthmian projects, deserves greater consideration than has as yet been accorded it in accounts of American politics of the dozen years before the Civil War. The conquest over nature which would necessarily be involved appealed powerfully to the imagination of the generation. The stakes involved in the solution of the problem were supposed to be, and were, enormous. Failure to provide proper facilities might result in estrangement and separation of the coast communities or their loss in a war with a strong naval power. The choice of route for a transcontinental railroad would powerfully affect the future prosperity of cities, states, and strong railroad interests farther east. It would largely give direction to the colonization of the coast and of the great plains, and that, in turn, would have important bearing on the balance of political power between the sections engaged in the struggle over slavery and other issues. A decision in favor of a railroad built and operated by the government might go far toward altering the character of our govern-

---

18 These matters are discussed satisfactorily in Lewis H. Haney, *A Congressional History of Railways in the United States* (Madison, 1906-10), I and II; and John B. Sanborn, *Congressional Grants of Land in Aid of Railways* (Madison, 1899).

19 See especially *Cong. Globe*, 27 Cong., 3 Sess., 154, 198-200, 227; 28 Cong., 1 Sess., Appendix, 224, 622; 29 Cong., 1 Sess., 1214-17; 29 Cong., 2 Sess., 356, 367, Appendix, 127-28, 132; 30 Cong., 1 Sess., Appendix, 337-40, 350, 370, 383-93.

mental system. The interest in this issue was, therefore, great and general, the rivalry over routes and termini was intense.[20] Professor F. H. Hodder has shown what can be done toward illuminating one famous episode in our history, the Kansas-Nebraska Bill, by sketching in this Pacific railway background.[21] The real dignity and importance of our ante-bellum isthmian diplomacy would be better understood if we should more often discuss it along with the Pacific railway issue[22] rather than as a detached episode in our history.[23]

Then there is the matter of sectionalism. Of course, we must cease writing our history as if sectionalism of the North and South were the only important fact in the ante-bellum period and every other matter turned or waited upon it. We have allowed sectionalism to obscure somewhat the story of the onward march of democracy, industry, culture, and even nationalism. Yet when all is said by way of correcting emphasis, sectionalism was one of the greatest facts in our history and had most tragic consequences.

We cannot ignore it or exorcise it away. We must understand and explain it. All factors bearing upon it should be analyzed. The effect of improved means of transportation and communication upon sectionalism has by no means been neglected,[24] but it still awaits satisfying analysis and summarization.

Orators and political philosophers before the Civil War fondly pictured railroads, steamboat and telegraph lines as bonds which were operating to bind the Union together, remove prejudices and misunderstandings, spread common ideas, and establish a community of interest. But sectionalism was not allayed, the war came. What was the matter? Were there not railroads, steamboats, and telegraph lines enough? Or were there too many? There were more in 1861 than ever before.

---

20 These ideas are somewhat amplified in R. R. Russel, "The Pacific Railway Issue in Politics prior to the Civil War," *Miss. Val. Hist. Rev.,* XII, 187.

21 F. H. Hodder, "The Railroad Background of the Kansas-Nebraska Act," *ibid.,* 3-22.

22 John B. McMaster, *History of the People of the United States* (New York, 1909-1918). However, this account is incomplete.

23 Separate discussion has too often led authors to emphasize jingoistic assertions of the Monroe Doctrine or a restless search after more land for cotton and negroes as the prime motives of our isthmian diplomacy. See, for example, M. W. Williams, *Anglo-American Isthmian Diplomacy, 1815-1915* (Washington, 1916).

24 For examples see Chaning, *op. cit.,* VI, chap. xiii; C. R. Fish, "The Decision of the Ohio Valley," American Historical Association, *Report,* 1910, pp. 153-64; Phillips, *op. cit.,* 386-96; and T. D. Jervey, *The Railroad the Conqueror* (Columbia, 1913) and *Robert Y. Hayne and His Times* (New York, 1909).

The net effect of improved means of communication down to 1861 seems to have been actually to augment sectionalism rather than to allay it. Improved means of communication made the North and South somewhat better acquainted, but this better acquaintance did not remove prejudices in the North against slavery nor in the South against abolitionists; rather it seems to have increased them. Better facilities of travel encouraged the northern people to become excessively addicted to the convention habit, the southern people at least moderately so. Intersectional conventions, however, were comparatively few. Northern conventions nursed generous enthusiasms for various reforms, striking the shackles from the slave for one; southern conventions nursed a feeling of southern wrongs. Nor, before 1861, did better means of transportation even tend to bring a community of interest between the sections. Such facilities enabled the southern people, more readily than before, to get their manufactured goods and a portion of their foodstuffs from the East, or from the Northwest, or from Europe by way of the East, while they devoted themselves more exclusively than ever to growing their great staples for export to the North or to Europe, chiefly in northern ships. Northern people regarded this intersectional exchange of goods and products as mutually advantageous. A large proportion of the southern people came, especially when cotton prices were low, to look upon their commercial and industrial dependence on the North as "degrading vassalage," and economically disadvantageous.[25] Futhermore, northern commercial and industrial interests and southern agricultural interests demanded different policies on the part of the federal government, and bitter quarrels ensued.

Steamboats, canals, and railroads also contributed to the development of northern sectionalism in another way, by assimilating the Old Northwest to the economy and culture of the East. Thus they made possible a political alliance between the two as against the South. The fact has been frequently cited that they developed a considerable trade between the Northwest and the East and between the Northwest and Europe through the East. In fact, this trade soon came to exceed greatly the trade between the Northwest and the South. The East looked upon this trade as mutually advantageous and came eventually to lend support to western measures designed to increase it, while for various reasons, there was not the same disposition in the Northwest as in the South to regard commercial and industrial dependence on the East as degrading vassalage. For one thing, the Northwest never became so exclusively devoted to staple agriculture. However, there was an econ-

---

[25] Russel, *op. cit.*

omic basis for political alliance between East and Northwest much
more important than a mere large volume of trade. Canals, steamboats,
and railroads, together with great natural resources and the energy and
thrift of the people, brought prosperity to the Old Northwest. They
brought towns, cities, merchants, packing-houses, carshops, ship-yards,
prospects of iron and coal mines, eastern capital, and the prospect of
more employers and wage earners, in short, an economic order which,
by 1860, began to resemble that of the East. In one respect the two
sections had never been widely different; in both, small farms and free
labor everywhere prevailed. In this similarity of systems lay chiefly the
economic basis for political alliance. But the basis for political co-
öperation between East and Northwest was not solely or even primarily
economic. It was cultural. The majority of the early emigrants to the
Old Northwest were of southern stock, but when railroads, steamboats,
and canals came they gave the section a population preponderantly
eastern in origin and, therefore, preponderantly eastern in ideals, beliefs,
and prejudices.26 The new facilities for travel and communication were
an influence making for continued and greater homogeneity throughout the North in these respects.

Likewise, better means of transportation and communication helped
to develop southern sectionalism by assimilating more and more of the
South to a uniform type of economy and culture. They did not develop
a great internal commerce within the South.27 Most of the trade continued to be with the North and Europe. Rather, improved connections
with the outside world made it possible for similar physiographic and
climatic conditions to support in the larger area the same sort of
economic and social system, namely, plantations, slavery, and staple
crops produced for export. Culturally the newer parts of the South
were the offspring of the older and there had been little time to stray
from the paternal pattern. The new means of communication and
travel brought greater uniformity in this respect. Thus was the way
prepared for the acceptance of the tenets of the South Carolina school
(so vigorously propagated) by a sufficient number to precipitate the
cotton states into revolution when an exclusively northern combination
threatened to gain control of the national government.

It would seem, therefore, that in the period before secession, improved means of communication, as far as they had developed, had

---

26 This statement is well supported in the case of Illinois in A. C. Cole,
The Era of the Civil War, 1848-1870 (Springfield, 1919), chap. i; also F. J.
Turner, *The Frontier in American History* (New York, 1920), 135-42.

27 Phillips, *op. cit.*, 386-96.

actually tended to augment sectionalism. There can be no doubt, however, that in the long run they have been nationalizing factors. If armed conflict could have been avoided by compromises for another decade or so, it would have become impossible, and the railroads would have played a large part in determining the issue.

Already, by 1860, railroads were beginning to draw sections of the border slave states into the current of national life; the influence of railroads, built or prospective, upon the decision of the border states in 1861 has often been remarked. Railroads would soon have become numerous enough to give the South some internal trade, thus giving an impetus to the growth of towns and cities. They would have taken more northern men South, and many more southern men North. They would have brought in their wake repair-shops, carshops, and locomotive works. They might have given an impetus to the lumber industry. They would have penetrated iron and coal fields and aroused southern people to the prospect of their development. They would have put southern water-power sites on transportation lines, thus giving another incentive to manufactures. They would have put isolated rural communities in touch with the currents of commerce and thus would have began the transformation of backwoodsmen into moderately prosperous farmers. In these several ways they would have contributed to the formation of a class of capitalists who were not plantation owners, of free laborers with class consciousness, and of independent farmers not directly and primarily interested in slavery. The grip of the planting class on southern politics would have been weakened, possibly broken, and the influence of classes less antagonistic to national policies would have been correspondingly increased. With such changes slavery itself would have become difficult to police,28 and, therefore, less earnestly defended. Within a decade several more north and south roads would have crossed the intersectional boundary line, and with both northern and southern stockholders and personnel, would have strengthened the bonds of union, in one respect at least. When secession came, Texas was on the point of becoming the scene of railway struggles and land speculation and settlement, the like of which the South had not yet seen. Within ten years or less a railroad would have extended across her plains from New Orleans, another from Vicksburg, one from Memphis by way of Little Rock, another from Cairo with Chicago connections, and still another from St. Louis through Springfield and Fort Smith. Texas cattle would have been going to St. Louis and

---

28 Russel, *op. cit.*, chap. viii.

Chicago markets. Ten years without armed conflict would have been sufficient for the construction of a Southern Pacific railroad. Texas interests might have become too varied to be conducive to revolution.

Likewise, another decade or two of uninterrupted railroad building would have influenced powerfully northern sectionalism. Railroads would have helped to colonize the territories with a free labor population; and this done, the North might have become more willing to let the South solve her labor and racial problems without interference. Nor is it certain that the new West thus created would have had such a community of interest with the East as to permit its joining a northern political combination against the South.

Considering these signs of the times and others which it is not within the province of this paper to discuss, it would appear that, whether it was so understood at the time or not, in 1861 secession was a matter of then or never for the old order in the cotton states. It is extremely improbable that in the sweep of social forces the peculiar combination and play of factors and conditions so conducive to secession sentiment would have persisted long. It was the task of national statesmanship to interpret the trend of the times and to make the compromises, concessions, and adjustments necessary to prevent conflicting interests and ambitions from resulting in an attempted dissolution of the Union.29 Statesmanship failed. Secession and civil war came. But we are not entitled to lay the flattering unction to our souls that the Civil War was an inevitable conflict.

---

29 Dodd, writing of the state of the Union at the opening of Franklin Pierce's administration said: "A new era had begun . . . . and all the social tendencies seemed to be working out a national life which was no longer parochial. It was the business of politics so to guide and regulate the varying activities of the people that sectional hatreds should pass away and that the resources of the country should not be squandered," *op. cit.*, 206.

Index

About the Author

Robert R. Russel is Professor of History, Emeritus, Western Michigan University, Kalamazoo, Michigan. He received his M.A. from the University of Kansas and his Ph.D. from the University of Illinois. Professor Russel has written numerous articles for scholarly journals and is the author of the following books concerning American sectionalism and economic history: *Economic Aspects of Southern Sectionalism, 1840–1861* (1924), *Improvement of Communication with the Pacific Coast as an Issue in American Politics, 1783–1864* (1948), *Ante-Bellum Studies in Slavery Politics and the Railroads* (1960), and *A History of the American Economic System* (1964). .

Critical Studies
in Antebellum Sectionalism
was printed by offset lithography
and bound by Litho Crafters,
Inc., Ann Arbor,
Michigan.